P9-CKS-113

WITHDRAWN

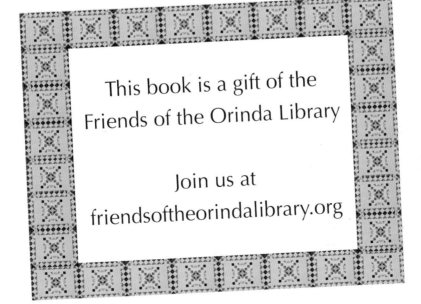

This book is a gift of the
Friends of the Orinda Library

Join us at
friendsoftheorindalibrary.org

Dangerous Rhythm

Dangerous Rhythm

Why Movie Musicals Matter

RICHARD BARRIOS

OXFORD
UNIVERSITY PRESS

OXFORD
UNIVERSITY PRESS

Oxford University Press is a department of the
University of Oxford. It furthers the University's objective
of excellence in research, scholarship, and education
by publishing worldwide.

Oxford   New York
Auckland   Cape Town   Dar es Salaam   Hong Kong   Karachi
Kuala Lumpur   Madrid   Melbourne   Mexico City   Nairobi
New Delhi   Shanghai   Taipei   Toronto

With offices in
Argentina   Austria   Brazil   Chile   Czech Republic   France   Greece
Guatemala   Hungary   Italy   Japan   Poland   Portugal   Singapore
South Korea   Switzerland   Thailand   Turkey   Ukraine   Vietnam

Oxford is a registered trade mark of Oxford University Press
in the UK and certain other countries.

Published in the United States of America by
Oxford University Press
198 Madison Avenue, New York, NY 10016

© Oxford University Press 2014

All rights reserved. No part of this publication may be reproduced,
stored in a retrieval system, or transmitted, in any form or by any means,
without the prior permission in writing of Oxford University Press,
or as expressly permitted by law, by license, or under terms agreed with
the appropriate reproduction rights organization. Inquiries concerning
reproduction outside the scope of the above should be sent to the
Rights Department, Oxford University Press, at the address above.

You must not circulate this work in any other form,
and you must impose this same condition on any acquirer.

Library of Congress Cataloging-in-Publication Data
Barrios, Richard.
Dangerous rhythm : why movie musicals matter / Richard Barrios.
pages   cm
Includes bibliographical references and index.
ISBN 978-0-19-997384-2 (hardcover : alk. paper)
1. Musical films—United States—History and criticism.   I. Title.
PN1995.9.M86B36   2014
791.43'6—dc23
2013037273

1 3 5 7 9 8 6 4 2

Printed in the United States of America
on acid-free paper

FOR MY FATHER
whose favorite movie was *The Jolson Story*

Contents

A Note of Explanation

....

The title of this book, along with all its chapter names plus those of the Introduction and Epilogue, derives from the titles or lyrics of songs performed in or written for films. The following is a list of the songs and films and creators and singers.

DANGEROUS RHYTHM
From "The Continental," in *The Gay Divorcée* (1934). Music by Con Conrad. Lyrics by Herb Magidson. Sung by Ginger Rogers, Erik Rhodes, and Lillian Miles. Danced by Rogers, Fred Astaire, and chorus.

[AND] ALL THAT JAZZ
From *Chicago* (2002). Music by John Kander. Lyrics by Fred Ebb. Sung and danced by Catherine Zeta-Jones, Renee Zellweger, and chorus.

EVERYTHING'S BEEN DONE BEFORE
[A.k.a. "Ev'rything's Been Done Before"] From *Reckless* (1935). Music by Jack King. Lyrics by Edwin Knopf and Harold Adamson. Sung by Allan Jones, danced by Jean Harlow (and dance double Betty Halsey), and chorus.

WHERE DO THEY COME FROM (AND WHERE DO THEY GO)?

From *Murder at the Vanities* (1934). Music by Arthur Johnston. Lyrics by Sam Coslow. Sung by Kitty Carlisle. Danced by chorus. [It should be mentioned that *Murder at the Vanities* was a loose—*very* loose—adaptation of a Broadway original.]

SEEING'S BELIEVING

From *The Belle of New York* (1952). Music by Harry Warren. Lyrics by Johnny Mercer. Sung and danced by Fred Astaire.

PEOPLE

From *Funny Girl* (1968). Music by Jule Styne. Lyrics by Bob Merrill. Sung by Barbra Streisand.

THE ART OF THE POSSIBLE

From *Evita* (1996). Music by Andrew Lloyd-Webber. Lyrics by Tim Rice. Sung by Antonio Banderas.

MUSIC MAKES ME

From *Flying Down to Rio* (1932). Music by Vincent Youmans. Lyrics by Gus Kahn and Edward Eliscu. Sung by Ginger Rogers.

WITH PLENTY OF MONEY [AND YOU]

From *Gold Diggers of 1937* (1936). Music by Harry Warren. Lyrics by Al Dubin. Sung by Dick Powell.

I GET THE NECK OF THE CHICKEN

From *Seven Days' Leave* (1942). Music by Jimmy McHugh. Lyrics by Frank Loesser. Sung by Marcy McGuire.

TURN ON THE HEAT

From *Sunny Side Up* [a.k.a. *Sunnyside Up*] (1929). Music by Ray Henderson. Lyrics by Lew Brown and B[uddy] G. DeSylva. Sung by Sharon Lynn. Danced by chorus.

PAINTING THE CLOUDS [WITH SUNSHINE]

From *Gold Diggers of Broadway* (1929). Music by Joseph Burke. Lyrics by

Al Dubin. Sung by Nick Lucas and chorus. Danced by Ann Pennington and chorus.

[I'VE GOT YOU] UNDER MY SKIN

From *Born to Dance* (1936). Music and lyrics by Cole Porter. Sung by Virginia Bruce (and evidently not dubbed).

PUT 'EM IN A BOX [TIE 'EM WITH A RIBBON, AND THROW 'EM IN THE DEEP BLUE SEA]

From *Romance on the High Seas* (1948). Music by Jule Styne. Lyrics by Sammy Cahn. Sung by Doris Day. Performed by the Page Cavanaugh Trio.

DREAM DANCING

From *You'll Never Get Rich* (1941). Music and lyrics by Cole Porter. Performed instrumentally. Recorded by Fred Astaire and the Delta Rhythm Boys.

Dangerous Rhythm

Introduction

All That Jazz

....

O ver nine decades, the musical film has had an existence that might best be termed preposterous. From the pre-Depression 1920s to the post-millennial now, these movies have lurched from times of glory to times of scorn, greatness to ignominy, abundance to extinction, *Gigi* to *Glitter*. Where other genres simply pass in and out of style, musicals soar and career and nosedive. Intended to seem effortless and diverting, they are, beneath those gleaming surfaces, complicated and contradictory. Small wonder, then, that they divide audiences like nearly no other kind of film: one person's Astaire will be another's anathema. The peculiarity extends as well to their history, which has been a thing less of evolution than recurrence, often regression. Their timeline is so rocky, in fact, that conventional chronology does not truly grasp exactly what musicals are about. Nor would it account for why their existence has been so odd, nor why or how they might continue to be vital and meaningful. Thus it is that *Dangerous Rhythm* seeks to explore the musical film experience less as chronicle than as reflection. A meditation, perhaps, that takes into account the musical's aspects, tendencies, strengths, and weaknesses. As its subtitle indicates, it proceeds from the viewpoint that musicals—when done right—can be pretty damned sublime. But there are no illusions or misty outbursts in these pages. Instead, it is a look, respectful yet clear-eyed, into how it can be, exactly, that musicals

can be so wonderful—can matter so inimitably—and then, with ballet deft-
ness, lose touch and turn useless.

For all their outward accessibility, movie musicals can be so riddled with
paradox that it becomes difficult to comprehend them. They can be insubstantial, trivial even, but are costly and require massive engineering. At their best
they transport, even exalt, offering up a spectrum of fantasies that appear as
compellingly real as the screen upon which they unfold. Then, and on a steady
basis, they forget their viewers and lessons and achievements and history and
era, and when this happens they deserve everyone's scorn. This wide range is
what is known as the gamut, one these films run with a force that belies their
glistening veneer. How, and why, have musicals been so extreme, touching
greatness and then failing so massively? Why do some musicals made more
than eight decades ago still enchant while others made very recently were stale
before they opened? Why do musicals remain prone to sudden bouts of cluelessness, even repellence . . . and yet continue to be important and special to so
many people? There are always answers, even as they often come in odd and
nonstandard ways. This book, in considering these issues, celebrates and questions musicals in the light of their achievements and failures, their relevance
and expendability, their pertinence and, OK, their impertinence. Most important, threading through it all like some insistent theme song, there are the rever-
berations of the musical's heritage and history. Sometimes remembered, often
forgotten, never insignificant.

Like the people who love or hate them, musicals are balanced unsteadily
between the sublime and the inane. It could be said that, with most of them,
there's only been the intention to bring, in the words of the jerk diva in *Singin'
in the Rain*, "a little joy into your humdrum lives." They can indeed bring that
joy, yet it is their fate and nature to be precarious, with vastly rewarding rhythms
that are ceaselessly in danger of failure. When undertaken by those who care,
they can be transcendent, even while tottering on the edge of total absurdity—
wonderfully hazardous, seldom safe. Wrench a musical film from its context or
audience and it's trouble; take a good one on its own terms and there may be
magic. Either way, the same extreme qualities that make them treacherous and
open to ridicule also can make them magnificent. When too safe or too oblivious, they can be khaki-colored sludge; when they go far and take risks, they can
be Technicolor-marvelous or *Moulin Rouge!* or, on especially blessed occasions,
Singin' in the Rain. They've been stolen from for many years—music videos
would not have occurred without them—yet remain unique and irreplaceable,

if constantly on the verge of extinction. This, then, is an exceedingly odd saga, and one way to begin to examine it comes with a visit to the Academy Awards ceremony held on March 23, 2003.

It was supposed to have been the ultimate Oscar show—the Academy's seventy-fifth anniversary, with untold panoply, stratospheric layers of self-congratulation, and the best-laid plans. Then, as sometimes happens when musicals are popular, a war started. This time it was Iraq, and the Bush administration's just-declared war against Saddam Hussein and his purported nuclear weapons had nabbed the lion's share of world attention and curtailed some of the Oscar excess. Presenters and winners were warned to keep the protests out of it, some of the more effulgent moments were eliminated and—sacrifice of sacrifices—necklines were raised on some gowns. Since the Academy Awards are nothing if not shameless, there did remain a great deal of the usual gloss, along with the hairdos and red-carpet gush, and something of a rare and unintended moment of candor as well: the big winner that year did not lay claim to the "seriousness" of a stirring drama or historical epic, and the kind of uplift that concerned it had far less to do with inspiration than with cleavage. It was glossy and flashy and filled with song and dance. It was *Chicago*. It was a musical.

At the end of those wartime Oscars, *Chicago* had tallied six statuettes, including Best Picture. While other things that evening seemed more immediately momentous or strange—the Best Director award given in absentia to a fugitive Roman Polanski, Adrien Brody as an unguardedly elated Best Actor winner, a nonplussed Barbra Streisand announcing that Eminem won the Best Song award—those of broader perception knew the chief significance. It had been thirty years since a musical film had done well at the Academy Awards, and thirty-four since one had been given the top prize.[1] Perhaps history was acting upon its weirdly persistent habit of recurring: back in 1969, *Oliver!* won the top award while a controversial war raged, and song-and-dance Dickens did seem particularly off-kilter during Vietnam. At any rate, that was a time when musicals were still the coin of the realm. They had been so for forty years, and they were about to vanish.

---

[1] This recounting of Oscars past does not mean to testify to the award's artistic status; a quick look at some winners and runners-up of any year will extinguish that notion pronto. Even so, Oscars offer an easy guide to the movie equation: profitable = popular = valid = worthy. In such a world, a Costner can win over a Scorsese. *Only* there.

Getting off with a bang: Catherine Zeta Jones and chorus, showing what "All That Jazz" is about in *Chicago*. For most musicals, this much heat and impact would have spelled climax—but here it was just the opening salvo.

When *Oliver!* received its award, no one thought the event to be anything extraordinary; it was, indeed, the fourth time in seven years that a musical had taken the top prize, which has to be some kind of record. All four—the predecessors were *West Side Story*, *My Fair Lady*, and *The Sound of Music*—were adapted Broadway shows, expensive, prestigious, conventionally well made. After *Oliver!* there would be a couple more big good musicals—*Fiddler on the Roof* and *Cabaret*—then silence. The movie musical had been an American institution, in some minds an essential popular art, and from 1972 onward it would die many deaths. The graveyard calm would occasionally be interrupted by flops big and small and the rare non-flop, plus one bona fide hit (*Grease*) and a few compelling novelties. Still, thirty years is a blasted eternity where film is concerned, and the period between *Cabaret* and *Chicago* was of such desolation that any attempt at resuscitation could make the corpse seem all the colder. *Chicago*, as it happened, was on the drawing board for much of that thirty-year down time. It was that extreme rarity: a planned film suffering decades of reversals and false starts, then both happening and succeeding. Again, it could only have been with a musical. *Chicago* was a special kind, sure—a dark vaudeville requiring a great deal of skilled staging, a nightmare to adapt to

the screen in any sort of cohesive manner. It was, in the event, good and successful enough to revive musical films for a time and inspire hopes for an
ongoing renaissance. Eventually that time passed, and hope was tempered
with much sober reflection. The truth is that in an age of media saturation and
virtual realities and immediate gratification, musicals do not always fit in well.
Think of it as the newest incarnation of a conundrum musicals have been
presenting, endlessly so, ever since their inception: they are vital, they are necessary, and they are impossible.

All types of films go in and out of fashion. Westerns, historical epics, and
romances all have their ins and outs, and there are even phases of wax and
wane for those that always seem to be around: mysteries, horror, action thrill-
ers, and low comedy. So it is also with literature, music, religion, politics, civility,
and much else in the known world. But musicals—the official notice of *finis*
has been hung on them at least six times: loudly in mid-to-late 1930, mutedly
in the television-sated mid-1950s, and emphatically in every decade since
1970. The odd *Les Misérables* glitch will surface to give the illusion of life, and
then silence follows. For such quintessentially American entertainment, they
have often been disdained in their own country, even as overseas they seem to
manage better. Formerly, they were a bread-and-butter staple that movie companies could do, sometimes well, in their sleep; then suddenly they were out
of the question. They were hooted off movie screens even as they continued to
thrive on stage and on television. When it became fashionable to admire some
of the older musicals, the new ones became sparser and crummier. All these
issues form the concern of this present fantasia, and the lion's share of its
scope will be confined to American musicals. Granted, this choice is arguable
and idiosyncratic; musicals are obviously part of a world stage, with countless
striking examples that come from everywhere. Nevertheless, they originated in
the United States and at their core remain uniquely American. The cinema of
German operetta or French experimentalism or Bollywood or anywhere else—
all worthy of their own multiple volumes—will always harken back, intention-
ally or no, to the stateside progenitors. Crass or philistine or mechanical or
soulless they may be, and in all this they manage to embody American optimism, American enterprise, American taste and exuberance and vulgarity. Predictable and formula-bound without question, and also frequently surprising
and surpassing to the point of occupying an unshakable bomb shelter in the
collective heart. Many have loved to criticize what they have accomplished and
what they have delivered, while others only realized how good they were, the

best of them, after they were dead and gone. Nostalgia is habitually a perilous slope, and while the musical documentary-cum-obituary *That's Entertainment!* was too rosy in many of its particulars, it did manage one clear-eyed observation. During an insanely skillful 1940 production number, it was with a gentle kind of rue that Frank Sinatra and the screenwriter noted, "You know, you can wait around, and hope, but I tell you, you'll never see anything like this again." The past can, after all, be an especially ornate prologue.

For diversions that can specifically be termed *Follies*, musicals raise controversies as endless as the colossal divisiveness they inspire. Assemble a group of knowledgeable people, and bring up the subject of the film version of *My Fair Lady* or *An American in Paris* or *The Broadway Melody* or *West Side Story* or, again, *Chicago*. The pros and cons come out in dense and heated and irreconcilable array.[2] There is also the quandary posed by an unknowable future. Are musicals too innocent for a time of contentious politics and hard economic truths, of "reality" "entertainment" and commercialized sex and apocalyptic fantasy? Does their kind of analog escapism retain any kind of currency in a digital age? Does *Nine* count for more or less than *Les Miz*? These are valid issues to raise at the time of this writing, just as similar questions were being asked at many other points in musicals' history. If there are not always steadfast answers, it might be possible to grasp why, like that tree falling in the forest, musicals sometimes keep on singing even when it appears that no one is listening.

Musicals depend vastly on the public for their existence, and that relationship has swung crazily through the years from exaltation to disdain. At the very beginning of the sound era, back when no one was sure exactly what a musical film was or would be, they were highly respected. Then the public became oversaturated—musicals, remember, seldom leave well enough alone—and began to look at them with a condescension that has never entirely gone away. "It's really good," one would hear, and the unspoken qualifier would finally drop, "…for a musical." Certainly, over the long haul, they would seldom acquire major prestige (and when they did, the results weighed tons); nor would they generally acquire, save in rare pockets, the reverent patina of respectability

[2] Even a formerly disreputable genre like martial arts is now given a more consistent respectability than musicals. (Note that they are both choreographed.) Since musicals seldom reside in the realm of the au courant or trendy—except when made by someone like Lars von Trier—their lot tends to be one of haughty contempt. Too safe or fey, too conventional or insubstantial—the rap sheet is as endless as the uncut version of *South Pacific*.

given by cinéastes to westerns or film noir. Part of the problem is that musicals are seen as a collaborative endeavor, one that does not permit an individual artist to leave a signature. The directors who inspire rabid devotion or shelves of books seldom turn to musicals—there's no body of Ford or Ozu musicals, and the one time Hitchcock did one, he regretted it forever after. Godard's sole musical is mainly *hommage* and stunt, while Bergman's *Magic Flute* is a record of a stage production. So-called respectable serious directors dabbled in musicals only reluctantly, and often with misguided zeal—William Wyler, Billy Wilder, John Huston, Francis Ford Coppola, Martin Scorsese. The directors who really took off in musicals—Vincente Minnelli, Rouben Mamoulian, Busby Berkeley, Gene Kelly and Stanley Donen, George Sidney, Bob Fosse, even René Clair—do not always earn the respect of the serious-minded, never mind that they usually should. Only Ernst Lubitsch, among the high-tier directors, seems immune, and few deem his musicals prime among his biggest-bang efforts.

So musicals have the auteur strike against them going out of the gate. That seems to indicate that they somehow bypass elevated criticism to communicate directly with the larger public. Well, yes and no. In some of their lushest periods, they did rake in huge grosses; a later chapter, examining the economics of musicals, includes some genuinely staggering financial figures. But does a film's huge financial success truly indicate that its makers have captured that producer's Holy Grail, the public's imagination? Not always and not anymore. When the dynamics of filmgoing changed in the megaplex boom of the 1970s, the marketing of a movie began to, and continues to, take strange precedence over its intrinsic quality. In so event-driven a culture, a film may double as huge success and profound artistic letdown. Many superhero opuses fall into this category, and it's worth noting that these big-screen comic books channel the same dynamics of many musicals: propelled less by substance than impact, relying on preset gimmicks to get their effects, intensely clued-in to formula and keyed response. (What's the difference, really, between a chorus line and an interplanetary explosion?) So, in some ways, big dumb action films are the twenty-first century's equivalent of the big dumb musicals of the late 1930s: both of them disposable, of-their-time products existing to fill up screen time and make money, then go away. And just as the likes of *Thor* will never be reclaimed as a lost gem, so also will *Rosalie* not receive or deserve more than furtive affection from a couple of misguided buffs.

No less than any other kind of movie, and more than many, musicals can be, for lack of a less polite term, utter dreck. In 1929, some observers went on about their excessive frivolity, their seeming to not mean very much or be about anything. The complaints continued through the years, moving across the scale from irate dudgeon to faux-indulgent patronizing that holds even the best movie musicals to be lowbrow. Especially after the "serious" musical took off on Broadway in the mid-'40s, movies were deemed the gauche and inferior dauphin to stage royalty. It helped that some good shows were truly botched in their movie transfers—*Anything Goes* (twice), *One Touch of Venus*, *Kismet*, too many others to count. That made for two demerits—some people were just not going to accept musicals under any circumstances, and others were and are forever going to find them way below the Broadway standard. Even when people accept some musical movies—*West Side Story* is a good "serious" example—there is a tendency to look down on them as genial time-wasters, as insubstantial as the scenery in a dream-sequence dance. They can be fun, but don't confuse them with anything truly worthy.[3] It's unreal in the wrong way, it's not life, it's not art, ultimately it's not worthwhile. An acolyte will argue "But...*Love Me Tonight, Cabaret*..." in vain. Diversion can be so banal.

They can be crass, they're not always respected, they're virtually extinct—formidable truths all, which makes it fortunate that they are balanced by equally solid verities on the positive side. It can be far too easy to underestimate musicals, in part because they can give vastly more than can usually be comprehended. At their greatest, they commune with the hearts and minds and souls of their viewers in a way that puts into actual sounds and visuals things normally not a part of waking hours. They cover all temporal bases: reminders of the past that bring joy and comfort in the present, and through film's permanence guaranteeing a long future. As a result, they are retained and treasured and loved such as few works are. Once the good ones are here, they stay. "Over the Rainbow" will never go away, and Fred and Ginger dancing cheek to cheek will always be a moment of the most chic sort of rapture. The

---

[3] If expressing devotion to musicals draws a look down the nose from many, imagine the reaction when people learn of a book being written about them. Or, worse, a book about their beginnings.

It should be noted that while few serious (or captious) observers care to ascribe genuine relevance to musicals, *Chicago* prompted a superb *New York Times* Op-Ed piece by Frank Rich. Entitled "They Both Reached for the Gun," it equated Roxie Hart's lying assertions of innocence with the trumped-up charges then leading the United States into Iraq. By making such a brilliantly succinct point, Rich showed how a giddy piece of entertainment can impart even more meaning and significance than its creators could have intended, even apart from the O. J. trial.

big-studio system of the 1930s and 1940s was called The Dream Factory for a reason, and the craftsmanship and resonance of its finest product are, ultimately, as precious and lasting as literature or music. Leave the detritus to ghouls and mavens and confront the feast that comes with the greatest of these intricately wrought delights. Not to hector with a favorite title here, but what the hell: baldly put, does anyone wish to know someone who truly believes that their life was not made better by the existence of "Over the Rainbow"?

Perhaps the word "beguile" is too loose and too weak a description of the effect of the best musicals. Let a particularly wonderful moment in their existence serve as an example of their capability. In the spring of 1933, with the inauguration of Franklin Roosevelt, the United States was hoping for some kind of relief after three years of financial and emotional blight. Somehow, it was a movie musical that framed this national mood better than anything else. The movie was *42nd Street*, and forget about all the clichés of Let's-put-on-a-show and you've-got-to-come-back-a-star and the delirious overhead Busby Berkeley camera angles. *42nd Street* was a rallying cry for the New Deal and an authentic American miracle, offering up equal portions of hope and frivolity. Ruby Keeler's homeless nobody who becomes a star stood in for every spectator wanting to make it out of the Depression, and Warner Baxter's desperate and ailing director was a constant reminder that even the lightest fluff comes at a price. With this much awareness and skill, song and dance could seem germane. It did so as well in the 1940s, when extravaganzas bearing titles such as *Star-Spangled Rhythm* took the national mind off fear. There was no art, nor even that insinuatingly artless way in which musicals can illuminate deep feelings and hidden cravings. It was a very particular type of escapism being offered, one that acknowledged what was going on in the world, refracting it through the Hollywood lens, and having it come out in terms of swing music, Technicolor, and Betty Grable.

After the war, a disconnect became steadily more apparent. Even as a film like *Singin' in the Rain* embodied the musical at its absolute apogee, there were too many changes for musicals to bridge the gap. By the time of *Gigi* in 1958, it was clear that while musicals could occasionally rise wonderfully out of the old routine, they had somehow become less essential—equivalent to canvases that are sublime but must necessarily be placed in the isolation of a museum setting. There then followed, as a sort of rebirth, the huge grosses and Oscar stockpiles of *West Side Story* and *The Sound of Music* and the others. Even as the self-congratulation continued, something false was going on. These movies owed their allegiance to footlights, not cameras, reflecting the film musical's past far less than the enormous popularity of Broadway musicals in those years. On the screen they were liked and attended—even, in the case of *Sound of Music*, inspiring faith-based devotion bordering on fanaticism. But there was nothing else going on in movies or in American life or in the world—notably, Southeast Asia—that would give these movies genuine consequence. Besotted with their own prestige, these big-gun singing epics tried to pretend that musicals were not essentially an unpretentious art, a thing of honest craft and sweat and barely articulated finer feelings. For some, the refinement of a *My Fair Lady* came off, in an age of Beatles and antiwar protests and freedom marches, as a lack of simpatico. Then came a bunch of lavishly petty blockbusters to finish off the job. *Camelot* and *Paint Your Wagon* pretended to be relevant, but their mien was zillions of light years away from the genuine cool of, say, Astaire and Rogers dancing to "Smoke Gets in Your Eyes" in *Roberta*. The times and the musicals had changed, and no one had bothered to coordinate one with the other.

Cabaret, in 1972, was not the last successful American movie musical before *Chicago*, nor the last good one. There were, in the intervening thirty years, some worthy tries as well as some things that could truly be counted unspeakable. But, to many, it felt like the end of the line. Over about four years (1970–74) the musical film died, in effect, completely, and MGM's survey of its former glories, *That's Entertainment!*, was the eulogy. The initial effect of *That's Entertainment!* was the regretful nostalgia of "They don't make 'em like that anymore"; yet in a larger sense it showed not only why musicals were extinct (cynicism, economy, rock music, faddishness) but why the best of them were transcendent. It could be said, while warily skirting a pun, that they had legs. They weren't only wistfully brassy reminders of lost innocence or the stuff of campy excess. Many of them were unmatched reminders of the effect made when talent and showmanship and well-spent money find the right point of collusion.

When *That's Entertainment!* was released in 1974, it had been a generation since the last golden time for original film musicals. *Gigi*, the final great one of that era, had come out in 1958, so there had been enough time for them to have, in effect, gone out of fashion and back in again. The impact was startling—almost nothing in that documentary drew laughs, even though derision was encouraged at the sight of Joan Crawford's maladroit dance stylings and those pomp icons Jeanette MacDonald and Nelson Eddy. Even, or especially, Esther Williams's world of undersea rococo drew gasps. People began to think about what earlier had been taken for granted. The growing appreciation was abetted by television and retrospective screenings, a few books, and, in time, the home video market. The secrets were out: Fred Astaire was a god, Gene Kelly was sexy, and Judy Garland could be loved by straight people too. Adding to it all were the occasional modern-day forays into musical filmmaking. If *Sgt. Pepper's Lonely Hearts Club Band* didn't make one appreciate even a mediocre Betty Grable vehicle, what would? Seeing Gene Kelly trundle geriatrically through the dire *Xanadu* served less to elicit pity than, fortunately, to remind everyone of his former greatness. As each new abomination came out, more millions realized the quality, even the relevance, of the old ones.

So...musicals are wonderful, musicals are trash. Both are accurate, and this holds true not just because *Singin' in the Rain* is a masterpiece and *Paint Your Wagon* belongs in a litter box. They can be art and garbage, and they deserve the arguments. What cannot be disputed is their achievement and their importance. *42nd Street* and *Gold Diggers of 1933* are not only major parts of the musical canon but of American sociology. *The Broadway Melody*, the first real movie musical, is a historically vital originator of a new kind of American pop art. So, in its way, is *Snow White and the Seven Dwarfs*. As for *The Wizard of Oz*, a shelf of books could be written about its impact on the movie and television industries and on gay and straight culture. That musicals were popular and liked can be proved by sheer numbers. But there's more to a movie than its being a hit, let alone winning an Oscar. Whenever a movie comes out, it is part of a vast channel of history and culture and aesthetics. Sometimes it has a reverberant impact and sometimes very little. Either way, it will be swept along by trends and currents established by everything that's come before, yet ultimately it will end up in a unique destination. What those currents are, why they can be both good and otherwise, is the main topic of consideration here.

Dreams are by definition the most evanescent of things. Gone with the morning, never to be touched, seldom recurring, not even so tangible as to be remembered. Small wonder that movie musicals are often held to be an accurate actualization of dreams and fantasies. And, as with dreams, close inspection can help make their presence more comprehensible. They do not evaporate when examined—on the contrary, they welcome an examination that seeks to understand why they've danced in so many brains for all these scores of years. Not all the magic can be totally captured; no one, not even Arlene Croce, has completely explained the full enchantment of Fred Astaire and Ginger Rogers. However, scrutiny and understanding are still possible, even desirable. Enough remains, for example, to help explain why Busby Berkeley's "Lullaby of Broadway" sequence is a truly masterful piece of cinema. Enough may remain, too, to account for a great singer like Bing Crosby making so many dull and flimsy movies yet retaining immense popularity. Or to account for the numerous occasions when the musical lost its magic even as it kept making money. Or why some of the best musicals are those not featuring live performers. Or why African American artists were able, back in the day, to get just a little more of an even break in musicals than elsewhere in films. It might even be possible to fathom why the musical-film terrain of the 1960s began to resemble the elephants' graveyard. The answers are usually present, and they do not come through a web of preconceptions. These films don't necessarily conform to normal standards of greatness, and far too many of them are prone to shoving wonderful moments in between sections of stolid compost. Like dreams, like human beings, like life, there's a great deal of inconsistency here. Fortunately, for those whose hearts go that way, there is also an inordinate amount of bliss, plus rewards that are without parallel. And, as a connoisseur knows while sampling an especially fine champagne, a closer look at the bubbles does not lessen the sparkle.

Chapter 1

Everything's Been Done Before

....

Musicals have, in a way, been eternally accidental. While they are usually vastly dependent on precision and calculation, it should also be remembered that it is not always in their nature to make perfect sense. Thus, they emerged far from their creators' initial intent and, ever since, have been medleys of happenstance and collision, nestling celestial details within an overall devilish kind of chaos. If they come out, the best of them, like wondrously polished and superbly well-oiled machines, a great deal of blind uncertainty is always hovering just offscreen. First and last, there is their ever-present history, which is rich and often ambiguous. It swirls about, bears down, and forms an overlapping cluster of inescapable truths. Consciously or not, musical films will always operate within them:

1. There is no such thing as a sure thing.
2. The musical is a vibrant, incestuous cannibal, relentlessly feeding off itself, repeating itself, forgetting and then remembering what it does. Every good or great musical is built on a foundation of the good qualities established through previous musicals. On rare occasions when something new or innovative happens, it is added to the mix.
3. Any part of a musical will find causes and equivalents in other musicals, before or since. Janet Gaynor is the direct ancestor of Johnny Depp, triumphing in spite of a lack of song-and-dance experience. *The Desert Song*

or *Les Misérables*, Morton Downey in *Mother's Boy* (1929) or Kelly Clarkson in *From Justin to Kelly* (2003)—it's all, almost, the same.

4. Musicals enjoy a mutually admiring kinship with their audiences. The bond is special and precise, unintelligible to outsiders, and quite fragile. When either side violates it, crisis occurs.

5. Because of the musical's once-and-future nature, its past remains a live and immediate thing. Al Jolson, believe it or not, like it or not, is still singing.

As binding as these precepts are, musical film has always picked its way through an existential minefield. These movies try to be new at the same time they regress and reconstruct. They are uncannily self-referential, yet they sneer at their past while celebrating it. They are fragmented and oddly cohesive, predictable and variable, nostalgic and current. Their history, too, is both straightforward and serpentine, a progression that constantly digresses. The capsule account of their lifespan recounted here, then, will follow history's lead and at times dart back and forth through the years to connect the dots, just as the films do themselves. The echoes of their earliest years are still being felt today, the viewers matter as much as the films, and one way or another the same damn things keep on happening. There's also that brilliant, confounding trump card: just when it appears that musicals don't count, they prove their worth.

"It's always best to start at the beginning," Glinda the Good Witch observed, and that beginning is not Al Jolson and *The Jazz Singer*. Because of the florid power of his iconography—the big voice and ego and black-painted face—it can be easy to zero in on Jolson rather than search out the more mundane truth. (That, unfortunately, is how history sometimes works. Also movies and politics. That's entertainment.) This is where *Singin' in the Rain* does something of a disservice. Let it be beside the point for a moment that possibly the greatest of all musical films is about how musical films began—could the circle be closed more ecstatically?—and embraces its history with sublime zest. With all its glory and smarts and affection, *Singin' in the Rain* does propagate that old Warner Bros. myth about Jolson blurting out "You ain't heard nothin' yet" and changing movies forever and causing song and dance to spring up overnight. At best, this is a gross oversimplification, dramatically efficient yet about as similar to what really happened as Kathy Seldon's voice is to Lina Lamont's. The less magnetic truth is that the initial push to bring sound to movies was not about musicals or talking pictures, and that Jolson was less a cause of the revolution than an unintended by-product.

In the mid-1920s, silent film was at such a peak that few thought of it as an incomplete art. It was not the stage, nor did it try to be, and while dreamers and delusionals had been working for years to come up with a valid way to add sound to the projected image, few were unhappy with silent film as a commercial and creative enterprise. Movies, most felt, were a universal art, fine as they were. Where they were finest, quite clearly, was in large metropolitan theaters, accompanied by full orchestras and even sound effects. At that time Warner Bros. was a second-rank movie company and like other studios owned a chain of theaters that played the films it produced. Sam Warner, the imaginative brother, began to wonder about the attention Warner films might get if they could be screened everywhere with the same musical amenities as a big-city presentation. Then, as an afterthought, he envisioned another big-theater staple in addition to the orchestra: vaudeville acts to run between the feature showings.

After much technological toil, plus anguish from Sam's cash-minded brothers, the Warner Bros./Western Electric sound-film system, Vitaphone, made its debut in a legit Broadway house on August 6, 1926. It was a triumph, and not for the intended reason. The hit was supposed to have been the feature, a silent swashbuckler: John Barrymore IS **DON JUAN** !! But New York crowds, snarky and particular then as now, were used to hearing orchestras play for movies, and Vitaphone—phonograph discs played over big speakers—could not compete with live sound. The sensation came instead with the prologue, a series of musical acts, mostly classical and prestigious. Watching Barrymore fight a duel while hearing an orchestra plus clank-clash sound effects was fun; seeing and hearing esteemed artists in big-screen proximity was exhilarating and relevant. The *New York Times* was so excited that it gave the Vitaphone acts (not *Don Juan*) an awestruck editorial, and Warner's intentions quickly took a sharp detour.

Jolson comes in around this point, not entirely deliberately. The second Vitaphone program, in October 1926, was pop-oriented instead of classical, and the star spot was given to actor/comedian/singer George Jessel. He had created the title role in the successful play *The Jazz Singer* and was set to star in the film version, so Warners was indulging in promotional synergy. Unfortunately for Jessel, the program also featured a short titled *Al Jolson in A Plantation Act*. Performing three songs in the trademark makeup that now disqualifies him from millions of people's regard, Jolson became the second big accident of sound film. No wonder: when the short resurfaced after being lost for nearly seventy years, it showed a Jolson more magnetic (and subtler and less over-bearing) than in his feature films, and infinitely more exciting than the earth-bound Jessel. While Jessel was still slated for the *Jazz Singer* film, some months later he dropped out. It was, or claimed to be, because he demanded more money when it was decided to add sound sequences; most likely it also in-volved backstage maneuvering plus a dollop of fate.

So it was that Jolson came into *The Jazz Singer,* a mostly silent drama inter-rupted by occasional songs, as Jessel's replacement. This was felt at the time to be a personal triumph, as opposed to a bold leap—not the beginning of the musical film—and seemed to many less a cohesive work than some Vitaphone shorts patched into a mute feature. Nevertheless, Jolson's force in the sound portions was unlike anything film audiences had ever witnessed, and after *The Jazz Singer* had been running for some weeks the implications finally became clear. The notion of songs entering a film narrative was fresh and captivating, and "Blue Skies" and "My Mammy" tied the music to the drama in an affecting way never before possible. And, over it all, there was that close-up projected image, giving an immediacy not possible in live venues, the world's greatest entertainer singing directly to you.[1] Sound would have (and did) come to movies without Jolson, yet his particular talent made the transition more urgent.

Jolson and Jessel, time and again. A hallowed part of musicals' history is that it is never possible to know with certainty how a performer will read onscreen. It involves instinct and timing and shrewd presentation and luck, and while brilliance on a stage or television does not always translate, mere adequacy might blow up to Astairean proportions on a movie screen. Pop singers, for example, tend to fare unevenly. In 1929, Rudy Vallee's *The Vaga-bond Lover* was so unfortunate that no one took Vallee seriously again in film until much later. His immediate successor as a radio idol, Bing Crosby, took off like a shot on film, his success echoing down the years to Frank Sinatra (big in musicals, if not always happily so), Elvis, the Beatles, and Eminem. Contrast them with the children of Vallee: Lanny Ross, Frankie Laine, Peter Frampton, and the unforgettable Vanilla Ice. In another realm are the actors, nonsinging yet undubbed, who find ways to pull it off—Gloria Grahame in

[1] From *The Jazz Singer* to *Funny Girl* to *Les Miz,* a solo filmed in close-up can be a sure-fire way to grab an audience. At least it can when not overused (*Les Miz* again) or misused (*Camelot*). Even in the musical's world of compelling excess, more is sometimes less.

Oklahoma!, Jean Simmons in *Guys and Dolls*, Peter O'Toole in *Goodbye, Mr. Chips*, Renee Zellweger in *Chicago*. (Tom Cruise, in *Rock of Ages*, smacked of Autotune.) Back to the beginning: the first musical comedy star signed for sound film after *The Jazz Singer* was Fanny (sometimes Fannie) Brice. If she was a more all-around performer than Jolson, a better actor, and more subtle singer, her quality didn't read on film in the way of Jolson. Or Streisand. On a related high note are the opera singers who sometimes come to film. Lawrence Tibbett and Grace Moore did well, while Mario Lanza's opera stardom was chiefly onscreen. Many others, from Ponselle to Pavarotti, were far less successful.[2]

The suitability of the players is one part of a question asked and anguished over from the dinosaur time to the twenty-first century: how, exactly, does a musical function on film? Will it be like the stage, or might it be, as some thought early on, the intersection of silent movies and radio? The answer has taken many forms and the medium has ultimately followed its own muses, to the extent that a beloved film like *Lili* can be a musical to some and a drama to others (including the Academy). Warner Bros., in any case, was ill-equipped to provide solutions, regardless of the vast technical edge it owned at the start of the sound era, before other studios could come up with their own sound-film processes. That frantic time of sound transition, alleged by myth and *Singin' in the Rain* to be mere weeks, stretched in reality over two years. Even Warners was caught unaware by the success of *The Jazz Singer*, so much so that it had no planned follow-up. Finally, after something of a down time in late 1927 and into 1928, it resumed production with sound films that were often stopgap and halting. One surviving exhibit of this is the transcription ("film version" is too liberated a term) it made, in the fall of 1928, of the Broadway operetta *The Desert Song*. The first musical feature to be shot, it was in essence a play printed on celluloid, and since Warners made the mistake of delaying its release it seemed even more dated by the time it opened. Because of this delay, MGM took the lead and, in one of film history's major spasms, set the tone for all musicals to come.

If *The Broadway Melody* is at all famous today, it is as the second film to win a Best Picture Oscar. Some will also recall that, courtesy of MGM's publicity

---

[2] Geraldine Farrar was a smash too, but in silent movies. Opera stars in European films often had a better time of it, yet even there some real disappointments could turn up. This could be attested to by anyone who's seen Maria Callas in Pier-Paolo Pasolini's *Medea*.

department, it gave posterity the legendary slogan ALL TALKING! ALL SING-ING! ALL DANCING! To the relative few who have seen it in recent years, it is known as a charming, numbingly primitive museum piece, with clumping musical numbers and a backstage plot so rudimentary that the writers can be heard figuring out just how people in movies should talk. Such are the tricks that history can impose on major innovation. In its time, *The Broadway Melody* was a sensation, in most ways the birth of its genre, a work of genuine signifi-cance. Jolson's triumph—his second film, *The Singing Fool,* was a far bigger hit than *The Jazz Singer*—had been forged from personality plus novelty. *The Broadway Melody,* in contrast, was seen *at the time* to have worked through nearly all the problems of sound film: story, songs, performance, technique, design, dance, even Technicolor. The fact that it was a musical was hardly co-incidental, for it was a shrewd demonstration that only one type of film had not been possible in the silent era. Nor was it a stagebound *Desert Song,* for in its crude way it managed to look and act like a film.[3]

The effect of *The Broadway Melody* was to give musicals a syntax they have owned ever since. Even as technique changes along with participants and ma-terial, the musical heritage that began here has remained. This is what proto-types do, from *The Great Train Robbery* to *Spider-Man:* when they spawn good films, the tropes are rethought with wit and grace; in lesser films, that sad majority, they are recycled and regurgitated with one eye on the box office and the other on expedience. Accordingly, a flood of fake *Broadway Melody* back-stage tales tumbled out of the Hollywood factories in 1929 and 1930, dozens of Xerox putting-on-a-show imitations filled with ambitious hoofers and inno-cent chorines. In 1933, *42nd Street* reinvigorated the clichés and joined *Broadway Melody* as a backstage-film template that continues all the way to the present. The incidentals vary and the basic idea does not: *Dancing Lady, Alex-ander's Ragtime Band, Cover Girl, The Band Wagon, White Christmas, Cabaret, Fame, Showgirls* (God help us), *8 Mile, Hustle & Flow, Rock of Ages.* Also, *Singin' in the Rain,* which took from *Broadway Melody* songs, a producer (lyri-cist Arthur Freed), and a warehouse of memories and details.

---

[3] Tradition holds *The Broadway Melody* to be less sensational than *The Jazz Singer.* Leave it, then, to the British to nail its effect properly. In the 1944 film of Noël Coward's family chron-icle *This Happy Breed,* one character tries out the new 1929 talkies and comes home enrap-tured. No, not Jolson: it's *Broadway Melody,* and they went so far as to lease a clip from MGM, the black-and-white looking quaintly dynamic in an otherwise color film.

Nothing but the truth: Some of the original poster art for *The Broadway Melody* stressed the "all" nature of the talking, singing, and dancing. Here, along with idealized depictions of the three costars, MGM was content to stress quality, not quantity. Meanwhile, drama is compelled to take a decided back seat.

Not that backstage stories have been the sole progenitors. *The Great Zieg-feld* showed how easily music could bolster a faux-authentic biography, as did the later *Yankee Doodle Dandy*, *The Buddy Holly Story*, *Ray*, and far more. The Jeanette MacDonald-Nelson Eddy operettas, themselves a slicked-up version of a staple from earlier on, brought dozens of imitators and in some ways remain, as do the fantasy spawn of *Snow White* and *The Wizard of Oz*. For *Meet Me in St. Louis*, the primacy of the original became even clearer with such inferior copies as *Centennial Summer*. Much of the rest is drawn from Broadway and previous movies, the mercy being that a fresh approach can usually make rejuvenation possible.

One of the more perverse truths about musicals is that they were most daring and original at their very beginning. The lack of an entrenched sense of identity caused them to traverse the entire map: dramas and comedies that didn't need songs, westerns, gangster pictures, even science fiction.[4] Many, naturally, were halting and derivative, yet there were also major indicators of potential. In *The Love Parade* and *Monte Carlo*, master director Ernst Lubitsch slyly upended the clichés of both operetta and film romance. So did the little-known *Sweet Kitty Bellairs*, which was, of all things, a witty pastiche of eighteenth-century ballad-operas. In the mood-piece *Hallulujah!*, King Vidor portrayed an evangelist's fall and redemption with the use of songs and spirituals, and Rouben Mamoulian used a tawdry backstage yarn, *Applause*, as a testing ground for a startling amount of virtuosity. More conventionally, there was *Sunny Side Up*, a smash-hit love story with charm and a fine score, plus the spectacular Technicolor revue *King of Jazz*, the dancing of Broadway's Marilyn Miller in *Sally*, and the striking operetta *The Vagabond King*. Many others as well—too many.

One factor fully on display in the early years was trial-and-error. Trying things out is a venerable part of the musical's tradition, and some filmmakers were able to find their own route to effective problem solving. *The Broadway Melody*, for example, sounded better than earlier talkies because director Harry Beaumont ran a print in an empty theater to calibrate acoustics, sound levels,

---

[4] Yes, sci-fi. Eons before *Rocky Horror*, *Just Imagine* was a million-dollar musical comedy set in the far future of 1980, with futuristic gadgets, a trip to Mars, and a *Sleeper*-like shlub waking from a fifty-year coma. Unfortunately, and not infrequent in 1930, the good ideas were mitigated by workaday routine, a wan score, and not quite enough wit. It starred a Swedish-dialect comic called El Brendel. Remember the name and tremble.

and general audibility (obvious step now, keen innovation then). Months later, MGM did an all-star variety show called *The Hollywood Revue of 1929*. No one knew, or ever would, how to make a filmed revue work, so the studio blindly shot a big bunch of songs and skits that seemed, not surprisingly, pointless. Then someone realized that a star-filled sock finale would make it fall into place. Since everyone was working on other movies in the daytime, MGM set up a special night shoot and hauled out the Technicolor camera. Weary stars like Joan Crawford and Jack Benny donned rain-slickers and (except for Buster Keaton) big smiles to run through a final chorus of the movie's hit song, "Singin' in the Rain." They did it only ten days before *The Hollywood Revue* opened. It worked like a charm, and still does.

This tailoring, in which creators divine how best to serve their public, can be brilliant or common-sense or plain luck. In 1933, the gritty conviction of *42nd Street* and *Gold Diggers of 1933* was the precise reinvention the musical needed, and that same year also saw the film advent of Fred Astaire, to whom precision and care were bywords; in a *Swing Time*, only the most grinding labor could make the near-impossible look so easy. This is the sort of craft evident when, during *Meet Me in St. Louis*, Vincente Minnelli grappled tooth and nail with technicians over the insanely complicated scene where Judy Garland walks through the house extinguishing the lights. Busby Berkeley and Bob Fosse could take similar, if more intimidating, control, and on and on through movie-musical history: a favorite moment probably has a story behind it about someone's push and battle for detail, individuality, quality. Or, in the case of "Over the Rainbow," to fight to keep it in the movie. It's about commitment, about being determined to divert, exhilarate, comfort, and provoke, without letting the strings and seams show. Musicals, all other things being equal, are no place for sissies, and require astonishing inspiration and sweat to stave off the empty and the tedious. Imagine, for instance, the *American in Paris* ballet in less imaginative hands; it might have come out like ooh-la-la candy from tripe like *April in Paris*. This isn't the standard assembly-line way in which movies were and are made, back then in factory times and now through the relentless maw connoted by the word "franchise." It's a lesson that should be perpetually heeded and often is not: to make one of these work, it's necessary to assemble a group of artists who are aware that musicals are not like other movies. This is when the magic may happen.

Unfortunately, the good ones, or the ones with great parts, have always been surrounded by the filmic equivalent of foam peanuts—the empty product that insistently fills a void. In the harshest times, when musicals are not properly attuned to their viewers, the quality work fails along with the garbage. This is what occurred in mid-1930, when people stopped going. The collapse, which came just as the country was beginning to feel the effects of the stock market crash, carried an absurd paradox: by the time more musicals were beginning to get it right, no one was interested. With the Depression starting to hit home, something like *Sweet Kitty Bellairs* seemed far less tempting than a story with unwed mothers or gangsters. Very few musicals produced during the down time did at all well, and a genuine masterpiece like Mamoulian's *Love Me Tonight* (1932) had no chance to recoup its cost or reach the audience it deserved. The moratorium remained in effect for three years, at that time an eon in the industry; when a similar oversaturation happened again forty years later, it would be for three decades.

In 1933, *42nd Street* made musicals current once again, in large part because of the ministrations of two strong men: Franklin Roosevelt and Busby Berkeley. The thirty-fourth president promised change and encouraged optimism, and Warner Bros.' erratic and often brilliant dance director refracted that new confidence through a kaleidoscopic lens. Warners went so far as to advertise *42nd Street* with Roosevelt's slogan—"Promoting a **New Deal** in Entertainment!"—and timed it to open just as he was inaugurated. The unknown dancer played by Ruby Keeler was, in effect, One of Us, despite (or because of) her heavy-footed taps and scratchy singing, and the musical numbers supplied the escape the moment demanded. Berkeley, who combined the job of dance director with those of movie director, cameraman, and editor, created sequences so self-contained as to be stand-alone short essays on geometry, rhythm, style, and sex. (Also, on less savory occasions, violence toward women.) In *Gold Diggers of 1933*, Berkeley's depiction of a breadline filled with ex-soldiers—Roosevelt's "Forgotten Men"—was so heartfelt and virtuosic that it seemed far less a trivialization of a national crisis than an earnest call to action. At this mid-1933 time, the musical attained rare stature: propaganda piece, social document, escapist distraction, morale-rouser, national panacea. While the financial figures were staggering, it was the centrality within the national mood that counted most.

Shortly, the immediacy would be yanked away. A year after the arresting peak of "Remember My Forgotten Man," musicals were subjected to the wholesale whitewashing of the notorious Motion Picture Production Code. Propelled by the vehemence of true believers—think Tea Party—masses of moral crusaders and church leaders planned a movie boycott, after which the federal government threatened to step in. Sex and crime, essentially anything seen as "harmful" to impressionable viewers, would be the target; the movies were forced to police their own content, and the effects were massive. The Mae Wests and Jimmy Cagneys and Jean Harlows of movies were denatured, gritty vitality became a memory, and Shirley Temple became film's belle ideal. The crackdown, extending for well over thirty years, hit musicals especially hard: the randy give-and-take of backstage stories was flattened, the gay characters frequently popping up were forcibly closeted, costumes showed less skin, and lyrics were inspected for anything even remotely suspect. (This is how New York New York was downgraded from being a helluva town to, in 1949, merely wonderful.) It all made for less immediacy and far less edge, and the old vitality was increasingly replaced by gloss and noise. That odd mooring in reality (or something like it) that was one of the musical's most appealing features was now gone. Seldom, moving forward, would there be the subversive touches of frankness and truth that had made the Warner films a smash and Berkeley a king. People who don't like musicals take them to task for being idle-minded schlock, oblivious and dishonest; here is where the charges begin to ring true.

Their boisterous rough edges removed, musicals began to focus on form. Soon they were the acme of Hollywood professionalism, things of numbing excess, dreary repetition, empty largesse. Such a world was exemplified by the 1936 Oscar-winner *The Great Ziegfeld*, which for all its top-heavy song and dance was not so much musical or even biography as a consumerist-driven plunge into sledgehammer magnificence. In this factory-tooled setting, innovation would count for little and fine performers and marvelous songs were placed within workaday, imitative conformity. There could be showcases for tenors or ice skaters or comedians or ciphers without detectable talent, and nothing mattered so long as everything stopped every fifteen minutes for a song with a dance break. No thought about connections between story and music, let alone between content and recognizable feelings. In a world of *Ziegfeld*s, musicals were a steady part of a moviegoer's diet, and with few exceptions they were expected to be competent, formula-driven, and essentially empty. They might awe, but not move or surprise; most often, the material was so derivative that in effect it was the same old song.

The major exception to the routine came through the efforts of Fred Astaire. Overt seduction was no longer permitted, so Astaire, with his talented associate

Hermes Pan and the stunningly apt partnership of Ginger Rogers, did it through dance. "Night and Day" (*The Gay Divorcée*), "Cheek to Cheek" (*Top Hat*), "Let's Face the Music and Dance" (*Follow the Fleet*), and the other rapturous duets never needed to contain anything explicit; movement combined with great song made clear what was going on. By *Swing Time*, in 1936, Astaire's art had attained such refinement that one masterful number, "Never Gonna Dance," climaxed the film by encapsulating its entire plot. This work would have repercussions later—*An American in Paris*, again—yet at the time could be owned by Astaire alone. Not that others would not try: as with Berkeley, or Shirley Temple for that matter, imitators were conspicuous, plentiful, uninspired. Such unoriginality is, alas, the lot of a majority of musicals, from then to eternity. Vaudeville routines in 1929, Hollywood overproduction in the 1930s, big-band in the 1940s, rock'n'roll in the '50s and '60s, and even, in later years, unto disco, break-dancing, the Lambada, and hip-hop: all different and all essentially the same. How much effort, after all, would it take to string a few songs and routines together with some shreds of "story" and extraneous comedy? It filled time and made money, and Bing Crosby would always play Bing Crosby. Ditto Betty Grable, then Elvis. This was what musicals were, for the most part—one pretty much like the other.[5]

Such was also the case with filmed Broadway shows, which in the 1930s and '40s looked as hollow as the made-for-movies material. Perhaps even more so. Between the crimp of the Production Code and the studios' penchant for heedlessness, little was done to retain what had already worked well, let alone translate the shows into filmic terms. Prime material was habitually denatured, ravaged, and trivialized, with outstanding songs giving way to clunkers: something called "Shanghai-De-Ho" was crammed in alongside the tattered remnants of Cole Porter's *Anything Goes* score. The casting could be desultory as well: the competent and likable Ann Sothern would not be a valid substitute for Ethel Merman, not in the vapid wreck MGM made of *Panama Hattie*. Ages before that pitiful *Chorus Line* film, or the dutifully plodding one made from *Rent*, Hollywood was giving Broadway far less than its due.

---

[5] How interchangeable could they be? Marilyn Monroe found out in 1954 when 20th Century-Fox announced that she would star in something called *Pink Tights*. After repeatedly asking for and not receiving a script, she got hold of a press item asserting that *Pink Tights* would be "a remake of a Betty Grable movie—or two!" Grable's films were the most standardized of any star short of a cowboy, MM said no, and *Pink Tights* was never filmed. Or refilmed.

Thank God, then, that the exceptions to the clones and dross were sufficient to make this part of the story a paean instead of a lament. There was Astaire, and Ginger too, making it look so blissful that no one could guess the truth just beyond camera range: he was a nerve-wracked perfectionist who worked her until her feet bled. There was Jeanette MacDonald, and forget "When I'm Calling You-oo" jokes—at best she was the real thing, not a mere prima donna on celluloid. There were also the songwriters, doing peerless work: Irving Berlin and "Cheek to Cheek," Al Dubin and Harry Warren with "Lullaby of Broadway," Jerome Kern and Dorothy Fields writing "The Way You Look Tonight." Untouchable, all of it—the *best*. The rare work of distinction or innovation also turned up. *Show Boat*, in 1936, was in many ways a model for transferring a stage show onto film, its lyricism and sensitivity emanating from a director (James Whale) of great idiosyncrasy and zero musical experience. With Disney's *Snow White and the Seven Dwarfs*, the inherent musicality of short cartoons segued effortlessly into a larger structure, with human characters operating alongside figures of fantasy, the whole of it propelled seamlessly by music and movement. Such a context was far more gratifying than the "live" formulaic likes of George Murphy or Sonja Henie and looks ahead to the time when the only good movie musicals would be those, like *Beauty and the Beast* and *The Lion King*, made of ink and paint. The *Snow White* formula could translate into flesh and blood as well, at least when done with MGM's budget, an Arlen/Harburg score, and an irreplaceable cast: *The Wizard of Oz*.

If *Snow White* and *Oz* first seemed to be ends unto themselves, their influence reached far, albeit less in "integrated" musicals à la *Oklahoma!* than in innately self-propelled cinema. Mamoulian, Astaire, and Berkeley had already intuited this notion, which Minnelli, Stanley Donen, Fosse, and others would expand on. It was governed by that most forgotten (then and later) basic truth: musical film and musical theater are cousins, not siblings. Equal but separate, using similar tools to different ends, propelled by dissimilar dynamics, each brokering a unique pact with its audience. With all his stage fame, Astaire was a different, greater performer on film, his bent for the medium so innate that he created a new dance language. By shooting numbers in one long take, he was less attempting to duplicate theatrical continuity than to present movement that scaled momentary heights only a camera could make permanent. Berkeley, crass as he was, had equal affinities. For him, the camera was participant, not spectator, even or especially when it involved overhead floral patterns or close-ups of legs. His best work is of such pure cinema that attempts to reproduce it in a live context, as in the stage version of *42nd Street*, are implicitly doomed. He was the least self-conscious of creators: to him, art was more a matter of how erotically he could pose a chorus girl. At that, he was ahead of most of the other directors of his day; Warner Bros. would compel a Michael Curtiz to treat a musical as interchangeable product, to be shot after a western and before a swashbuckler. The only specialists on a musical project were those who saw to the songs and choreography, and even their work tended to blur together. This is why so many musicals seem so earthbound—essentially, they're staged and designed identically to any other film, with songs and dances added. They may be diverting, but they're not intrinsic. They lurch, not flow, and they're meant to be forgotten in an hour.

By the early 1940s, the manufacture of musicals was a set procedure that few felt a need to improve. Why should they?—Lord knows they made the money, and with people like Betty Grable in them they were starting to make more. Still, just a few observers began to see that they could be special, and around the time *Oklahoma!* was spurring some changes on the stage, these same people began to rethink how a musical might function.[6] Here must be invoked the phrase "The Freed Unit," for lyricist Arthur Freed, an MGM employee since *The Broadway Melody*, became one hell of a good movie producer. As associate producer for *The Wizard of Oz*, he evidently laid a fair amount of groundwork for the final, miraculous result, after which, as a full producer, he and Busby Berkeley made *Babes in Arms* such a smash that it absorbed most of the red ink seeping from the costly *Oz*. *Babes* was far more a Mickey Rooney- Judy Garland vehicle than a replica of Rodgers and Hart's Broadway original, for Freed was not above that philistine habit of eviscerating stage material. Nor was his work consistently good: some of his movies—*Panama Hattie* again—were hits without any merit at all. (He himself was no prize either, with that notorious casting couch.) Yet, like other rough-diamond types, he knew talent and, far rarer, how to use it. He was generally a sound judge of material, usually knew the value of money well spent, and had a gift for hiring people who could work together.

Anyone who believes Freed's talent as a producer to be of small import should turn elsewhere—specifically, to *The Goldwyn Follies*, produced in 1938

---

[6] Stage and film musical tended to operate independently, yet the *Oklahoma!* juggernaut was such that it inspired a number of movie imitators, particularly *Can't Help Singing* and *The Harvey Girls*. Even so, good cinema will out: *The Harvey Girls*'s wondrous "Atchison, Topeka, and Santa Fe" sequence could only have happened on film.

by someone whose name is in the title. There was the money (at more than $2 million, the most expensive musical yet made), there were names (Gershwin and Balanchine, among many others), and there was detail and lavishness everywhere. The result was a molehill: a groggy divertissement, full yet empty, the extravaganza as Bermuda Triangle. Freed, who had high-price calamities as well, also had a knack that Goldwyn didn't have, that Darryl Zanuck at Fox didn't have, nor Paramount's Buddy DeSylva. Having been there, with *The Broadway Melody*, at the very beginning, he had seen it all, done most of it, and knew how a movie could soar. By 1942, even with successes like *Lady Be Good* and *Babes on Broadway*, he knew that there might be more. When he began to gather a specific coterie of artists to create musicals—Vincente Minnelli, musical stylists Roger Edens and Kay Thompson, designer Irene Sharaff, Fred Astaire and Judy Garland and Gene Kelly—he was, perhaps unwittingly, reforming the movie musical as it had been known up to that time.

The results could vary and the old formulaic schlock never stopped completely, but the finest of the work by Freed and his worthiest rivals was spectacularly beyond price. *Meet Me in St. Louis*, *Gigi*, the *American in Paris* ballet, many moments of *On the Town*, *The Band Wagon*, and *Cabin in the Sky* and others, plus the non-Freed *Seven Brides for Seven Brothers* and *Kiss Me, Kate*. And every frame of *Singin' in the Rain*. Even otherwise shaky films, at MGM as elsewhere, had superlative moments: the Astaires and Garlands and Kellys, the Doris Days and Dan Daileys and even Howard Keels, plus talents such as choreographer Jack Cole, might make musical gold transcend mediocre material. Take a titanically ordinary MGM tidbit from 1953 called *Small Town Girl*. Amid many minutes of small-town/small-time dross, two virtuoso sequences popped like grenades. In one, Ann Miller's manic tap staccati were set, with surreal illogic, amid disembodied hands playing musical instruments; in the other, Bobby Van hopped—*hopped!*—through an entire town as intricate staging and a prowling camera crane imparted an air of unbridled elation. The force responsible for both of these: Busby Berkeley, professionally a has-been but still in peak form. The past alongside the present, yet again.

The triumphs might have continued longer without television. In the 1950s, with TV as a major culprit and economics and changing tastes as significant factors, decline came. Musicals either became more faithful/less imaginative copies of Broadway (*South Pacific*, *Guys and Dolls*), or else continued to decant the old tired wine of formula and convention. *Gigi* was one of the last to succeed in terms of cinema and content, and even it was

King Arthur: Mr. Freed on the set of his most personal and likely greatest project, *Singin' in the Rain*, in the company of one of its supreme assets, Jean Hagen. (How talented was she? That's her voice speaking when Kathy is dubbing Lina.)

accused by some of being merely *My Fair Lady* with tacked-on Gallic élan. By the 1960s, the discrete molds had been cast. On the one hand, prestige direct from Broadway, high in budget and generally deficient in cinema; on the other, *Beach Blanket Elvis*, high-energy and low-everything-else. Both groups had roots in those first musical attempts in 1929, and seldom did either of them act as if they knew about the good movies that had expanded the rules in the meantime.[7] As it had been at the dawn of the talkies, stage hits and pop singers would earn automatic tickets to Hollywood, where a

---

[7] For an arresting glimpse of these two worlds in collision, look to Annette Funicello in Disney's unfortunate 1961 version of *Babes in Toyland*. The most modest bubble-gum pop is one thing, and operetta, no matter how scaled-down, is quite another. Poor Annette, and even poorer Victor Herbert.

dying studio system was still attempting to operate as if Mary Pickford was queen of the world.

The pop-and-rock stuff came and went like fast food, and no one cared much, except when the Beatles were involved; it was Broadway, in this time and mindset, which held all the good cards. When the *My Fair Lady*s and *West Side Story*s of the world were faithfully filmed, the respect rolled out like a red carpet. (One original exception to prove the rule: *Mary Poppins*.) The huge budgets were allotted, the stage people would fly west to work their magic, the voice dubbers donned their earphones, and the Oscars stood in wait. It seemed, to some, like the age of Freed writ even larger. Musicals were *finally* worthy of esteem and respect, and no more of that Busby Berkeley-type nonsense. This was art, direct from Manhattan. Not coincidentally, except for the most vital moments of *West Side Story*, it paid scant attention to all the outstanding things that musical film had been working toward years earlier. It was lushly canned theater, for the most part, not cinema, entirely forgetful of the ways in which a '36 *Show Boat* or a *Cabin in the Sky* or even a *Best Foot Forward* might be adapted to film and retain its theatricality even as it behaved like a true film. It was, in short, back to the Square One of that prehistoric *Desert Song*. On the occasions when a filmic sense was retained, as in the superbly crafted *The Sound of Music*, the falseness of the content camouflaged the truth of the cinema.

Falseness and honesty: what is a musical if not a phony way to tell the truth? Tricks and tinsel and deception can, in the right hands, be steered toward some sort of authenticity—honest emotion, a sincere assessment of humanity, a simple acknowledgment that people need diversion and each other. The absence of these is what makes bad musical films so offensive. Those big Broadway things plodding out of the dying studios in the 1960s were so fixated on surfaces—the trappings, the stage roots, the by-rote song cues and dance breaks—that they lost their sincerity and their ability to resound within a viewer's heart. A good musical forges an empathetic bond with its public; a poor or ignorant one is all merely show-and-tell. *The Broadway Melody*, for all its primeval clank, had done it the right way, eliciting discovery and delight, intimating unlimited possibility, allowing more emotional involvement than most works of musical theater. *42nd Street* had the hard-boiled integrity to offset its Berkeley ostentation. And down the line with the usual suspects, those great works that managed to shore up that top layer of filigree with plainer truth-telling and substance. In the '60s, the veneer began to matter so intensively that the moviemakers could not see how times and spectators had changed. By decade's end, the disconnect had become grotesque: assassina-tions, riots, Vietnam, and . . . *Paint Your Wagon?*[8]

The contract, then, was beginning to expire. More acutely than most film, musicals must heed their spectators. When they don't, they lose their bearings along with their timing, and shutdown occurs. They cease to matter. It had al-ready happened in 1930, with Ernst Lubitsch's elegant *Monte Carlo*. That film failed in part because most musicals were flopping and because it lacked star power. An equal contributor, though, was the specific frivolity on display. If a musical farce about madcap gamblers would have played well in 1929, it alien-ated people who saw it a full year after Black Tuesday. A quarter-century later, *It's Always Fair Weather* was in some ways a dream project: the *Singin' in the Rain* creators reuniting for a funny and bitter look at postwar mores and disen-chantment, almost *The Anti-Ike Story*. Unfortunately, it was not a time for iron-ically titled satire, and people preferred watching TV to seeing a movie that made sport of it. *Monte Carlo* and *Fair Weather* were financial losers, not ar-tistic failures, out of sync with their time, able to find redress in the form of retrospective esteem. In the 1960s, when musicals forgot about their era and their audience, the artistic wing would be let down as much as the fiscal. *Hello, Dolly!* and *Camelot* and *Doctor Dolittle* were so focused on production and pedigree that they failed to reach out to those who were expected to see them. Pure razzle-dazzle, when it lacks an emotionally genuine core, is an arid and spiritless thing. Escapism is necessary—in the late '60s there was plenty to escape—but being oblivious atop glossy was an insult. The parade in *Hello, Dolly!* was one of the largest-scale sequences ever shot in the United States, intended to give viewers a double-barreled charge: spectacle plus Streisand equals the musical equivalent of the chariot race in *Ben-Hur*. There's so much surface, and so little beneath it, that anyone in 1969 with a conscience might have flinched; the lyrics, instead of "Before the Parade Passes By," might be "Let them eat cake." Even a circus needs a soul.

By 1972, the situation was clear. Times were different, and musicals couldn't or wouldn't accommodate them. *Cabaret* came out early that year, and its fast-edit chic and mordantly frivolous allusion to dead-serious themes showed how

[8] Let it be confessed: *Paint Your Wagon* is a favored whipping child, Exhibit A of how musi-cals died. It pretended, hard, to be with-it and fresh, cloaking its fusty heart in a welter of flower-child trappings. It does this so expensively, and to such a desperate degree, that if it's not the worst musical ever made it may well be the least honest.

a musical could be simultaneously dazzling and alert. *Cabaret* was as far as a movie could be from the likes of *Doctor Dolittle*, and those who wanted to keep making and seeing musicals were hopeful. Such hopes were cruelly dashed, then, with *Lost Horizon* and *Mame*. In the year of Watergate, what could be less apt than a miscast television icon trying to sing and dance and be Auntie Mame? When out plugging *Mame* on television and press junkets, Lucille Ball went on about how her movie could give people sunshine and hope. While a good musical might have done something like that, *Mame* could only coalesce every apprehension about musicals being over. They were, in fact, so out of fashion as to seem cursed: Barbra Streisand moved on to dim comedies and an atrocious *A Star Is Born*, Julie Andrews to television and career moratorium. Liza Minnelli and Diana Ross could not choose suitable material, and someone like Joel Grey couldn't fit in anywhere. Bob Fosse preferred dark movies and Broadway, and Minnelli *père* had no successors. *That's Entertainment!* showed people what had been, and then *The Wiz* showed what remained. Small wonder that "movie musical" became a synonym for nostalgia.

The one silver lining was that in this time of past yearning and current dross, the realization grew, then grew some more, that musicals had been wonderful and important, perhaps even necessary. While many of them fit better into a more innocent time, the best of them could transcend the years. Sometimes, even, they had a few new moments: if John Travolta in his white disco suit was more nervy than Fred Astaire in his tux, he was equally kinetic and valid. *Saturday Night Fever* was good old wine in a brand new bottle, filled with unconscious reminders of the past. Clearly, connections were still possible between what had been and what was current, between a script and a song, between the movie musical and the modern spectator. History was not only resonant; it could also be pertinent.

So, even in a dark time, the musical form per se was not the problem. As much difficulty lay in finding the way to make it all meaningful, even comprehensible. Besides a basic skill set, it takes a sharp awareness of who is being performed to at any given time. Look again at *Mame* and Watergate. Hearty diversion in the face of national crisis is well and good; as *42nd Street* proved, it's one of the things that musicals do best. But understand what you're doing and why, and how it will be viewed. Shortchanging the material won't cut it, and neither will underestimating the audience. If musicals are in some ways about make-believe, they must be made at least in part by someone with a sense of hard-assed reality. In the 1930s and 1940s, most musicals were directed by run-of-the-studio guys who showed up ready to shoot and did it. It wasn't art, and it needed more inspiration, but at least these hacks knew what a public expected. By the 1980s, there would be the occasional disaster—above all, *A Chorus Line*—made by people who didn't know from musicals or audiences or even, sometimes, cinema. As the 1990s beckoned, music videos became so entrenched in the popular taste that musicals seemed to many an elongated and insufferable parody, not the other way around. When a big live-action musical finally did come out, it was the near-unbearable *Evita*, which looked like a music video with two hours of outtakes spliced in. Except for a few animated films, there was little else . . . and, frankly, who's to know if it's not to this same dust that we shall return?

Musicals, then, must know their heritage and their times. They must also know how to elicit the proper response—which, baldly put, must entail a viewership of sufficient amount to make a profit. Making a musical into a financial success is a risky game, for such a film does not run up the grosses of a *Titanic* or *Avatar*. *The Sound of Music* was a whale of an exception, as was *Grease*, but there are few other examples—which didn't stop studios from running through Versailles sums to make a *Hello, Dolly!* or *Camelot*. The bigger-is-better hubris of such efforts failed to heed an unalterable dynamic: because of their particular demands, musicals are more costly than most movies, and care must be taken to keep those costs in some kind of proportion to a projected gross. It needs to be remembered that these movies, even those with potentially wide appeal, are not for everyone. The creators of *Chicago*, for example, pinched every penny they could to keep the budget down. The gamble can be as extreme in cinema as in a Broadway catastrophe like *Dance of the Vampires*. For further verification, ask the producers who recklessly turned the 1982 movie version of *Annie* into the most expensive American film up to that time, then saw the worldwide gross fall far short of expectation and break-even.

If history broadcasts some cautionary notes about financial figures, it does so also in terms of timing and volume. Broadway and London, with their constant influx of tourists and visitors, can handle a large musical load; movie screens cannot, and excessive familiarity does not breed affection. The musical pileup of 1930 was so intensive and awful that few could tell the good from the ghastly, and in 1968 there was the disaster that befell Julie Andrews when she undertook to play the Broadway star (and musical-film flop) Gertrude Lawrence. As it turned out, there were two big musical-star-lady bios opening within a few weeks of each other. No question, *Funny Girl* was the one with the advantage; but without such nagging, unshakable comparisons, *Star!* might have had a slightly less grim fate.

Some simply won't respond to musicals at all, no matter how many or few are coming out. From 1929 onward, there has always been a core of people who simply say "it's a musical" and stay away. All sorts of rationalizations can be made to explain why some people just don't like musicals. "Unreal" will always be a complaint, as if all *cinéma* is *verité*. Others will zero in on perceived triviality or the ingrained inferiority of film to stage. For some, a major problem has been the great split in American music. Show music used to be the common coin, so perfectly in line with the pop music of the day that a score like *The Pajama Game* sounds like it was taken off a juke box. Then came rock, and the equation shattered. When rock took over pop, musicals were effectively taken out of the mainstream and removed from relevance. Sure, rock music has been used to make musicals, occasionally with arresting results (*The Who's Tommy, The Rose,* parts of *Hair, Hedwig and the Angry Inch*). Generally, rock and movie musicals are uneasy partners, except in documentaries and concert features as well as music videos. The best musicals, in film as on Broadway, usually won't rock out. For some audiences that makes them automatically outdated, new or old, or at least alien. A Madonna may try to bridge the gap between rock and, say, Marilyn Monroe, but irony is no substitute for ability, and few with any sense can accept the result unquestioningly. For many, the changes in music have forcibly robbed musicals of their currency, which is another reason they aren't much on screens anymore. When a *Moulin Rouge!* compacts together any number of musical styles into a gigantic old-and-new synthesis, the result is fascinating in part because it acknowledges how much things have changed. In 2003, when it gave an Eminem rap number the Best Song Oscar over a new tune added to *Chicago*, even the Motion Picture Academy conceded what had happened.

The disconnect from the late 1960s onward will never be completely eradicated, and it's hard to envision that there will ever again be a large number of new musicals—nor many good ones. So they have less opportunity to shine and need to work hard to bridge gaps that once did not exist. Fortunately, there will always be a However: there are still, on occasion, people who can understand what musicals have been and are able to translate that past into a newer syntax. The personnel have changed and there are vastly different ways to move from story to song, but ultimately it's still the same movie, and all the predecessors exist to show the way—*The Broadway Melody* for the basic setup of script and music; Al Jolson for rampant star power; *Love Me Tonight* and the films of René Clair to show how the rhythms of music and film can intertwine; *42nd Street* for grit and nervous energy; Astaire's work for its intuitive understanding of storytelling through movement; *The Wizard of Oz* to show how smoothly a musical can set off the intersection of ordinary with fantastic; *Meet Me in St. Louis*, with its sensitivity to time and place, décor, and emotionality; *Singin' in the Rain* for showing that a script can matter as much as song and dance, and for taking such sheer delight in being a musical film about musical films; *Cabaret*, with virtuosic editing as the link between song, storytelling, and commentary. Many others as well; these are among the most basic, the ones giving abundant lessons and inspiration.

Not many of the musicals stemming from these ancestors will be great, since pallid recycling will always be an inevitability. As Marilyn Monroe divined when she balked at *Pink Tights*, the same buck-minded people will eternally try to fool the public with the same script over and over again. Providentially, more important recurrences are also at work here—those of inspiration striking twice, or witty *hommage*, or good lessons wisely taken to heart. For all the rank imitations they spawned, neither *The Broadway Melody* nor *42nd Street* nor *Meet Me in St. Louis* could be genuinely replicated. Nevertheless, in some fashion, they can be honored. By establishing what musicals could be and could achieve, they and the worthy others became not merely historical signposts but ever-present forebears. Nor is that history a dead thing, like minstrel shows or flower power or civility in politics. It lives and it transforms. Look, once again, at *Singin' in the Rain*: can loving acknowledgment—and active deployment—of one's ancestors be taken any further? *Chicago*, the movie, alluded to Astaire and Marilyn and Fosse and dozens of others. *Nine* had its own references as well, albeit in a markedly less inspired fashion, and so did *Les Misérables*, love it or hate it. As for *Moulin Rouge!*...well, there was little that it didn't quote. One way or another, musicals keep finding ways to engage their viewers while connecting the past with the future. Those ways can be new at the same time that they're very, very old. From *The Broadway Melody* to *Rock of Ages*, from Jolson to hip hop, it's all of a piece. Any musical on stage or film that says it doesn't look to its progenitors is deliberately lying, or else it's fooling itself. Either way, the audience will always know better.

Chapter 2

Where Do They Come From (and Where Do They Go)?

T he first Broadway musical made into a sound film, *The Desert Song*, was shot in 1928 and released in 1929. How primitive is it? The visuals recall old newspaper photos and the sound is like two cans and a string. One latter-day viewer described it as "the oldest movie ever made," while another claimed to have spotted a pterodactyl traversing the desert sky. It's not unwatchable, in the manner of some early sound films, because of the music and some game performers and the way Myrna Loy, as a lurid half-caste, wipes the floor with everything and everyone. What is most remarkable about it is that neither the primitive Warner Bros. technology nor the archaic material is what makes it so alien: that comes, instead, with the jarring fashion in which stage conventions collide with the needs of cinema. Lines, blocking, cues—all, when projected onto a screen, are more obvious than ever. The very first of its kind, and it instantaneously raised all the issues that have loomed ever since.

Original versus Adaptation is an argument central to musical films, and it should be said upfront that, from pre-*The Desert Song* to post-*Les Miz*, there are no clearcut answers. Cinema will never leave musical theater alone, and the path from one to the other is perilous, just as the relationship between movies and stage is symbiotic and inevitable and often torturous. Without theater, cinema might still be a matter of peepshows and ninety-second documentaries of Herald Square. Musical theater, and opera and vaudeville, were necessary components of musical cinema at its birth and afterward, and the models they set up have been both troubling and seductive. The temptations are nothing if not irresistible—the famous titles, the loved songs, the memories of those who saw them onstage, the grosses of *The Sound of Music*. Then, at the end of it, there can be the feeling that film and theater should be kept as far away from each other as spouses waging a messy divorce.

Filmed shows are the biggest single reason some otherwise sympathetic folk decry the entirety of musical cinema. It seems, often enough, that these films offer an infinite cluster of damnable things that connote the medium at its most philistine: the cut songs, slashed and dumbed-down scripts, wan casting, dormant imagination, low energy. It feels, with some shows, that every good onstage quality was systematically amputated en route to the screen. *Man of La Mancha* and *Lady in the Dark* and *A Little Night Music*. *Anything Goes*, twice. The color filters in *South Pacific*. Such titles are as a cudgel used to argue that movies never get it right. The bungled scripts and dubbed voices. Not using Julie Andrews or Ethel Merman. The entirety of *A Chorus Line*. A *Can-Can* with only a vague offscreen reference to "I Love Paris." The color filters in *South Pacific*, worth mentioning twice.[1] When the mind strays to *Cabaret* or the 1936 *Show Boat* or *The Pajama Game*—outstanding movies by any standards—thoughts of *The Wiz* may make it snap back. Yet and even so, it continues.

Adapting a stage musical for film is never not a tricky proposition. The artifice that works on the stage can quickly become most peculiar on camera, as can many performers in these works, especially when observed singing in close-up. It is never clear how much a play should be opened up, or kept confined. And how, exactly, does a film move from its script to its music? Song cues onstage may be an accepted convention, especially in the looser musical theater of the 1920s and 1930s that could drop a song in from nowhere; pulling this off on film is trickier dramatically and even technically, when the sound might change disorientingly from live to prerecorded. Small wonder that movies are often more comfortable with having a song done in a performance, as opposed to an offstage, context. There would also be, for more than thirty years, the hazard of censorship. Also, right at square one, is the question of length: except for some of the heavyweights, a movie musical will have a

---

[1] To be fair, there are reasons for most of these. The exception is the near-total elimination of "I Love Paris," unless the people in charge of *Can-Can* were seeking one more way to make their film dumb and wrong.

shorter running time, meaning that songs and script are cut, not always wisely.[2] Some differences lay in the variance in the audience. Stage spectators tended to be urban, relatively sophisticated, accustomed to how musicals operate; movie audiences were of a more egalitarian common denominator. For people who worked on the stage, the crassness of film, and of those who produced it, could seldom serve any good purpose other than financial, while filmmakers deluded themselves into believing that nearly anything that succeeded on the stage could be made into a movie, no matter that it might involve the dilution necessary to draw in a far larger audience. When the relationship between the two powers was satisfactory, one might supply what the other only implied. Unfortunately, in many cases, a wholesale dumbing-down would be involved. The perils were and are constant, and vultures always circle in anticipation.

Joan Crawford, that least oblique of movie icons, never sang "Indian Love Call," so far as anyone is aware. Nevertheless, she did traipse through some faux-Canadian MGM pines as *Rose-Marie* in 1928. This was part of a long silent-film tradition of filming just about any big musical show that had a strong or at least coherent plot. There were versions of *The Merry Widow* and *Sally* and *Kid Boots* and many more: money is money, and music needn't matter very much. Nor would words, for that matter, since the arrival of sound lessened none of the tension between film and theater: writer Samson Raphaelson, for one, hated what Warner Bros. made of his play *The Jazz Singer*. As for *The Desert Song*, whose hero-in-disguise plot played like an over-the-top silent romance, bombastic dialogue and major song cues and florid music made it a compellingly escapist fantasy on the stage. In that prehistoric movie version, it clung to its stage roots with such obsessive fidelity that it seemed too literal, too candid in the wrong way, the camera diminishing the property and the performers. This was what mattered most about *The Desert Song* on film, and even though it was a huge financial success one puzzled review after another said the same thing: "Something different is needed."[3]

---

[2] People wonder about why movies would sometimes replace older stage songs with new ones: surprise, it was about the money. Studios bought into music publishers, new songs were part of the profit machine, and quality was a secondary priority. Some things don't ever change.

[3] One grandchild of that first *Desert Song*, sporting the same weird authenticity, was the film of the Phil Silvers show *Top Banana*. It tried to give the impression it was actually shot in a theater, stage sets and all. In, good grief, 3-D.

The other Broadway-derived smash of 1929, *Rio Rita*, managed the transfer more graciously. Indeed, it was so skillful in filtering its stage protocol through cinematic resources that it was long considered the gold standard for filming a show. Viewed today (sadly, in a cut-down version) it looks to be neck-and-neck with *The Desert Song* in the primitive-cinema division: such can be the whims of history. When it was new, it was widely acclaimed as a graceful marriage of theater and filmmaking. The former involved a relatively intact translation; the latter encompassed location shooting, early Technicolor, and a sound example of movie-star casting in Bebe Daniels, who could both sing and interact suavely with the camera.[4] Here, then, is the ancestor of the high-powered Broadway-on-film work that otherwise began in 1955 with *Oklahoma!* and continues up to the present: well-crafted and beholden to its source, playing it safe while, if the audience is lucky, holding a few wild cards.

As sound film settled in, the faithfulness to the original became so less prevalent that, until about the mid-1950s, the resemblance could be as fleeting as to border on the coincidental. This wasn't, at the time, quite as onerous a practice as it now seems, since even on the stage few musical comedies were considered to be set in concrete. The scripts and songs could be changed as frequently as the casts, and even the greatest musical of its time—*Show Boat*—was altered and cut down at will, scenes and songs dropped or curtailed. On film, it became less a matter of how faithful a film could be than how much of a show's original spirit might be evoked or violated. From 1934 to 1936, for example, there was a quintet of movies made from Jerome Kern shows, three done in collaboration with Oscar Hammerstein II: *The Cat and the Fiddle*, *Music in the Air*, *Sweet Adeline*, *Roberta*, and, best for last, *Show Boat*. Kern's work had long been a dominant force on Broadway, not least because the scripts for his shows tended to have a little more edge than the usual fare. Even *Roberta*, which is little more than fashion parades punctuated by great songs, gave its characters some definition through what would later be termed story arcs—"Smoke Gets in Your Eyes" acquires even more stature if you care about the woman who's singing it. Save for *Music in the Air* dropping "The Song Is You" and the rather drab *Adeline*, these were films that respected both their sources and their audiences. Quibbles over changes are in large part

---

[4] Daniels was selected over Broadway's original Rita, Ethelind Terry, who then proved the aptness of the call by starring as an imperious diva in MGM's *Lord Byron of Broadway*. Ever see a performer do *everything* wrong?

compensated for by astute casting and a good deal of smart filmmaking—two factors that would be less in evidence over the following years.

Unlike Kern, Cole Porter wrote shows that constantly had trouble making it onto film, and the 1936 version of *Anything Goes* goes a far piece in explaining why. In a way, this is a film that doesn't exist—not lost (albeit retitled for TV purposes as, go figure, *Tops Is the Limit*), but an oddly milquetoast distortion that drops all but three and a half songs, much of the plot, and nearly all the exuberance and charm. This happened despite what seems to be some good intentions, or at least a lot of cash. As the show had been Porter's biggest hit to date, Paramount was required to pay a near-record $100,000 for the rights and spent an additional million or so on production. Since it included some ace talent from the show itself (Ethel Merman, plus writers Howard Lindsay and Russell Crouse) and from Hollywood (Bing Crosby and director Lewis Milestone), it should, even if slightly denatured, be dandy fun. Should. Certainly there have been less faithful adaptations—including, in a putrid 1956 sort-of-remake, *Anything Goes* itself. There have been less well-cast films, with stranger production concepts than that weird moon-swing-thing Merman has to sit in while singing "I Get a Kick Out of You." There have been more egregious additions than that "Shanghai-De-Ho" number near the end, and feelings even more sinking than the one that comes on as soon as Merman blares out "Staaaars over Shaaanghaaaiii."

All this should lead, correctly, to the inference that this *Anything Goes* is not a terminal fiasco. So why, exactly, is it so bloody dispiriting? Why does it seem, with tiresome efficiency, to sum up the entire fractured relationship between Broadway and Hollywood? Some, many, of the specifics came from an expected place: the Production Code. In 1934 the Code had leaned so hard on Porter's *Gay Divorce* that even the title needed changing: while a divorce is never happy, Code logic went, there could be such a thing as *The Gay Divorcée*. With *Anything Goes*, neither script nor songs escaped intact: deletions included much of the title song (sex), "All Through the Night" (ditto), "Blow, Gabriel, Blow" (sacrilege), and the cocaine of "I Get a Kick Out of You," supplanted by "perfume from Spain." Countless lines and situations were laundered from raucous into merely energetic, with vapid talk about not much in particular vaguely spotting songs here and there. The casting, at least, had promise, since Crosby replaced the stage's coarser and older William Gaxton, who starred in lots of hit shows without managing to be indelible—something

Shanghaied: Few films point out Hollywood's distortion of Broadway more thoroughly than the 1936 *Anything Goes*. And few moments in it do so more jarringly than the "Shanghai-de-Ho" number, with Ethel Merman and Bing Crosby, plus a bewigged chorus. Lots of gestures, lots of fans, and absolutely no Cole Porter.

Crosby could do without breaking a sweat. Again, unfortunately, there's that script, enlarging Crosby's role over Merman's to no useful end save to supply him with new, non-Porter songs.[5] As the would-be Public Enemy No. 1, the expert Charlie Ruggles cannot bumble with the beatific lunacy of the stage's Victor Moore, and only Ida Lupino—crisp casting for a nonsinging ingenue— seems to genuinely give herself to the situations.

Censorship and casting, then, can assume part of the blame for *Anything Goes* turning out as it did. So too can Milestone's slack involvement with the material, plus the generic insouciance that was beginning—likely but glaringly—to standardize Bing Crosby's performance style. More than all these,

---

[5] One of the new songs is called "Moonburn." Really. Reportedly, Crosby had wanted his wife, Dixie Lee, in the Merman role. That might account for his non-chemistry with Merman— it's almost as if they're in different movies.

there is something that can, for lack of a better term, be called the Hollywood Machine. Call them dream or glamour factories, each of the major American studios operated under a series of guidelines and aesthetics that would not necessarily treat a Broadway property in a different way from a movie original. At Paramount, this assembly-line approach was so efficient that the movie *Anything Goes* was in theaters less than ten weeks after the show *Anything Goes* closed. It also meant that it would be, in effect, just another Bing Crosby picture, with Merman's presence in the cast due far less to Paramount's wanting to capture the show's essence than to expedience and availability. All this is why *Anything Goes* often seems indistinguishable from *The Big Broadcast of 1938*, another gleaming Paramount musical set on a boat. Like so many other filmed shows, it forgets its roots, acts like a movie original, and betrays its source.

Forgetting, it must be noted, is not always a bad thing, because it's not always easy to recall just how many shows were making it onto the screen in the later 1930s and through the '40s. In one way or another most of the big ones were filmed: *On Your Toes, The Boys from Syracuse, Babes in Arms, Too Many Girls, Hellzapoppin', Louisiana Purchase, This Is the Army, Lady in the Dark, Knickerbocker Holiday, One Touch of Venus, Up in Central Park.*[6] Plus a whole lot of Cole Porter—*DuBarry Was a Lady, Panama Hattie, Let's Face It, Something for the Boys,* and *Mexican Hayride. Babes in Arms* was a huge hit, but it is not the show—not without "My Funny Valentine," it isn't—and of the others, really, what is remembered? Mainly that they were changed, eviscerated, laundered. That most of the original music would be cut—in the case of the dowdy *On Your Toes,* everything except the "Slaughter on 10th Avenue" ballet. That what could be a delight onstage (*Syracuse, Venus*) became doltish or wilted as filmed. That people like Ethel Merman (*Hattie*) and Bert Lahr (*DuBarry*) should not be replaced by Ann Sothern and Red Skelton. Plus, notoriously, that a work as provocative and inventive as *Lady in the Dark* could—with much money and miscalculation—be made banal and over-accessorized.

---

[6] There was also the decidedly odd case of *I Married an Angel*. Rodgers and Hart wrote it in 1933, while under contract to MGM, as a vehicle for Jeanette MacDonald. After it was scuttled by script problems and censorship, Rodgers and Hart successfully reconfigured it for Broadway in 1938. When it came back to the screen in 1942, again with MacDonald, it was every bit as denatured and distorted as any of its other adapted fellows.

The boorish expedition of that Hollywood Machine might lead to the wish that there had been some kind of moratorium through the later '30s into the '40s. This was a time when many film musicals, originals as well as stage properties, possessed craft without inspiration. The people making them were great, indisputably: their names are a litany repeated through these pages. Yet it's hard to not hold on to the regret for the wasted talent and missed opportunities. Instead of more works like *Swing Time* or *Show Boat*, there was a whole armada of *Anything Goes*–type pieces, time-passers with high production values and great music and occasional fine numbers along with ragged scripts and little resonance. With routine at this level, it's no surprise that the originals and the filmed shows tended to blur together. It might be summed up by the title of one of the least of the many B-musicals made at workaday Universal: *Sing a Jingle*, it was called, and that's what it all seemed to be.

During World War II, with musicals proffering cheer-up diversion worthy of a Nobel, their profit margin skyrocketed. Such success did not necessarily supply incentive to make musicals different or better; it would seem especially unlikely that a stage work would come to the screen as something other than generic pablum. Thus it was with stark relief that two 1943 films from MGM managed to stand out. Both were supervised by that same Arthur Freed so often sneered at by revisionistas. And, verily, Freed was not a genius any more than he was a first-rate lyricist. Still, these two films, both adaptations, tell something about the work he could sponsor. It's not that *Cabin in the Sky* is consistently great, nor free from cringe-worthy moments and stereotypes. But look at it alongside other musicals made around the same time, whether an original like *Song of the Islands* (Betty Grable, hula, Technicolor) or a filmed show like *Panama Hattie*, with its miscasting and truncated score. *Cabin in the Sky* had been far more an artistic than a financial success on Broadway, and there had been only a tiny handful of big-studio films to have an all-black cast. With both factors, Freed was taking some chances and expending some clout, which the show clearly warranted, and he oversaw any number of wise decisions: retaining Ethel Waters and Rex Ingram from the original cast, supplementing them with Eddie Anderson (Rochester) and Lena Horne from the Hollywood ranks, tossing in such plush add-ons as Louis Armstrong and Duke Ellington, and giving a major chance to a new director, Vincente Minnelli. Even the lamented practice of cutting and replacing songs was upgraded with Harold Arlen and Yip Harburg writing "Happiness Is Just a Thing Called Joe." Condescension and compromise are still present—come on, it's white 1940s

Hollywood—but alongside them are a conviction and a hand-crafted individuality that seem far removed from that usual assembly line. The palpably warm feeling when the lights (or commercials) come up after *Cabin in the Sky* is not simply because of Ethel Waters's greatness or Lena Horne's purring insinuation or the way the script and songs balance each other, or even the meticulous way Minnelli handles his cast and his camera. It's because, from Freed on down, they all cared and wanted to do it right.

It was more through coincidence than anything else that Arthur Freed filmed three more shows immediately after *Cabin in the Sky*. *Girl Crazy* was another of Freed's Mickey Rooney–Judy Garland duets, using enough of the Gershwin score (the show's strength) and jettisoning enough of the book (its weakness) to make a satisfying end to that series. *DuBarry Was a Lady* was another of the Cole Porter transfers, in this case a show with so much dirt that there was no way it could escape being mangled. While it was less insipid than *Panama Hattie*, neither Red Skelton nor a dubbed Lucille Ball could compete with the stage's Bert Lahr and Ethel Merman. Ball also figured (as a replacement for Lana Turner) in the most interesting of the trio, *Best Foot Forward*. That show had been notable for its zippy score and youthful energy, and both somehow survived the transfer in fair measure. Again there were welcome contributions from members of the stage cast (blessedly, Nancy Walker), and even the usually film-averse William Gaxton was on hand, though he was not in the original show. While there were tweaks and changes—the original high school setting was turned, for wartime purposes, into a military academy—an amusing, not-great show was being respected, and made into a better film because of it. Even a mid-range piece of fizz can benefit by treatment that goes a little beyond the usual, simple drive to get it done.

Original musicals tended to dominate the later part of the 1940s and, considering the way things like *One Touch of Venus* turned out, this was just as well. Freed came back to the fore in 1949 with the oddly paradoxical *On the Town*, a success far more on its own terms than as a version of something else.[7] Then, soon enough, came another Merman-without-Merman piece, *Annie Get*

---

[7] A case can be made for *On the Town* being the first successful reimagining of a show. If the new songs were inferior to the Bernstein originals, it was, on its own terms, first rate. The same is true with *Cabaret* and *Hair* and even *Gentlemen Prefer Blondes*, all successful as films if not records of their shows. As Ann Miller sang (wonderfully) in the rare good film of a Cole Porter show, *Kiss Me Kate*, one is true in one's fashion.

Your Gun, which managed to be both cinematic and occasionally stiff, done with reasonable faithfulness to the show and with an unquestioned if controversial star at its center. Betty Hutton tends to divide audiences—some can't forget that she replaced Judy Garland, some love her, some can't forgive her for not being Merman, some find her plain exhausting. Like her or not, she holds the screen with such ferocity that *Annie* is boosted past the realm of another-big-MGM-musical to being an event. With its splash and spectacle and color, *Annie Get Your Gun* was one of the hits that pointed the way by which film could compete with its new rival. And, no question, television hit musicals hard: with Ed Sullivan offering blue-chip singers on Sunday night, how was it better to get dressed, leave the house, then pay to see something that might be mediocre? There were even Broadway shows on the home screen: as early as 1950, Martha Raye appeared in a live-broadcast *Anything Goes.* Cut down and constricted, but convenient and available and free. Film, in order to survive, was going to need to adapt, and this notion would be expanded figuratively with bigger films and literally with the new wide screens the musical would be required to fill.

Just as crucially as the wider screens, the entire experience of going to see a movie musical grew bigger as well, and adapted shows were central to that expansion. It's easy to forget, in the today time of wide openings and an all-important first weekend, how different moviegoing has become in the past half-century. It has, in truth, changed as much as movies. More so, perhaps. Marketing and access now make film attendance almost an extension of television or the Internet, with overpriced junk food added, and this is a world away from how big movies, musicals in particular, were presented in the 1950s and 1960s. During that heyday time, roadshow engagements were the first-class travel of cinema, given to only the most elite or expensive of films. They had been present in major cities since the silent era, and early musicals like *The Broadway Melody* started their runs in this fashion. After the Depression called an end to such things, only a top-tier piece like *Gone With the Wind* would buck the trend, but in the 1950s it all resumed being an especially ritzy alternative to television. The key to the whole notion of roadshows was that going to see a film could be made as deluxe as, *the same as,* a trip to the theater. The buildup began long before the movie opened, with large newspaper ads that included a mail-order form. The seats were reserved and high-priced, and for a much-anticipated film, there might be a months' long wait before there was any availability. The film would open in New York and slowly roll out to other cities, running twice per day in theaters kitted out with lavish decor and a uniformed staff. Audience members were expected to dress for the event, men in coat and tie and women with hats and gloves. A glossy souvenir program was available for purchase, the washroom attendants expected tips, and the feature would not be accompanied by the crass likes of a cartoon, newsreel, or trailers. For a movie good enough to hold up under the presentation, a roadshow run could last for months, or in a case like *The Sound of Music*, years, and bring in huge profits. If it was a hit, the regular-priced continuous showings would not follow until much later, then finally move on to the smaller towns and drive-ins.

In the mid-1950s, Broadway adaptations became the cornerstone of the roadshow film experience, which made the rivalry with their theatrical forebears more intense than ever. Since they were expected to provide bang for buck, it was little surprise that they became (as a later, irreverent movie musical film would term it) bigger, longer, and uncut. *Oklahoma!* was the first of them, filmed under the watchful eyes of Rodgers and Hammerstein in the impressive Todd-AO widescreen process. Faithful it was, and beautifully shot on location, with an Ado Annie and Will (Gloria Grahame and Gene Nelson) to die for, everyone singing in his or her own voice, and not off the rails in any particular way, save possibly for Rod Steiger's conflation of Jud Fry with Stanley Kowalski. This was a correct, enjoyable production, and between those lines it can be read that no, in certain ways it wasn't terribly exciting. Perhaps the presence of Rodgers and Hammerstein enforced the heaping of reverence atop faithfulness, making what seemed exhilarating on the stage oddly earthbound on that big screen. Somehow the cornfields and surrey rides and Agnes de Mille ballets didn't astound as much as they should have, and this munificent placidity would be an increasing problem as roadshow musicals continued their expensive reign.

The concurrent *Guys and Dolls* was hobbled by other factors, notably overproduction and an approach that evoked neither stage nor film nor anything viable in between. Visually unprepossessing, it had an annoyingly overlit stylization that included the most spotless sewers in history. People flocked to *Guys and Dolls* to see how Marlon Brando would fare in a musical—not terribly, all things considered—but, Jean Simmons excepted, there was even less Broadway magic up on the screen than in *Oklahoma!* Two key choices, made with an eye toward movie audiences, pointed up much of the problem: a big name (Frank Sinatra) completely miscast, and a prestigious director, Joseph L. Mankiewicz, with no detectable affinity for the genre.[8] What was most germane, and befitting the whole roadshow era, was that *Guys and Dolls* and *Oklahoma!* and the forthcoming *South Pacific* and *Porgy and Bess* were the most expensive musicals, and among the priciest studio films, made up to that time.

By the early 1960s, musicals were the designated hitters of the whole blockbuster mentality. A certain elephantiasis, respectful yet pernicious, was beginning to creep in, and more and more of these films would fall under that spell. There had still been, in the '50s, reasonably scaled film versions of *Where's Charley* and *The Pajama Game* and, less happily, *Brigadoon* and *Kismet* and *Pal Joey*. In the '60s, *The Music Man* and *Gypsy* and *Bye Bye Birdie* were all "big" films in one way or another, yet marketed conventionally, without the high pressure and higher risks of the roadshow experience. As such, they were a vanishing breed: it would soon be all or nothing. This fact was cemented after all the attention and Oscars bestowed upon *West Side Story*. Again there were casting problems—Natalie Wood was understandable, but Richard Beymer as Tony?—and fortunately there were also the vitality and imagination that come when filmmakers extend themselves. Any number of parts of *West Side Story,* the dubbed voices and compromises and aura of self-importance, could be quibbled with; at its best, though, and at its core, it was valid and important—a work that many had loved onstage made into a movie that many more love equally.

My Fair Lady was, of course, the official grand coronation of the whole process. On Broadway it was such an event that there was a whole subgenre of jokes about how hard it was to scare up tickets, and the pinnacle was of such height that Warner Bros. was compelled to pay a fee higher than a studio had ever paid for any property.[9] The immense production cost atop that initial sum was felt to necessitate the movies' best-known example of name-recognition casting: Audrey Hepburn as Eliza Doolittle instead of Julie Andrews, and gamely attempting to do her own singing. In the end she was dubbed, while Andrews

---

[8] Even a mundane studio workhorse might have done better, as with Walter Lang, who helmed the following year's *The King and I*. The peculiar issue of directors is discussed more in a later chapter; suffice it to mention here that assigning Joshua Logan the *South Pacific* film seemed like a good idea at the time. He had directed it on Broadway and already had movie success with *Picnic* and *Bus Stop*. Look what happened.

[9] Few have paid it since, either; $5.5 million—in 1963 dollars, yet—is still almost unheard-of for a stage property. Imagine paying the inflation-adjusted sum of $75 million or so. Not even Harry Potter books could ask that upfront.

earned underdog glamour and an Oscar for *Mary Poppins*. Except for the back-lash, *My Fair Lady* turned out exactly the way its makers intended: lavish (the costliest musical up to that time, once again), elevated, Oscar-laden, and her-metic. It looked beautiful, it sounded fine, and Hepburn's Ascot hat nearly rated its own sequel. Every frame of film seemed emblazoned with a command for the audience to genuflect; accordingly, few dared say aloud what some felt—that Warners should have fitted the auditoriums with windows to let in some air, that any number of smaller works owned more musical-film integrity, and that it had been far more zesty and warm and likable on the stage. With a *Cabin in the Sky*, a creative team on a small budget created something close to magical; with *My Fair Lady*, the goal was to stick close to Broadway while making it bigger, so Jack L. Warner and his people just kept throwing money at it.

Poses: The singularly formal stylization of *My Fair Lady* on film is adored by some and irksome to others. Here, an on-the-set shot of Audrey Hepburn and Rex Harrison gives a good representation of many of *Fair Lady's* components—the style, the stiffness, the wit, the calculation. Also the money—not least that this Cecil Beaton dress and hat fetched millions in a 2011 auction.

Certainly the ploy worked, for *My Fair Lady* was a big hit. What, then, could *The Sound of Music* be called? Anyone not alive when it came out might have difficulty grasping just how much this movie meant to people. At least to some: seldom since 1865 had the nation been so sharply divided. The show had not been one of Rodgers and Hammerstein's finer hours, for many thought it treacly, well below the standards of *Carousel* or *The King and I*. The movie, conversely, was phenomenal: inescapable, immune to brickbats and carping, an all-devouring leviathan. If *My Fair Lady* equated moviegoing with theater attendance, this one replaced Mass for many people. It had a lark learning to pray, a flock of nuns who foil the Nazis, and Julie Andrews, who seemed touched with some kind of divine spark. The jokes came out in full force, as did the outrage of critics like Pauline Kael, but nothing could hide the fact that as a film, *The Sound of Music* was devastatingly well made. Not only technically impeccable, with some of the best location work this side of *Lawrence of Arabia*, but with a minutely calibrated ability to produce every desired response from an audience. What the songs and Andrews didn't do, director Robert Wise did. The kids were darling, the nuns roguish and cute, the Nazis out of an operetta. All this, plus "Do Re Mi"! None of that hoity-toity-Shaw *Fair Lady* nonsense here. This was schmaltz as Olympus, the movie that 1965 America wanted, and it was a musical. It was also, for a while, the top-grossing film of all time. The movies had finally trumped Broadway.

My Fair Lady and *The Sound of Music* made studios more enthusiastic about musicals, or more properly about the potential profits of big musicals, as opposed to the pop-driven cheeseballs yet being made with Elvis or Annette or even Herman's Hermits. The budgets went up, the demeanor grew more confident, the marketing more insistent, and it all devolved into a latter-day rendition of "What shall it profit a man, if he shall gain the whole world, and lose his own soul?" Busby Berkeley composed his musical sequences while sitting in his bathtub or on his camera crane; the people in charge of these created them while calling their stockbrokers. The aesthetic was so pervasive that when a *Doctor Dolittle* or *Happiest Millionaire* was made from original material, it seemed as much stage-derived as any of the others. Razzle and splendor took precedence over all else, and studio backlots were graced with ever-more-colossal sets depicting Camelot or 1890s New York, or Dickens's London. Soon, the entire roadshow experience began to feel off-kilter and anachronistic. *Camelot*, enormously expensive and uniquely turgid, was the first major post–*Sound of Music* disappointment, and after a respite in 1968 with *Funny*

Girl and *Oliver!*, some $15 million chickens began to come home to roost in the decayed remnants of the old studio system. *Hello, Dolly!* offended a few by casting Barbra Streisand, and many by the tons of cash and meringue it used to inflate a nice musical comedy into the biggest epic this side of *War and Peace*. When *Sweet Charity*, billed as "The Musical Motion Picture of the 70's," failed to run past the fall of 1969, the end was at hand.

Besides the change in times and tastes, the big musicals were killed by their unwillingness to stretch, as Broadway was slowly learning to do in the 1960s. There was the rise of rock music in shows—a stiletto that could cut both ways—and there were also the concept shows of producer-director Harold Prince and others. By the late 1960s, the usual literalism was being deserted in favor of work that might allude or imply or have surface and subtext so discrete as to plunge the audience into evening-long irony. It was tricky and it could be grim in the wrong hands; when done by Prince or Bob Fosse or Michael Bennett, it could be the experience of a lifetime. While this unified type of experience was harder to do on film, Ernst Lubitsch and Rouben Mamoulian had intuited, in their fashion, the workings of a concept musical; if *Love Me Tonight* isn't a full, complete-unto-itself work of musical-comedy art, name something that is. *Top Hat* and *Snow White and the Seven Dwarfs*, too, among others, found their own aesthetic and created their own world. Some of the better Broadway transcriptions operated this way as well: *The Pajama Game* and even *Bye, Bye Birdie* almost seem created for film. Still, with the firm entrenchment of the roadshow mentality, movies increasingly forsook the allusive for the concrete, and the effect was to rob musical films of their unique charm. When a movie implies that enthralling things are going to happen—visual music to go along with the soundtrack—and then the result is a *Can-Can*, an audience can feel cheated. Or, worse, like it's at someone's wake.

The creators of the big roadshows were not only tone-deaf to the times and the new directions on Broadway. They were also ignorant of their own history and past. Back in the Bronze Age of 1929, those clumsy people who made *Rio Rita* had been on to something. With capricious microphones and stiff cameras and every kind of problem, they grasped how stage and film could be coupled while keeping everyone happy. At the time, they were adjudged to have succeeded beyond all expectations, and their basic methodology, streamlined and vastly refined, was successful enough to be passed down to many successors. Nearly four decades later, when *Camelot* came to the screen, the lessons had been forgotten in an especially lavish fashion. The patina of *Camelot,* visual and aural, is largely beguiling—a retro-storybook look, with gorgeous musical arrangements by Hollywood pro Alfred Newman. All this, alas, is placed at the service of a glum and wearisome script, actors who can't sing, and a director, Joshua Logan, whose touch is as ponderous as it is oddly uncomprehending. Movie sorcery has come up against twelve-ton stage machinery, and no one wins.

With *Sweet Charity*, which he had also directed on Broadway, Bob Fosse attempted a resuscitation. He knew, as Busby Berkeley had, that film choreography is as much a matter of camera and editing as it is dance, and the camera in *Sweet Charity* was so hyperkinetic, with so much zoom lens, that many were annoyed. Nevertheless, Fosse had given *Charity* a point of view and some striking set-pieces that made it interesting in ways that other musicals were not. His second film was also an adapted show—*Cabaret*—and now all his ideas were in place. *Cabaret* was truly a film, and it made the movie musical feel like a more powerful experience than it had for years. Not that there had not been some quality and success amid the dinosaurs: *Oliver!* and *Fiddler on the Roof* were very well done, if in ways that seldom rethought the originals; *Finian's Rainbow* tried to act like a movie even as the show's socially conscious whimsy pulled it down; *Funny Girl* was a competent one-woman-band; *The Sound of Music* was what it was. *Cabaret* was more dynamic than all these—nasty, funny, thought-provoking, titillating, charismatically repellent. Most important, it was unified: every frame of film had a specific, reasonable connection with every second of soundtrack. Just like a precious few of its predecessors.

Cabaret could not be imitated, but it was reasonable to think that it indicated any number of new directions. Fat chance. While musicals did not exactly die, their effect soon became death-like. Fosse never directed another all-out musical film (*All That Jazz* is an arresting, ego-driven hybrid), and Hollywood followed with *Man of La Mancha* and *Mame*. When another Broadway master, Harold Prince, tried to put *A Little Night Music* on film, he was woefully compromised by everything and everyone. *The Wiz* and *Annie* were done in by misjudgment, unknowing direction, solemnity, and overspending. *1776* was smaller scale and, on its own terms, not bad; it really did belong on the stage, as did *Jesus Christ Superstar* and *Godspell*. Milos Forman's *Hair* was a rare exception, but then it had been an exception on Broadway. By the time a game Dolly Parton and a bored Burt Reynolds tried *The Best Little Whorehouse in Texas*, the balcony was empty. Then there was *A Chorus Line* . . .

There was also *Grease*, and no disputing what a hit it was. For decades, it was the record-holder for top-grossing movie musical of all time, so great a success that it requires a certain amount of framing. The show itself had been a Broadway departure, far closer to *American Bandstand* than *Camelot*, and as a movie it's equally disconnected, as much from the history of musical film as from the real 1950s. The effect is less of a traditional genre piece than a hybrid John Travolta vehicle/Hanna-Barbera TV cartoon, or else as a bunch of faux-retro music videos dotting shreds of plot taken from *American Graffiti*, *West Side Story*, *The Wild One*, and *Happy Days*. Yes, it's fun, as are Graciela Daniele's choreography and much of the cast, and it's a total detour—a soldier, one might say, in a different war. Such few imitators as emerged, like *Xanadu* or that sequel, showed how much of a dead end it was: the un-*Rio Rita*, a huge hit with no lessons to pass along.

Curiously enough, around this time, Broadway started paying Hollywood back for all the years of borrowing and stealing and defacing. For years, musical shows had used straight films as a basis—*Oh, Captain!* (based on *The Captain's Holiday*), *Sweet Charity* (*Nights of Cabiria*), *Carnival* (*Lili*), and such. Even *The King and I* was based far more on the film of *Anna and the King of Siam* than on the original book. In 1980, with *42nd Street*, a big-time Broadway musical called on musical cinema more directly: a less-than-imaginative idea, prone to condescension, perhaps a desecration of the Busby Berkeley principle of composing musical numbers specifically and only for the camera. Its saving grace came with director Gower Champion (whose extensive film résumé was mainly in front of the camera), who retooled the material sufficiently to make it seem dynamic and fun, at least to people who'd forgotten the movie. By and large, *42nd Street* behaved as much like a stage piece as it did a copy of something else, and it managed to be a Broadway hit twice. When other shows in New York and London began turning to similar sources, the results were stale and uninventive: *The Wizard of Oz*, *Singin' in the Rain*, *Seven Brides for Seven Brothers*, *Meet Me in St. Louis*, *State Fair*, *Mary Poppins*, *Footloose*, *Dirty Dancing*, and the especially dispiriting *Victor/Victoria*, in which Julie Andrews attempted to reconquer Broadway. Among the few successes in this line were the cutesy *Thoroughly Modern Millie* and the hilarious *Xanadu*, which deliberately sent up its silly source. One of the biggest movie-based smashes, *The Producers*, had not really been a musical on film, while the live shows drawn from Disney cartoons, especially the ingenious *Lion King*, were another ballgame entirely. On a different deck of the same ship, there were what seems to be an endless procession of pop-jukebox shows, which also have movie roots of a sort—they're the zippy updates of all those song-filled composer biopics Hollywood used to do.

Unfair as it might be, this ashes-to-ashes trade-off tended to leave the movies behind, essentially in the past and on home video. Good and lesser shows went unfilmed, although *Little Shop of Horrors* was a nice exception. It was almost as much of a cartoon as, say, *South Park*, and true to its scrappy roots, both the ratty Roger Corman film and the nifty off-Broadway show. Otherwise, there was grimness—a mediocre version of *The Fantasticks* that got virtually no release at all, and an animated *King and I* so stupid that some people still think of it only as an urban myth. *Evita*, for its part, took twenty years to get onto film—and perhaps might have benefited from more time. Its foundation was a stage property more stylized than literal: a fantasia with less connection to the real Eva Peron than *The Sound of Music* had to the Holocaust. Add, then, an ambitious director (Alan Parker) with movie musical experience (*Fame* and the endearingly creepy *Bugsy Malone*), plus a budget whose size all but guaranteed that anything allusive and symbolic in the show would be made numbingly concrete. Top it off with two stars, neither of them part of a musical-show tradition on stage or screen. Here they were halfway lucky: Antonio Banderas (as a non-Guevera "Che") was the rare movie star capable of building the necessary bridges from visual to vocal, from drama to music, from film charisma to stage savvy. So clearly did he know what he was doing that one could almost feel the warmth of Bebe Daniels's smile beaming from some heavenly screening room. Madonna, in contrast, offered poses and hauteur and grand gowns, superficiality excessive even for a Lloyd-Webber show, and an unawareness such as musicals have rarely seen since the heyday of Ethelind Terry. "You Must Love Me," this Evita insists on her deathbed, necessarily stating an imperative that few past the hardcore fans would yield to otherwise. Her director, for his part, held fast to a vision mindful less of the history of musicals than of Madonna's music-video past, as refracted through a *Masterpiece Theater* prism. Here, in sum, was an unwitting précis of all the misplaced mechanisms used to bring big shows to the screen since the dawn of Vitaphone, at once serious and insubstantial, bloated and wispy, music-filled and insufficiently lyrical. It was no way to craft a music drama or to film a show.

Chicago's journey to the screen was even longer and more fraught than that of *Evita*.[10] With Bob Fosse reunited with *Cabaret*'s John Kander and Fred Ebb, the

---

[10] Bob Fosse actually set up a meeting with Madonna to discuss a possible *Chicago* movie. That he died on the day this was supposed to occur surely qualifies as a tragedy. Possibly also as a tragedy averted.

show was the essence of concept—commentative, bruising, snide, so free from conventional literalism that it was presented as a vaudeville show instead of a narrative. While the original production had been well received, it took the 1996 revival—and the intervening spectacle of the O. J. Simpson trial—to bring fresh currency to the cynicism that lay at *Chicago*'s bitter, damaged heart. The director who was finally able to harness the beast and put it on the screen was from the stage and had done a television remake of *Annie* that vastly improved on John Huston's bleak original. Most important, Rob Marshall and his associates had both awareness and intuition regarding the transferring of shows to film. As Fosse had extensively retooled *Cabaret* for film, as Vincente Minnelli and Stanley Donen respected and rethought *Cabin in the Sky* and *The Pajama Game,* Marshall and screenwriter Bill Condon jiggered some of the material yet retained its essence. Here was the antithesis of the *My Fair Lady* reverence that sets the outlines of a show in stone, which filmmakers are then required to meekly trace. There were, as always, critical voices, with many insisting that Marshall's editing cheated his dancers. The charge was not unfair, although it was clear that Marshall employed the quick cutting as a way to make the show palatable to audiences raised on MTV. Other complaints bordered on the pious—that Marshall wasn't the demon-god that Fosse had been, and, most insistently, that all the flash ultimately signified very little. (An odd objection, this last, coming in a decade when the most expensive films were imitation comic books.) Some of the show's partisans also decried the deleted songs and the decision to cast movie actors instead of stage people, though Catherine Zeta-Jones certainly qualified as the best of both worlds. Whatever the flaws or quibbles, *Chicago* achieved a self-realization that seemed especially impressive at a time when *American Idol* belters were pummeling the masses and so-called pop divas were getting by on packaging and "sonic enhancement." The key to its success, ultimately, was that it was of both the stage and the screen: theater's immediacy and imagination and heritage, coupled with film's sorcery and dynamism and, sure enough, its own rich and rewarding traditions.

One result of *Chicago* was to make filmed shows seem more viable, which had not otherwise been the case since around the time the cinematic Von Trapp family left Austria. This time, they would be opening in a multiplex world far divorced from the dress-up of roadshows. *The Phantom of the Opera, Rent, The Producers, Dreamgirls, Hairspray, Sweeney Todd: The Demon Barber of Fleet Street, Mamma Mia!, Nine, Rock of Ages,* and, finally, *Les Misérables*— ten films in less than ten years, a diverse bunch in every way. With Andrew Lloyd-Webber ensuring a modern-day Rodgers/Hammerstein fidelity, *Phantom* was so solemnly overproduced as to make *Camelot* seem like a beach party movie. *Rent* and *The Producers* were faithful, dutiful, and boring, while *Mamma Mia!* was, as on stage, far more about ABBA than lyrical theater. With Bill Condon's *Dreamgirls* and Rob Marshall's *Nine*, worthy artists worked hard to imprint style upon second-rate material—a tabloid version of the rise of Diana Ross and an empty redo of 8½ with inadequate songs. *Sweeney Todd*, at least, rethought its unique source material in Tim Burton's own filmic terms—too much so for many admirers of the show, yet at the least arresting and imaginative. In *Hairspray,* director Adam Shankman replicated the energetic frivolity of the show in the precise fashion that *Best Foot Forward* had done so long before, although he fared far less well four years later when he tackled the hair-metal jukebox world of *Rock of Ages*. As for the mammoth film of the endlessly running phenomenon *Les Misérables*, it can be averred that most of those who liked the show cried reasonably happy tears.

In the parallel existences of the stage and the movies, there are rivalries, wars, and sometimes outright defeats. Seldom are there clear winners, and this is well and proper. There is room in the world for both, and for those filmmakers who make the effort to understand both the material and the media, pay attention to the forebears, and look to the models. If this involves learning from others' mistakes, then at least something positive will have come out of a catastrophe like *Man of La Mancha* or *A Chorus Line*. Those who seek to change a show wholesale had best have a more-than-decent cinematic equivalent in mind, and those attempting fidelity need to remember that there's a film being made. Plus, while directives are being handed out, a memo to theater producers: enough with those zillion-dollar retreads of old movies. There are interesting ways to put a movie on the stage—look at *The Lion King*—but don't abuse the privilege. Film and theater are, it has been demonstrated time and again, very different animals, and while it's OK for the lion to dance with the lamb, the choreographer in charge needs skill and sense. And, first as well as last, it will benefit everyone to be aware of the ones that got it right. From *Rio Rita* to *Chicago* and beyond, they've proved that such things are indeed possible.

Chapter 3

Seeing's Believing

....

The musical woods are riddled with might-have-beens, and one of them is Billy Wilder. His Viennese roots and sharp cynicism might have made him the heir to Lubitsch in creating unsentimental romances with commentative lyrical overlay—*Love in the Afternoon,* for one, could easily have gone that route. But no: after one early bout of Bing Crosby gemütlichkeit called *The Emperor Waltz,* he knew he'd never go there again. In 1962, in setting out to film the London and Broadway hit *Irma la Douce,* Wilder decided to retain only such parts of the score as could be worked in as nonvocal background. "I have nothing against music," he said, yet the greater truth lay in what his Irma, Shirley MacLaine, noted much later: he was uncomfortable with a musical format. Would *Irma,* as filmed, have been better if its characters occasionally broke into song? There's no way to know—although it has to be observed that the resulting flat comedy was not remotely one of the better works made by this supremely smart artist.

Billy Wilder removed the songs from *Irma la Douce* for the same reason that many audiences and a number of filmmakers won't go near musicals: the perception that they are based on the notion of people bursting into song. True, many musicals do not operate the way *Oklahoma!* does, or *The Sound of Music.* Backstage films, for example, thrive on the very point of avoiding that tricky moment; Wilder himself directed a couple of great films—*A Foreign Affair* and *Some Like It Hot*—that made excellent use of songs in a performance, as opposed to a story, context. Still, it's that intrusion of songs into life that seems to connote musicals to many people: nuns or gang members or urchins or the poor people of Paris, stopping speaking and starting with the music. In *Irma la Douce,* it would've been whores and their clients, and this Wilder could neither countenance nor stage. For him, and for many, this one crucial hinge point—the transition between talking and singing—marks the place where conventions and artifice spill over into phoniness. The greater the cynicism, generally speaking, the less the ability or willingness to make, or follow, that particular journey. From *Madam Satan* to *Mamma Mia!,* this is probably the single greatest reason that musicals can seem awkward and silly.

The phrase first coined by Coleridge, "suspension of disbelief," has gone out of fashion. Seeking to access truth by less handy routes, many theorists find it a dated and somewhat underpowered way to confront anything that transcends conventional depictions of "reality" or naturalism. In musicals, much of this comes down to the notion of people in ordinary situations expressing themselves in song. This does require a certain kind of indulgence from many, even those putatively sane folk who might find themselves bursting into song at certain moments. Some musicals avoid this concept like the plague; others revel in it and—like it or not, use it or not—aspects of the concept have been around since the very beginning. Al Jolson, who was always onstage in some sense, sang "Blue Skies" to his mother (*The Jazz Singer*) and "Sonny Boy" to his kid (*The Singing Fool*) in intimate, story-propelled settings. (Intimacy, with Jolson, will ever be a profoundly qualified concept.) "Sonny Boy," in fact, was as much a reason as Jolson or Vitaphone for the earth-shaking hit made by *The Singing Fool* in 1928. Jolson sang it both ways in the movie—onstage to an audience, and in a "life" setting, directly to the little boy himself, and the connection between drama and song made millions weep and made "Sonny Boy" the biggest sheet-music seller up to that time. The lesson here was that musical performance in film need not always occur on a stage, even with a Jolson. *The Broadway Melody* had it both ways as well, with most of its numbers done as theater pieces but with "You Were Meant for Me" as an offstage expression of affection. In a way, it was the aural equivalent of a close-up.

The issue, then, was there from the very start: how exactly do people in a movie musical express themselves? No one thought anything of songs and cues onstage; operettas were overblown laws unto themselves, musical comedies could move easily from a jokey script into a light ballad, and the epochal *Show Boat* charted a brave and successful path squarely in between. Stage audiences were accustomed to the conventions, which were part of that intriguingly rich loam in which theater could thrive: the interlock of proximity and distance through which viewers could feel simultaneously close yet detached. Movies offered the precise opposite, keeping an audience at a remove—this is a recorded medium, after all—while bringing it in close enough to see the actors' pores. It's a qualified intimacy, one in which a move from speech into music can sit very peculiarly. Small wonder that so many of the earliest musicals avoided the issue by having their songs and dances done on a stage. Much of this was in nothing-succeeds-like-success imitation of *Broadway Melody* and Jolson, with the added-ease factor of not having to deal with the troublesome moment of transition from a plain talkie to what was, in 1929, sometimes called a singie. The year's biggest hit after *Broadway Melody, Gold Diggers of Broadway,* was a good example, with most of the songs not actually performed onstage being done as party pieces. This was vivacious, diverting, and so completely disconnected from the script that the main singer, Nick Lucas, simply played himself, with no part at all in the plot.

Some of the more interesting 1929 films did try for some kind of resonant connection between the music on the stage and the drama off it—tiny foreshadowings of the same treatment Bob Fosse would give to the musical sequences in *Cabaret.* In *The Broadway Melody,* the title song alludes to show-must-go-on smiling-through-heartbreak, just as the central character played by Bessie Love is compelled to do the same thing. *Lord Byron of Broadway,* shot later in 1929 and not a particularly good film in most ways, did have at its core a novel premise directly connecting plot with music: a songwriting hero-heel finds inspiration for his hits by exploiting the misery of those around him.[1] The ante was upped in the fall of 1929 with *Sunny Side Up,* which mixed back- and offstage conventions. Instead of Broadway or cabaret, there were block parties and a society soirée with performance pieces and an unforgettably lurid production number aptly titled "Turn on the Heat." The one essential scene anchoring the entire story involved a song done not onstage but in character: alone in her tenement flat, Janet Gaynor reaches for her autoharp, settles into a comfy chair, and plays and sings "I'm a Dreamer, Aren't We All?" while looking out directly at the movie audience. (In later years, such frankness would be sidestepped by having the singer look past the camera instead of into it.) It sounds

---

[1] *Lord Byron* would have been far better, and more profitable, had it been anchored by a lead performer with any weight or strength. Instead, there was someone named Charles Kaley, in his first and last feature film. He and the aforementioned, appalling Ethelind Terry were blatant reminders that musicals are no place for wimps or poseurs.

weird and silly and possibly it is, what with the fourth wall being demolished, the strumming, and a vocal range just this side of Minnie Mouse. That it is also body-blow effective is due to the song and especially to Gaynor, whose stardom was founded on a strangely immutable kind of sincerity that could obliterate the resistance of all but the most foul churls. I have a right to my dreams even if I'm a fool, she sings, and it's impossible to not believe the moment and the notion that this character would be doing exactly what's she doing. From here to the end of the long movie, the audience never stops rooting for her.

Janet Gaynor was one of only a few performers possessing the particular effrontery to break down the wall and connect an audience directly to a song. The king of this particular domain, in the early years and much later, was Maurice Chevalier. Audience rapport could not come more intensive than with a man who mastered his craft in French music halls doing this exact thing and had no problem moving it onto the screen. In his first American film, *Innocents of Paris,* he prefaces the entire film with an introductory speech to the audience, standing in front of a curtain as if he were still on the stage. He's being himself, not the character in the movie, thanking people for letting him appear in the movies, with special reference to the sponsorship of Mr. Paramount. The effect is made more startling by having Chevalier then appear as a character in a silly plot, in which he's called upon to perform songs both onstage and off. (The latter include the classic "Louise.") Thus is the whole of *Innocents of Paris* placed at a uniquely bracketed distance, the implication being that Chevalier himself isn't taking any of it seriously. In a strange way, it's akin to the arrestingly surreal in-and-out-of-the-plot dynamic that George Burns would do in his 1950s TV show, being involved in the action while also commenting as he watched it on TV in his study—a part of *and* apart from—which was the main key to Chevalier's success in his earliest American musicals. In his first good film, Lubitsch's *The Love Parade,* Chevalier constantly looks out at the audience in amusement, incredulity, and especially frustration: he delivers "Nobody's Using It Now" straight on to the camera to complain that Jeanette MacDonald won't sleep with him. His direct-address was one of many ways Lubitsch could maintain operetta's conventions while slyly sending them up. (Another way: a chorus of one of the songs is barked by a dog.)

While Chevalier joined Jolson in being the most imperative presence in early musicals, the elaborate candor of his style would not be countenanced after those first try-anything years. He reached his apotheosis—artistically and in addressing viewers—with the sublime *Love Me Tonight,* after which musicals

Isn't it romantic? Putting two Chevalier faces on a *Love Me Tonight* lobby card allows for one to do his traditional look out at the audience and the other to be, perhaps, a little naughty. At the time of this film, Jeanette MacDonald was the lingerie queen of movies. Her image changed later on, while Chevalier's really didn't.

took a sharp enough turn that there was little room for him or his boundary-breaking ways. Chevalier was gone from American film after 1935, and musicals would maintain an entrenched protocol in which songs would happen on a stage or within some kind of plot, and address was seldom or never direct-on to the camera in that Pirandello manner. Then, in 1958, Chevalier came back for *Gigi,* and there it was again. He participates in the action even as he introduces and comments on the characters and their motives and backgrounds: the most insouciant Greek chorus imaginable. His climactic moment comes when he gives the audience some gracefully venerable perspective on *Gigi's* romantic conflict, on romance in general, and on his career. "I'm Glad I'm Not Young Anymore" is delivered, again, straight on. He's already shared his wisdom onscreen with Louis Jourdan, and now he's sharing it with everyone: if older may not be exciting, at least it's easy. Throughout the witty song he wears the straw boater that had been so much a part of his style in *Innocents of Paris* and

Love Me Tonight, and its sheer presence is cause for historical reverb. A knowing viewer will wonder "Will he?"—then, in the final bars, he does: rising from his seat, he pulls the hat low over his eyes and exits with the same music-hall strut he'd done all those years earlier. With this capsule retrospective of the art of Maurice Chevalier, he's blurring the boundaries one last time, and he *is* young, anymore and always. It's a past-and-forever moment of film history, and it's breathtaking.

Few performers, early on or later, match Chevalier's ease in connecting music with film with audience. The pivot-into-song moment continued to be a problem for filmmakers and audiences, and served as a central reason why the run of expensive film operettas in 1930 did so poorly. Again, *The Desert Song* had conveyed the wrong lessons. Operettas were big and outrageous in a way that plays on a stage far less clumsily than on a screen. They took history—the Russian or French revolutions, the Great War, medieval France—and somehow diminished and inflated it simultaneously. Big songs, big voices, big dramatics, and even less truth or dimension than usual. Few things could look more absurd than the act of singing in the midst of tense or fraught or earth-shaking situations...and no wonder that many find *Les Miz* to be nothing more than a latter-day operetta. In *Song of the Flame* (like many of the operettas a lost film), Noah Beery played a rudimentary amalgam of Lenin, Trotsky, and several Bolshevik leaders, who assumes the seat of power in a post-tsarist regime. Crude and corrupt, he revels in his new status by chasing women and, in a song called "One Little Drink," extolling the joys of vodka. Eventually he is brought down and, as he is led to the firing squad, requests a final boon—"One Little Drink," and of course offers a reprise. In some ways this was intended as serious, with just a jaunty edge, and who could accept it as other than parody? Songs in a musical should complement the drama. Enhancement, not sabotage.

For a while, in 1929 and 1930, filmmakers tried to sidestep the whole music-versus-drama issue by setting aside plot and characters completely. Revues were film's most concentrated grab to be exactly like the stage, then outdo it with stars who would never deign to grace a Broadway house. From MGM's *Hollywood Revue of 1929* onward, these unformed collections of songs and stuff charted the full spectrum between entertaining and wretched: Warner's *The Show of Shows, Paramount on Parade, Happy Days* (Fox), *King of Jazz* (Universal). They were all, in their blatant commerciality, the wrong shot in the wrong war. The Warner film, in particular, was so desperate to pursue the stage that it forsook all except the most rudimentary tenets of cinema grammar; imagine a film so crammed with seventy-seven star performers that it never takes the time to give any of them close-ups. *The Show of Shows* was so *not* a film, and so alien to the expectations and needs of a wide audience, that it played a major role in contaminating the market for musicals of all type. Disbelief needs to be suspended, not despised.

Operettas were troublesome, revues a dead end. So what exactly would work to illuminate music on film? One of the invigorating things about the earliest musicals is how blatantly they can be seen searching for answers. All the devices and clichés are sampled, then there is the occasional stab at something new. The main standby, no surprise, is the "in performance" option, even in stories not set backstage. With music as part of a stage show, or at a party or nightclub or saloon or classroom or church, film is spared any chance of crossing over into that troublesome zone where characters convey feelings through song.[2] For a director like Cecil B. DeMille, who probably should never have been allowed near any kind of a musical, the elision could be especially hazardous. In his one demented attempt in the genre, *Madam Satan,* DeMille kept most of the music in a loosely diegetic context—a rehearsal for a show and a huge masquerade party. At one point, however, Madam's maid is called upon to give her some spoken advice that segues into music: go out and grab the brass ring, have fun, "Live and Love Today." At the key moment, the pivot between speech and song, DeMille fumbles so badly that he can't help the performer by giving her anything in the way of a transition. It's simply speak *bump* sing. This is truly startling, shocking even, because movies and Rodgers and Hammerstein have accustomed us to this convention being so easily done that it can be taken for granted and internalized. Here, it doesn't happen, and even in 1930 DeMille's bosses could see the clumsiness. Between revues (stars doing party pieces) and operettas (huge musical apostrophes about anything, or nothing) and the awkwardness of a *Madam Satan,* it became clear that some options would not be viable and some mechanics would need to be better concealed.

With DeMille, the unreality of the musical form trips up a director who seldom could move beyond the literal. Occasionally, early on, a better solution would be to accentuate the absurdity of it all. The early Ernst Lubitsch musicals—*The Love Parade, Monte Carlo, The Smiling Lieutenant, One Hour with*

---

[2] The anxiety was such that for a couple of years, circa 1930–31, bringing in background scoring also became a problem. The daft solution: a performer would turn on a radio to give the music a "real" reason for being.

You—are all mockeries, in the most benign sense. The characters and their conflicts, usually sexual in nature, are drawn so wryly that they're practically in italics, so removed from literalism that their use of song can actually make sense. Chevalier, with his straight-on rapport, and Jeanette MacDonald, with her witty imperiousness, were Lubitsch's most conspicuous co-conspirators in this alternative universe where music and love overlapped furiously. It's hardly a surprise, in such a world, that MacDonald, clad only in a chinchilla coat and frilly underwear, could flee a ghastly fiancé, board a train, and sing of the new life awaiting her at the end of the journey. The film is *Monte Carlo,* the setup is so unreal that it's perfect, and it helps no end that the song—"Beyond the Blue Horizon"—is as good as the occasion warrants. So what can Lubitsch do to heighten the sense of breakaway ecstasy? He synchs the train's chugging wheels with the song's percussive momentum, and as MacDonald gazes out the train window he has peasants in the field sing the song back to her. While this may not be the only way for musical cinema to comport itself, for sure it's one of the best ways.

Even as backstage films solidified the in-performance option, more enterprising works would occasionally make worthy tries at connecting song to character. One was Rodgers and Hart's *Hallelujah, I'm a Bum.* A huge flop in early 1933, it's a film some people later grew to adore. A non-backstage Depression setting, speech segueing rapidly into song, satire alternating with romance: all worthy, if not commercial, and then there are two elements almost guaranteed to cancel each other out—Al Jolson and rhyming dialogue. If the result is an unparalleled and likable curiosity, it is also less an indicator of new directions than a genial, stand-alone artifact. Far more viably, there were the Astaire/ Rogers films, with their straight-arrow show numbers interspersed with solos and duets of deeper and more insinuating implication. In *The Gay Divorcée,* the ballroom bash of "The Continental" is more than balanced by the intimate rhapsody that is "Night and Day," with its elegant evocation of seduction and ecstatic consummation. "I have so many things I want to tell you," Astaire says to Ginger, and then he glides into Cole Porter's fervent words and surging melody. After the dance, when she gazes up at him with what is best understood as afterglow, he counters by acting the likable conqueror, brushing his hands off each other with a "Well, that's done!" air. The love between these two—the need and the attraction and all the rest of it—has been made so real through the singing and dancing that it transcends the characters' other, cardboard attributes. This is the key to the Ginger-Fred films: the drama, such as it is, seems about as real as the never-Venice confection in *Top Hat,* with its spotless white gondolas and sparkling water. It's the love, shown through what they sing and how they dance, that is solid and inexorable, be it "Cheek to Cheek" or "Let's Face the Music and Dance" or *Swing Time*'s audacious "Never Gonna Dance" which is nothing less than a recapitulation of the couple's entire blissful and unhappy affair.[3]

Since Astaire and Rogers operated in an essentially fantastic environment, it was oddly fitting that the other works of the later 1930s to succeed as words-and-music amalgams sidestepped plausibility and forsook reality altogether. Walt Disney had been at the vanguard of music-on-film since 1928, with *Steamboat Willie,* and with it and the other early Mickey Mouse cartoons, plus the Silly Symphonies series that started with *The Skeleton Dance,* dialogue and song and movement all operated as simple extensions of each other. Anything might sing, and if a chair wants to get up and dance, all the better. Disney's work was promptly an inspiration to the more creative live filmmakers, whether in Europe (Rene Clair, Erik Charell) or stateside (Rouben Mamoulian), and his cartoons were able to thrive in a time when no live-action film was permitted any kind of music. There were backstage Disneys, operetta and opera Disneys, movie parodies, and much more. The next logical step, then, was to extend the format to feature length, and *Snow White and the Seven Dwarfs* owed part of its sensation to the fact that it embraced a musical unity such as film had seldom done in years. Snow White and the Dwarfs are all as comfortable with song as with speech—save, of course, for Dopey—and the Prince is so much a creature of song that he is permitted only a few spoken words. Note, too, that only the good guys are permitted to sing: the Queen/Witch only has contact with music through the scoring that underlines her evil. The songs by Larry Morey and Frank Churchill are small, simple miracles of concision, easy for kids to absorb and ingratiating to adults. Like all of *Snow White* and all great musical films, they seem effortless.

Given its status as possibly the most beloved of films, *The Wizard of Oz* is even easier to take for granted than *Snow White,* in part because the Harold

---

[3] "Let's Face the Music and Dance" is, in the context of the film *Follow the Fleet,* not connected with the Astaire/Rogers characters. But, along with "Let Yourself Go" and "I'm Putting All My Eggs in One Basket," it is so much more resonant than anything else that it becomes the film's urgent pulse and center. Thus, one might say, the dim draggy script—with its awful Ginger-bicarbonate episode—is relegated to the status of a snarky, sniping footnote.

Arlen music and Yip Harburg words so seamlessly connect the visual to the aural, the fantastic to the genuine, the comedic to the poignant. "Over the Rainbow" truly does articulate the longing felt by someone trapped in a drab environment for a world of color and magic, and there's the added fillip of hindsight that applies this as much to Judy Garland as to Dorothy Gale. The entire Munchkinland sequence, from "Come out, come out" through "We're Off to See the Wizard," is a seamless blend of the spoken with the sung, the folksy with the fantastic, and comedy, drama, whimsy, and dance are all accounted for. And how better for the Scarecrow, the Tin Man, and the Lion to express their selves and desires than through song, with just a little dance tossed in?[4] Even the Lion's "If I Were King of the Forest," basically an in-performance piece, tells us things we want to know about this silly, wonderful beast, as well as incontestable truths about the utter marvel that was Bert Lahr's talent. Taken as a duo, *Snow White* and *The Wizard of Oz* were the first original musical films since *Love Me Tonight*—a fantasy of another sort—to present a consistently viable alternative to the standard backstage-film model. Other works, even the magnificent Astaire-Rogers films, did it in spots and moments; these three were the standard bearers. They still are.

The density of musical film production in the 1940s, plus the financial figures, might encourage the notion that they were at some kind of peak. In terms of talent and technical efficiency, this could be true. Aesthetically, the tally might be judged a shade more ambiguous. For one thing, the reliance on the backstage model was so ingrained that when characters sang to each other offstage, ostensibly under some sort of scripted auspices, the old worries about believability remained palpable. In Busby Berkeley's *The Gang's All Here,* nearly all the music occurs in the context of a nightclub revue, a party, or a charity show. (Never mind that Berkeley's irrational arabesques would not be possible in any kind of theater.) One song is given offstage treatment: Alice Faye sings "A Journey to a Star" to her beau (James Ellison) while riding on the Staten Island Ferry. The song is a slow ballad, so love is naturally in the air—yet how valid does it seem, even apart from its Fox-soundstage ferry? It comes off as Faye playing to an audience, not a character (or underwritten collection of traits) communicating some major feelings. The love in question

[4] As most Ozians know, there was more dance originally: Ray Bolger had a long solo after "If I Only Had a Brain," staged in part by no less than Busby Berkeley. At least, unlike the "Jitterbug" number, this cut scene survives.

is less of this woman and man than the audience's long-nurtured appreciation for Faye's endearing presence and rich contralto. Another of her songs, "No Love, No Nothing," is performed onstage in an apartment setting and could as easily have been done by the character in her own apartment. In fact, the two songs could exchange slots without anyone being the wiser. This immateriality is a hallmark of many '40s musicals, and *The Gang's All Here* stands out from the others only because of Berkeley's mad imagination and his collaboration with that dynamo of Brazilian bizarrerie Carmen Miranda. Otherwise it would be as forgotten as other wartime Technicolor sorties: *Something for the Boys* or *Riding High* or *Broadway Rhythm,* all of them designed to pass time and make money, not score expressive points or mean anything an hour after the end title. Many may call this the designated reason for musicals; others might note that more could be possible if their makers were clued-in or motivated enough to try.

In 1944, two especially worthwhile films did try, in ways as divergent as the companies producing them. At MGM, the industry's Grand Hotel, a group of artists consciously extended the boundaries with the surface-conventional/content-subversive *Meet Me in St. Louis.* Across town, the situation was quite different. Columbia was a small studio, nearly a mom-and-pop outfit, with Harry Cohn as its notorious pater terribilis. Musicals were not necessarily Cohn's preferred habitat, but with a newly emergent nova in Rita Hayworth he was compelled to enlist such prime talent as Fred Astaire, who partnered her twice; Cole Porter; and Jerome Kern. For *Cover Girl,* there would be Technicolor, more Kern music, and an expansive production. This was, on its surface, a backstage musical with stock situations, and at Fox with Betty Grable or Paramount with Dorothy Lamour it would have remained so. There were slots for specialty routines, a big title number and a nice ballad or two, and comedy fill-in for Phil Silvers, who could've been Jackie Gleason or any other buffoon. The difference began with Columbia's very size: close quarters and modest facilities that made every major film, be it *Lost Horizon* or *You Were Never Lovelier,* essentially a hand-tooled affair. This did not ensure quality, for many of the Columbia "A" films were oddly clunky in seams-showing ways unlike those at other studios. Indeed, the *Cover Girl* script had infelicities that might have been ironed out elsewhere, plus a director (Charles Vidor) who worked professionally yet without particular distinction. Its music was partly set onstage and part, as it were, in life, and the chores were divided between two contrasting hands. The show numbers were the domain of Seymour Felix, who had been plying his trade in Hollywood since 1929. This translates as half the music in *Cover Girl* reflecting the Felix aesthetic—attractive, dutifully kinetic, lots of girls, less imagination.[5]

Felix's was the part of *Cover Girl* that looked back and played safe; the other half, as staged by Gene Kelly and Stanley Donen, did neither. Harry Cohn had not originally wanted to hire Kelly, who was still new to film, as the leading man. He was fast proved wrong by Kelly's chemistry with Hayworth and his staging of three sequences. The most conventional, "Long Ago and Far Away," was a Fred-Ginger romantic duet done with grace, an aptly lush kind of tact, and a beautiful Kern melody. In "Make Way for Tomorrow," Kelly and Hayworth and Silvers joked and danced down soundstage Brooklyn streets with the kind of lithe exuberance usually confined to onstage numbers. Here, the energy and the staging were deployed less to exhibit a performer's skill than to delineate the optimism of three characters the audience cares about. Then, in the third number, came a major departure. If "Alter Ego," Kelly's premiere ballet on film, did not involve a song per se, it supplied as vivid a delineation as the most specific of lyrics. Kelly walks down a street late at night and reflects in voice-over on his feelings for Hayworth, her ambitions, and her possible interest in another man. Suddenly a shop-window reflection of Kelly pops out and joins him on the street, and the tension heightens while the inner and outer Kellys dance and spar as "Long Ago and Far Away" plays on the soundtrack in edgy dissonance. The effect is to make concrete clashes quite familiar to tortured artists, including Gene Kelly as both character and man. The reflection finally jumps back into a window and continues to jeer, at which point Kelly hurls a trash can to destroy the window and the doppelganger, if not the struggle.

While there had been dream ballets in film before, they were never this Freudian, nor so aggressive, nor with the artistic and technical prowess shown by Kelly, with Donen's assistance. While neither received onscreen credit for their *Cover Girl* dances, everyone knew who was responsible, and the acclaim enabled Kelly to continue to explore new venues for dance on film when he

---

[5] The workaday Mr. Felix may be allowed one truly Olympian moment. MGM's *The Great Ziegfeld* was so full of everything that little in it stands out—with the staggering exception of Felix's first-half finale. "A Pretty Girl Is Like a Melody" is less a lucid statement of, well, prettiness or melodiousness than it is an awe-inspiring piece of engineering and spectacle. Try, just try, watching it sometime with an undropped jaw. Not possible.

returned to MGM. For effect, virtuosity, and sheer nerve, "Alter Ego" still earns a major prize in his canon and far beyond. Shattering boundaries as well as windows, it took offstage performance into a new venue: inside the head of a conflicted character. There, in itself, is quite a conflict—a splashy, star-propelled homage to cover-girl beauty somehow finding the means to access the jangling intensity of film noir.

Meet Me in St. Louis was the opposite of *Cover Girl* in so many ways that the two films could do some kind of frenzied alter-ego dance down a studio street. Essentially, the only things they had in common were a major female star and Technicolor. Where one was the product of a small studio with spare resources, the other came from a massive plant with song and dance and design ever at the ready. One found its major impulses through dance, where dance to the other was incidental, if that. In one the director was an attentive, competent manager, while in the other he was, to put the most evocative point on it, Vincente Minnelli in peak form. One traversed and ultimately transcended the auspices of a timeworn backstage plot, while the other proudly did away with any kind of conventional storyline. Where one leaned heavily on star brilliance, another tamped down the voltage to create an ensemble. Most obviously, *Cover Girl* dealt with fame and ego clashes amid modern New Yorkers; *Meet Me in*

Times two: Gene Kelly, as dogged by Gene Kelly, performs the "Alter Ego" sequence in *Cover Girl*. This is a photographically tricked-up evocation, yet it still shows the scene for what it is—one of the most striking moments in 1940s musical cinema.

St. Louis was about a Midwestern family in sudden danger of unwelcome change. That both films worked then, and work now, is obvious—as is the fact that *Meet Me in St. Louis* is the greater. Still a marker and milestone, and in both script and songs one of the most graciously unified musicals ever. "The Trolley Song," "The Boy Next Door," and "Have Yourself A Merry Little Christmas," outstanding in any context, become all the more so for the ways they impel, comment, propel, and aid the Smith family in their journey from complacence to fear to, eventually, elation.

There are many ways to assess the achievement of *Meet Me in St. Louis,* and comparison can be one of them. Not so much with *Cover Girl,* though there is that, but from the promontory of everything it caused. In a sense, it was to movies what *Oklahoma!* was on the stage—an unprecedented jolt of Americana that let song and script move each other along in near-radical ways.[6] Few films give as much testimony to the importance, in a musical, of attentive and sensitive craftsmanship, and few musicals this side of *The Broadway Melody* and *42nd Street* have been so exhaustively imitated. While the pretenders—*Centennial Summer, State Fair, On Moonlight Bay,* many more—are not bereft of all merit, it is once again the first one that got it the most right. The cast and design. The interplay of character and incident, as opposed to plot. The simple rightness of the score. The sense of interconnectedness. Some of it comes down to the tension of how to present the songs—in a performance setting, or not. *St. Louis* balances the two—"The Boy Next Door" is a soliloquy, "Skip to My Lou" is a party piece, and "The Trolley Song" manages to be both.

The presentation of songs in *Meet Me in St. Louis* is perhaps best effected during a moment of crisis. The father (Leon Ames) announces that the family is moving to New York. No one's expecting this news, no one takes it well, and nearly everyone leaves the parlor in distress. The mother (Mary Astor), wise if wounded, remains and knows how to cope: go to the piano and begin to play. It's "their" song, this couple's, called "You and I," and her husband starts to sing it. (Ames was dubbed by Arthur Freed, and there's a charming moment when

[6] A more literal Rodgers-Hammerstein connection: a song of theirs was originally in *Meet Me in St. Louis.* "Boys and Girls Like You and I," written for and taken out of *Oklahoma!,* was recorded by Judy Garland and shot, then deleted. Four years later, Frank Sinatra sang it in MGM's *Take Me Out to the Ball Game* and the same thing occurred once again. Sometimes it's easiest to blame it on a jinx.

Astor has to lower the key to suit his voice.) By the time Mom joins Dad for the final chorus, it is clear that they'll work through the trouble. Minnelli holds the camera on the pair singing in the foreground while the family can be seen trooping back into the room into its accustomed places. A "performance" song has crossed over into life and brought healing at a fractious time. Changes are rough—unity is forever. Other moments in *Meet Me in St. Louis* are better known than "You and I" and get more attention: the trolley and the Halloween segment and Margaret O'Brien's hysteria after Garland sings "Have Yourself a Merry Little Christmas." But it's "You and I"—not a major part of the score and not written by Hugh Martin and Ralph Blane, who wrote nearly everything else—which occupies the center of this movie, and its heart.

It was as a direct answer to *Meet Me in St. Louis* that 20th Century-Fox made a musical out of an old hit, *State Fair.* Instead of the standard ranks of Tin Pan Alley guys the studio usually enlisted, the score was by Rodgers and Hammerstein, flush with the instant success of *Oklahoma!* Once again, there is a family and a fair, some romance and a crisis or two, and little of it is as reverberant in Iowa as in St. Louis, or in the first version with Will Rogers and Janet Gaynor. (Better, though, than that 1962 remake.) The opening sequence, borrowing from *Meet Me in St. Louis,* indicates that the music will go far to prop up the rather mild story: "Our State Fair" is sung and passed along among a number of characters, all the family members and a kibbitzing visitor plus the family's prize hog. Rodgers had already done something similar in *Love Me Tonight* with "Isn't It Romantic," and it works again here. It gets even better shortly afterward when the starry-eyed daughter (Jeanne Crain) wonders about love, gazes out of her bedroom window, and sings "It Might as Well Be Spring." If there is a letdown that this beautiful voice does not actually belong to Jeanne Crain, what remains is that languid elation possible in a musical that permits song and situation and setting a harmonious co-existence. Minutes later, as she suffers through a visit from an especially dreary beau, Crain reprises the song with new lyrics so sarcastic as to make it clear that her trip to the fair has to bring her something better. A reward, in fact, fit for the person delivering such a gorgeous ballad.

The family goes off to the fair, and the musical program gets phoned in for the rest of the movie. The fair has a band and a singer (Vivian Blaine), the family's son (Dick Haymes) gets to join in, and nothing is permitted to move past the older movie norms. It would happen similarly in most of the other clones of *Meet Me in St. Louis* as well: that old "on the stage" model didn't just belong

to backstage yarns or faux composer bios—it could work just as well at the
Iowa State Fair. The songs are nice, if hardly top-drawer Rodgers and Hammerstein, and since their connection with the plot and people are vague at
best, they act as a reminder of just how often that same by-the-numbers treatment has continued since 1929. *State Fair* becomes simply the latest model in
a long, frustrating procession of musicals with a few sublime moments padded
with a great deal of uninventive excelsior. Too nice to be inherently objection-
able, it proves again how hard it is to get past the rooted conventions. To be
imaginative is to court failure, in one form or another.[7]

Alongside the imitations of *Meet Me in St. Louis,* there continued all the
workaday stuff: stories with a show-biz setting and bogus bios of composers or
stars, all with songs making only tenuous connections with their surroundings.
The unvaried nature of the material became especially frustrating after Doris
Day made her film debut in 1948. She was the goods, no question about it, yet
Warner Bros. put her in a series of retreads with catch-all scores and scripts to
match—the kind of vaudeville that seemed especially decadent as the 1950s
proceeded. Only twice did Warners allow Day the opportunity to shine in properties where songs and script blended well. One was *Calamity Jane,* in which
her vibrant expertise made it easy to forgive the Xerox-*Annie Get Your Gun*
circumstances. Later, just before she started all the sex comedies, *The Pajama
Game* gave definitive proof that movie-star casting can sometimes be the best
thing to happen to a filmed version of a Broadway show. In both roles, Day's
natural physicality enabled her to move from speaking to singing not only
smoothly, but with a uniquely vigorous conviction that was exactly what musicals needed—if only they weren't either dying or giving way to the Broadway
behemoths lumbering in the wings.

Even backstage stories could acquire new luster when the creators cared
enough, and two MGM films brought the concept to its apex. One dealt with
putting on a Broadway show, the other with putting on a movie, and both used
mostly preexisting songs, done in and out of performance. *The Band Wagon*

---

[7] MGM, which made a mint off *Meet Me in St. Louis,* lost a piece of that fortune when it
tried to make lightning strike again. *Summer Holiday,* which set music to Eugene O'Neill's *Ah,
Wilderness!,* was sweet and intrepid, with a fine cast, a decent score, and, in Rouben Mamoulian, a sometimes-genius director. It's one of those movies to watch and appreciate while knowing that things are wrong and, darn it, no solutions come to mind. If good intentions were all,
Summer Holiday would be the *Potemkin* of musicals; sometimes, alas, magic is only evident
when it's absent.

and *Singin' in the Rain* work so well in large part because they were written by
Betty Comden and Adolph Green—eternally witty, observant, ineffably capable
of exploring all the venues along which script can connect with song. As with
nearly all backstage stories, the main characters in both films are performers;
the genius comes in structuring the plots so that it's necessary for them to sing
and dance offstage as well as on. Why shouldn't Fred Astaire filter a jaunty
dejection through "By Myself"? And why wouldn't he and Cyd Charisse find
they care about each other by riding into Central Park and "Dancing in the
Dark"? Nor is it surprising that Donald O'Connor should offer Gene Kelly and
the audience a slapstick primer on how to "Make' Em Laugh." As for Kelly:
given the situations of a salvaged movie career and a freshly minted romance
with Debbie Reynolds, how could he do anything other than doff his umbrella
and dance through that Hollywood downpour? That all these are indelible goes
without saying. What is pertinent here is the way that their setup and presentation make them all *inevitable*.

After 1960, there were few inevitabilities in musicals save the notion that
whatever worked on Broadway would work on film, preferably in bigger form.
Or, in the case of *West Side Story*, with Jerome Robbins dances taking place on
real New York streets. If the subsequent clash of stage art and film literalism
was something of a jolt, most audiences, and the Motion Picture Academy,
accepted it entirely. For a minority, there was the feeling that the stylization so
shattering on Broadway had transitioned onto film somewhat ponderously, and
these doubters respected *West Side Story* where others loved it. (See also *Les
Misérables*.) And no matter how well those pivot moments had worked on the
stage, the shifts from drama to song could only call attention to themselves
when they involved Natalie Wood first speaking in her own self-consciously
Puerto Rican inflections, then, with a high-fidelity shift of sonic perspective,
singing with the soprano of Marni Nixon. It was, for some, every bit as jolting
as the *South Pacific* movie, when people knew a song was coming on because
the absurdly misguided Joshua Logan would drench the screen in whatever
lemon or aqua filter he thought would convey the right mood.

In its formalized way, *My Fair Lady* was intended as more of an overt theatrical experience than *West Side Story*, but once again there was that whiff of
devotion in the air, plus those odd aural bumps when we went from movie star
to Marni. Effortlessness, after all, could be only a by-product of something this
costly and preconceived. So, ultimately, could warmth, which is part of the
reason *The Sound of Music* has endured for many more people, fairly or not,

than *My Fair Lady.* (Another reason is a less jarring sound mix to lead from script to song.) Monstrous it might be for many, fascist or heinous or mercenary or fake or schmaltzy; there hasn't been a single derogatory adjective that hasn't, at some point, been applied to *The Sound of Music.* It isn't simply a movie to love or hate, since active loathing can be part of the process of getting sucked into it and buying the whole nuns versus Nazis shebang. And, however complex or negative one's feelings, attention must be paid: despite the manipulations and the saccharine, it's as skillfully assembled as one of the windows in the nuns' abbey. From Julie Andrews's ecstatic opening spin through "Do-Re-Mi" and that final climbed mountain, it's been presented with the skill and wisdom that could only be accumulated through eons of skill and thousands of shows. Love it, despise it, criticize Rodgers and Hammerstein, criticize the whole musical idiom—it comes together here to a degree that has seldom been equaled.

One way in which it might be truly legitimate to abhor *The Sound of Music* lies less in its own self than, as has already been cited, its influence. Some of its emulators would have made it to the screen in any case—*Hello, Dolly!,* certainly, and *Funny Girl, Camelot* for its score and Kennedy-connected nostalgia. But likely not *Paint Your Wagon,* nor *Half a Sixpence* or *Finian's Rainbow.* As for *Song of Norway* and that grim child-of-Poppins *Doctor Dolittle*: not a chance. They kept getting bigger—*Dolly* most of all—and they grew more and more empty, with the seeming obligation or mandate for them to burst into song every so often for no other reason than the hope that the "Do Re Mi" firecracker might be lit once more. Onward they came, ever more irrelevant, alienating audiences with their relentless sugar content and their trivialization of the musical form. In their hollow penchant for conveying generic emotion through insipid song, they were a ludicrous if unintended reflection of Vietnam-era flag-waving. Who, really, could care about all those smiling people waltzing through the park in *Hello, Dolly!,* or those prancing miners in *Paint Your Wagon,* trying to look like Hollywood's notion of nineteenth-century hippies? Nor, when it turned up, did the backstager make anything better, not least because by 1968, no one cared a jot about Gertrude Lawrence, *Star!* or not, even with Julie Andrews playing her. If the songs in a film like *Gigi* illuminated and furthered the action, the songs in most of these seemed less necessary than stem-winding; a truly fine or germane musical sequence, like *Funny Girl*'s "Don't Rain on My Parade," was noticeable mainly by its scarcity. While all those *Big Broadcast* things in the 1930s had been as insubstantial as these, they had not been this bloated in intent, nor as out of step with time, tide, and taste. If a *Sweet Charity* tried to lasso a sense of hip relevance, the desperation was apparent and the effect lethally quaint.

When *Cabaret* opened early in 1972, people who cared about musicals gazed in wonder. On Broadway, the show had been an expertly effected mix of plot songs and onstage numbers, like a better *Funny Girl*. While the Kit Kat Klub sequences did sometimes connect with the offstage incidents, they did not further the plot in the way the other songs did, in a more acidic Rodgers-Hammerstein vein. Thus, it was a major step by Bob Fosse to throw out both the offstage numbers and, in large part, the characters who sang them. Everything, all the music in *Cabaret*, would be done in performance and directly comment on the action, be it the lead characters' sex lives or the rise of Hitler. And, in the insidious person of Joel Grey's Master of Ceremonies, there was, again, a Chevalier reaching directly out to the audience—this time with the cheeky insouciance positioned atop debauched malevolence.

When it was released, *Cabaret* did not attract unreserved critical rapture. Some missed the parts of the show that had been jettisoned, others were annoyed by the flashiness of Fosse's technique or the notion that Liza Minnelli's virtuosity could square with the deluded second-rater Sally Bowles. Pauline Kael, however, cheered vigorously at this anti-*Sound of Music*:

> After "Cabaret," it should be a while before performers once again climb hills singing or a chorus breaks into song on a hayride; it is not merely that "Cabaret" violates the wholesome approach of big musicals but that it violates the pseudo-naturalistic tradition—the "Oklahoma!"-"South Pacific"-"West Side Story" tradition, which requires that the songs appear to grow organically out of the story.

As was not uncommon with Kael's more sweeping prognostications, this did not quite come to pass. Whatever the marker set by *Cabaret*, the *Lost Horizons* and *Mames* that followed continued to do the very thing Kael reviled, and then there was silence. Occasionally a *Rocky Horror Picture Show* would make fine sport of the old songs-in-script formula, yet musicals were so close to extinction it lacked a larger context.

With the 1980s there was MTV and music videos, those micro-edited stepchildren of the old Vitaphone shorts. The songs in music videos could make reference—"sampling" is one later euphemism—to anything, and occasionally there would be the jeering reminiscence of old musicals that burst into song. Music videos were nothing if not cynical, albeit not in the artistically constructive fashion that a Fosse might offer. They were technically proficient, expert in merchandising music and performers, and usually quite ruthless in appropriating, then trashing, the musical past. In their complete self-containment, they had no cause to deal with a song's context or its connection with character, drama, truth, or anything. All that was needed to set off a song was a vague kind of scenario or "hook," and singing talent and content mattered far less than presentation. It was no wonder, then, that a film like *Evita* owed far more to the music video idiom than to the musical film heritage, with connections between music and story that seemed as stiff and synthetic as Madonna's many lacquered wigs.

For many, *Moulin Rouge!* was more viable, Baz Luhrmann allowing his VH1-Goes-Bollywood production trappings to pick out such shards of verity and drama as might be found amid the relentless italicizing. Beneath it all was a tiny wisp of a *Camille*-ish story, overlaid by a musical program so far-ranging as to make the word "eclectic" seem paltry, from musical comedy (including "The Sound of Music") to every '70s and '80s rock star worth knowing (Bowie, Elton, Sting, etc.), and at no point was Luhrmann in anything but total charge. It was as iridescent as the "American in Paris" ballet and as personal as *Cabaret*, a bang-up mash-up of sound and image quite less disciplined than the movingly updated production of *La Boheme* Luhrmann had staged for the Australian Opera. *Moulin Rouge!* created its own truth, musical as well as dramatic, that spoke directly to those who acceded to its director's choices. Among unbelievers, there were reactions such as that of one viewer well versed in musical traditions: "The horror...the horror." If musicals traditionally split audiences, this one did it more than most, which was surely a major part of Luhrmann's intent.

Chicago managed to address the musical past in a less chaotic manner. There were constant echoes of *Cabaret*—which seemed abundantly fitting, since Bob Fosse had conceived *Chicago* on Broadway as *Cabaret* gone vaudeville. That format had been the chief reason the show had resisted adaptation for so long, and director Rob Marshall solved the problem by careening the musical numbers back and forth between "real" offstage and imagined onstage. This permitted the story and the songs to interplay seamlessly—and was why Marshall shot and then cut "Class" when he couldn't fit it into the predetermined scheme. If the show's ultimate, coruscating ironies were softened somewhat in the retelling, there was still a fair measure of the original Fosse-forged hardness—even, a near-unknown quantity, pertinence. In spite of its effort to honor the musical's past while maintaining present-day relevance, *Chicago* may not be the ultimate movie musical nor, certainly, the last great one. Yet, given the stressful admiration society in which its script and music intertwine, it has a Tabasco kind of reverberation generally missing from its successors, which lack its upfront artificiality.

No doubt Pauline Kael would be aghast at the fashion in which the "organic" musical trend she so despised continues in varying forms—stultifying, as in *The Phantom of the Opera*; derivative, as in Rob Marshall's *Nine*; or, in the formidable case of *Les Misérables,* with its much-ballyhooed use of live singing, uniquely self-important. There is also, in *Mamma Mia!*, rather unfortunate proof that junk-food jukebox shows can play enjoyably in the theater and seem asinine onscreen. By using something like a crowbar to jam preexisting ABBA songs into a sitcom plot, it forces a virtuoso performer like Meryl Streep to strain for the conviction to make drama and song connect. The nebulous musicality of such things is only one step away from the concert films that, at least for a while, became so commercially viable. Miley Cyrus or Justin Bieber or Katy Perry or One Direction—even Michael Jackson, from beyond the grave—could do their standard lip-synch performances and display preciously Photoshopped glimpses of their offstage lives. Songs, meanwhile, are free-standing entities that need not compel pop or rock to function within a larger context. God in heaven: this is the full-circle return to the days of *The Hollywood Revue*. Past, meet future.

It would be reassuring to believe that the musicals yet to come will not be confined to the narrow pigeonhole of filmed concerts, nor even filmed shows. The enormous popularity of *Les Miz,* whatever else it may or may not mean, offers a twinge of indication that further life might conceivably remain. Even in the post-post-modern world of memes and YouTube, there exists the possibility that the spoken can be reintroduced to the sung without having it all fall apart in a self-conscious heap, or matter as little as a *Mamma Mia!* Even a failure like Irwin Winkler's *De-Lovely* made a worthy attempt to bring Cole Porter into the new century. If little of it worked, there was some thought at work, just as Julie Taymor's *Across the Universe* and Todd Haynes's *I'm Not There* were non-jukebox efforts on behalf of the Beatles and Bob Dylan. It's worth noting that these were less corporate than personal projects, a reminder that a musical works best when it has a strong authorial stamp, be it that of a Mamoulian or Minnelli or Marshall.

Add Woody Allen to the list as well. *Everyone Says I Love You* was his meditation on the musical's past and conventions, a retrospective carnival posited wholly on the ways music can intrude into life, the ways people can express their feeling in song, and the ways the musical's ethos has had permanent impact. The nexus for the whole film—the pinhead, as it were, that Allen and his angels danced upon—was that "bump" moment of bursting into song, the same one that causes so much dread in so many filmmakers, from *Madam Satan* to *Mamma Mia!* The entire Rodgers-and-Hammerstein ethos so despised by Kael was here limned by Allen with such genial self-awareness that the effect was neither too precious nor too awkward.[8] Along the way, Allen and his game cast delivered shocks almost worthy of the early talkie era, when previously silent performers like Gloria Swanson or Buddy Rogers showed that they could sing as well as speak. Who, for example, would have tagged the intense Edward Norton as an engaging song-and-dance guy in the Donald O'Connor tradition? Not to mention Tim Roth, with his mien of total grimness, as a softie with a song. The incongruity, of course, was what Allen was trying for, its effect his antidote to the enforced "logic" of *South Pacific* or *West Side Story*. Not all of it succeeded, but in the musically dark time it was released (just a few months before the big noise called *Evita*), *Everyone Says I Love You* was a bracing way to celebrate where musicals had been. Whether or not Allen intended it, it also served as something of a prescient essay on where they might then go. On the screen as well as off, it insists, speaking one minute and singing or dancing the next may be difficult but are possible. At least they are if one is a dreamer. And aren't we all?

[8] With two exceptions. Julia Roberts's discomfort and unmusical voice seemed almost an *hommage* to the "I don't really do this, you know" days of all-star revues. Drew Barrymore, for her part, so feared onscreen vocalism that she was the only cast member Allen was required to dub. It was, at any rate, notable that one of her silently mouthed songs came straight from 1929: *Sunny Side Up*'s "(I'm A Dreamer) Aren't We All?"

Chapter 4

People
From Jolson to Justin in Eighty-Five Years

....

The tenor Giovanni Martinelli was the kind of fortunate performer who could be taken seriously while weeping in clown pajamas, at least in performances of *I Pagliacci*. Onstage at the Metropolitan Opera, he gave off the competent sort of brilliance that too often is taken for granted— a silver luster, compared with the golden aura of his late rival Caruso. On a movie screen, in 1926, he was astounding. When Warner Bros. enlisted him to appear in the first Vitaphone program, it was playing things safe: "Vesti la giubba," the laugh-clown-laugh aria, was sure-fire, and everyone knew how well he could sing it. What was not expected was the impact of this one brief performance. He looked convincing, his emoting stayed within reasonable bounds, his phrasing was impeccable, and that ringing voice transcended the constricted loudspeakers better than anything else on the program. It was, in short, a capsule demonstration of how performer and material communicate to an audience.

Another Met star on that premiere Vitaphone roster was a vastly different singer. Marion Talley was the kind of performer who, eighty years later, would have rated a reality series: a teenaged soprano from Kansas City with little professional experience, unformed talent, and great publicists. Her Met debut earlier in 1926 had been far better reported than reviewed, and the Warner sages knew that her appearance on film would be more news than art. Talley's film segment, "Caro nome" from *Rigoletto*, was produced more elaborately and cinematically than Martinelli's and, by consensus, was the dud of the evening. The reasons for this lay less in her vocalism than her inexperience, plus Vitaphone's less-than-optimal recording and reproduction, yet she was full-figured as well as young and, thus, an easy target. Even in a pre-blog age, the snipers were rough: "Long shots—and good, long ones—were just made for that girl." Ultimately, "Caro nome" was axed from the program while the Martinelli aria was moved to the final climactic slot on the bill and remained in circulation for years.[1] This outcome, seasoned pro versus untested tyro, could perhaps have been predicted. Nevertheless, logic is far too earthbound to serve as a binding criterion where musical performance is concerned. The results are compelled to play out in all the divergent ways stage and film function, and on occasion it comes down to sheer luck. The veterans can work on film or not, the amateurs might be naturals, some get by through trickery, others try hard and remain earthbound. None of it is an exact science, as Madonna or Marilyn Monroe will attest. Presentation, material, photography, and the peculiar notion of a performer's generosity all play a role, and little of it is knowable until attempted.

Back at square two, the second Vitaphone program in October of 1926, there was a replay of the Martinelli/Talley dynamic, this time with a twist. The whole Jessel/Jolson business has already been recounted, and while Jessel's segment is partly lost (the sound exists), the relative impact of the two performances can still be divined. It was not simply about Jolson being the far better singer, though he was that; it was also about the ways a performer might engage with the camera and, thus, the audience. In *A Plantation Act*, Jolson reaches out, literally and figuratively, while Jessel would always be the kind of performer to remain within the frame. He was not a force-of-nature personality, while with Jolson there was no other option. This extroversion, at this time, was precisely the kind of hard sell needed to convince a suspicious public about the merits of sound film. The sell grew harder by the time of *The Jazz Singer*, with a Jolson whose style had coarsened into that of a stand-alone performer unwilling to adapt to the needs of conventionally integrated film. Characterization would not be an option for him, just as it would not be for

---

[1] Talley's short, finally exhumed after many years, proved a pleasant surprise—her voice and technique are better than adequate and it helps that sound reproduction has, to put it mildly, advanced a whole lot since 1926. Plus, for what it's worth, she's not *that* large. Even so, she could never equal Martinelli, whose aria remains magnificent.

many future performers. Of course, many will not now deal with Jolson under any circumstance, even apart from the blackface. If this is understandable, it also shortchanges history: Jolson is too seminal, too *immense*, to simply be ignored.

Certainly, *The Singing Fool* should never be ignored, tempting as that might be in a sane world. It, more than *The Jazz Singer*, was the phenomenon of the early-sound age, a success to make Jolson the most famous person on the planet. Now it's a prime example of a major work failing the test of time, as well as proof of all the things that can go to a performer's head. The acclaim greeting *The Jazz Singer* had clearly propelled Jolson's self-confidence to full-bore extremes well beyond the imaginable: his work in *The Singing Fool* might cause a Kanye West to skulk off in meek abasement. Musically, this translates as excess emphasis; dramatically, it's monstrous, Job in blackface. Sudden stardom, a divorce, a custody trial, career failure, and the death of a child, all of it set to renditions of "Sonny Boy"—a song held by legend to have been written as a joke but taken seriously. *The Singing Fool* is the essence of a film made for its time, after which technology and style changed so radically that nasty and pointed "Sonny Boy" jokes turned up in multiple films of 1929 and 1930.[2] Jolson's star dimmed with uncommon speed, and it became clear that film required something more generous, less "Look upon my works."

One of the lessons of Jolson has to do with the careful offset of self-regard. Confidence is necessary, arrogance can be tiresome or abhorrent, and the dividing line may be a hazard. Some profess to dislike the early Maurice Chevalier for this reason, though unlike Jolson he could interact generously with costars. Later on, the cosmic versatility of Mickey Rooney could seem overgenerous to some and monomaniacal to others: a performer's need to please should not stray into the arena of the insistent. Similarly, in the 1940s, there was Betty Hutton, whose sock-'em-dead style convulsed millions and repelled some, and Gene Kelly, who was and is too brash for some tastes. With Barbra Streisand, the balance was nicely maintained until her own production of *A Star Is Born*, which rapidly devolved into an insufferable carnival of all things Barbra. For Madonna, with a persona knowing no crack or vulnerability, film exposed the void behind the confidence. Then, in an unusually pungent

---

[2] In MGM's *Hollywood Revue*, comedian Polly Moran does a mean, funny imitation of Jolson doing "Sonny Boy," and the great man himself eventually joked about it in his film *Big Boy*. Few sensations go so sour so quickly.

example of latter-day self-deification, there was the bizarre task Kevin Spacey set for himself as writer-director-star of the Bobby Darin bio *Beyond the Sea.* Not only was he compelled to prove to the audience that, vocally and age-wise, he could play Darin—he also had to convey the message that Darin was worthy, as a performer and person, to rate an entire film in the first place. Heavy burdens indeed, as they would have been even for a film significantly better than *Beyond the Sea.* All these were Jolson's successors, even if they never quite approached his hail-the-conquering-me level.

For years, Jolson's ego-fueled fall from grace seemed to point to more circumspect paths for many performers. Except for Chevalier and an ace singing comic like Eddie Cantor (and his direct descendant Danny Kaye), the men could seem bland and generic, even sexless: John Boles, Nelson Eddy, George Murphy, and the young, relentlessly chipper Dick Powell. With women, too, glamour seemed to matter less than spunk, even before Shirley Temple. The key heroines of early musicals were Bessie Love and Janet Gaynor, whose appeal tended more to the sisterly than the alluring. A little later there was Ruby Keeler, in some ways the grandmother of camp. While she made an enormous impression in *42nd Street*, it was soon clear that a portion of her markedly loopy charm and appeal derived from some formidable limitations. Amid the crackpot Busby Berkeley extravaganzas for which she functioned as the unflustered axis, Keeler remained ever sweet, always engaging, constantly hardworking, and blissfully unaware.

The name of Jeanette MacDonald has acquired a number of camp accretions as well, not always fairly. She was seldom as opaque a performer as Keeler, nor was she one of the grand Broadway women, like Gertrude Lawrence or Marilyn Miller, who dropped into movies as a brief stunt. She came in at the very top, directed by the supreme Ernst Lubitsch and costarring opposite Maurice Chevalier, and the odd thing about *The Love Parade* and several of her other early films is how they and she kid the conventions that her later work would then take seriously. At Paramount, opposite Chevalier and others, Mac-Donald was lithe and funny and oddly haughty, given to running around in her underwear, ever and always in on the joke. Then, with MGM and censorship, the panties were replaced by miles of petticoats and she was compelled to adjust. Even while retaining her sense of humor and expert soprano, she promptly became associated with the art of the stolid—a lofty Rose Marie deigning to raise her voice alongside the unbending Nelson Eddy, "When I'm calling you-ou-ou" sung with glistening solemnity. For some back then and most later on, the ornate prima donna ways and high notes quickly became an arrant caricature of romantic accessibility, and the iconography overpowered the talent. MacDonald's ability, as presented in a film like *The Firefly*, could reach nearly to infinity, yet few performers with this much talent have become so retroactively hemmed in by changing taste. How frustrating it is when an artist of gracious gifts begins to connote things that seem absurd.

For many, especially those not disposed toward dealing with the early years, it all starts with Astaire. And, at the conclusion, often returns to him. Oversimplification is inaccurate and unfair, but how reasonable Astaire makes it seem to regard him as the center and the launch pad. "Easy," that central unflappable tenet of musical cinema, is the whole point with him, concealing every bit of the effort and making him endure as others fade. In his own way, he encompassed realms: unsentimental yet sincere, callow yet romantic, homely yet magnetic, theatrical yet inherently cinematic. Always, too, there hovers the legend of the assessment made of his screen test by some myopic producer—"Can't sing. Can't act. Balding. Can dance a little." Whether it really happened—at least one biographer states No—it remains that Astaire was, at the beginning, one of those veteran stage performers not seen to possess the traits associated with conventional film stardom. He was bone-thin, his face had some odd angles, his hair required augmentation, and his ears were a shade large. In affect he could seem bloodless, a hoity-toity denizen of a social class unwelcome to most Depression audiences. It was all, naturally, part of that marvelous concealment—the unassuming look masking unparalleled grace and the ability to connect with any partner, almost any audience. Dance on film, pre-Astaire, had been finite and self-contained, more for groups than solos or duets, a toilsome thing not connected with life or emotion or anything other than exertion. For Astaire, who worked harder than anyone, the idea was to make it float and dazzle, be about anything other than the effort, make a viewer want to emulate him even as it was clear no one could do what he did. Since he was also a musician—a pianist and composer, and he made those look pretty easy, too—his singing quite resembled his dancing, not as virtuosic but equally adept in conquering that troublesome hinge between talk and performance. He had, after all, long since mastered the ability to speak one second and sing the next and turn even the most mundane walk into a dance without any discernible transition.

Since a major part of Astaire's art lay in his ability to partner, it's illogically fitting that the first person he danced with onscreen was his complete antithesis.

For Joan Crawford, whose every effect needed to call attention to itself, effortlessness was an unknown, and dance was a particularly stark battlefield on which to play out her Kabuki spontaneity. *Dancing Lady* is the title of the film, Astaire's first, yet it is the most averse of musicals, one far more eager to focus on Crawford's ascendancy in love and couture than in song or dance. If this seems odd, in that musicals-are-bigger-than-ever year of 1933, it becomes comprehensible when Crawford is called upon to dance. To call her work effortful is certainly accurate, yet incapable of evoking the resolute slog she makes of something that should evoke airy grace. The epic shoulders are curious ballast for a thrashing upper body, the elbows eternally tense linchpins for arms that flail without cease. The feet, meanwhile, stomp ever harder and heavier as she looks down, Keeler-like, to see if their movements chart anywhere near the right way. All that is missing, amid this determined exertion, is the sweat spattering onto the camera lens.[3] Then, some minutes later, Clark Gable calls out "Freddie," and enter Astaire into the movie and the movies, from screen left. ("My gosh, I look like a knife!" he said, upon first seeing his profile on film.) He has a couple of lines with Crawford and then they start—he on the left, she on the right, with spins and arm-waves that approach the ungainly. The effect is repeated when the somewhat peculiar number (a mashup of "Heigh-ho the Gang's All Here" and "Let's Go Bavarian") is presented in its final form. It seems strenuous and utterly non-Astairean, and for a great reason: he's being generous, aligning his style to her limitations to make her look better. Enhancement, not condescension.

The initial workout with Crawford set the tone for everything afterward—the ten films with Ginger Rogers, the pairings with trained dancers like Eleanor Powell and Cyd Charisse and Rita Hayworth, and non-dancers like Paulette Goddard and Joan Leslie. If they were capable, he would bring them up to his level; if not, he'd adjust. Sure, his solo numbers are past virtuosic: "Say It with Firecrackers" in *Holiday Inn*, the dance around the room in *Royal Wedding,* "Bojangles of Harlem" in *Swing Time*.[4] Yet it's the duets that are the most

---

[3] Append that with "if said camera stayed on her dancing for any length of time." Overly plentiful reaction shots—the kind Astaire rarely used—tend to denote a performer in trouble, being an attempt to invite the audience to focus upon the supposed magic effect, not the inadequate substance.

[4] Speaking of Bojangles, Bill Robinson's dance with Shirley Temple in *The Little Colonel* is another example of virtuosic accommodation—a genius solo dancer with over fifty years of experience finding the precise way to work with a gifted six-year-old partner. Plus, incidentally, helping to break down some barriers in the process.

Enter smiling: In *Dancing Lady*, Fred Astaire spent a fair amount of his first film working hard to be a proper partner to Joan Crawford. Here, in "Heigh-Ho the Gang's All Here," the strain almost shows.

effective, in part because his long years onstage with his sister Adele taught him that a duo succeeds only if both parts set each other off. One fails and both fail—and Astaire, exacting perfectionist that he was, abhorred failure. As practical and nonaltruistic as his generosity might be, it gives his talent a gallant aura that Jolson, with his demolish-the-folks ethos, could not attain. Two prototypical musical gods, Astaire and Jolson, and the one who leaves a more Olympian wake is the one who knew that a musical will always be some kind of collaboration, even when the performer is working as a solo.

Where Jolson conquered, Bing Crosby convinced and charmed, and like Astaire, Jolson too for that matter, he did not possess the physical gifts of a standard leading man (angles and ears and hair, yet again). Also like Astaire, he made it all seem easy, with the laid-back acting and the unforced way that devastating baritone could pour out and swing out. In one crucial sense he was more beholden to Jolson than Astaire, being primarily a solo performer who sang to people more than he sang with them. Recall: who was Crosby's only steady partner on film? Bob Hope, in a partnership based in jokey rivalry. Other singers in Crosby films, besides Hope and Dorothy Lamour, seldom counted. Nor did most of Crosby's films. Paramount, his home studio, was a formula-bound factory for most of the 1930s and '40s, and the golden goose of the Crosby films did not countenance feather-ruffling. One after another, they were amiable time-passers, relaxed escapism that made a mint and sold tons of records and sheet music. For many then and some now, these vehicles offered unthreatening comfort—few chances taken, little deviation from formula, a likable guy ambling through some minor plot and singing mostly great songs. On occasion there was something as glaring as the ridiculous *Dixie*: as composer Dan Emmett, Crosby speeds up the title song into an uptempo hit only because the theater's caught on fire. Generally, his films lacked even that cuckoo invigoration, which is why posterity dotes on *Holiday Inn* and its splashy, inferior semi-remake, *White Christmas*, and few of the others. While it would not be accurate to view Crosby as another megalomaniacal Jolson type, he lacked Astaire's forceful imagination. Greater professional curiosity might have made his films—not simply his singing—transcend time and circumstance.

Elvis, the new wave that brought down the previous generations of Crosbys and Sinatras, was similarly self-enclosed. Non-devotees tend to forget how many films he made or how popular they were, and especially for those living in the South—the smaller the town, the better—Elvis was as much movie star as cultural phenomenon. As vehicles, his movies regressed past Crosby to Jolson territory: what could they be about, after all, other than Elvis? Whether a GI or boat captain or race-car driver, he always played a nice guy. Such other actors as appeared in his films—sometimes very good ones, like Angela Lansbury doing her best as his mother in *Blue Hawaii*—were as irrelevant as those pretty blondes who gazed at Bing Crosby while he sang. Nor were the songs of much import, let alone capable of bearing a substantive link to plot or character. Early on, a few times, Elvis showed edge and potential, and once—*Viva Las Vegas*—he stretched to accommodate a powerhouse costar, Ann-Margret. Always, though, he was at the mercy of a juncture of limitations: the career-limiting judgments of the Presley puppetmaster, Colonel Tom Parker; the notion (primarily American) that pop and rock would be spotlighted in only the cheesiest of movies; and ultimately his own phone-it-in disinterest. Thus, there was no way these films could be anything other than parched and small, proof that charismatic soloists need care and interaction and offset. For many of them, it's not worth the effort, which is why Neil Diamond and Eminem had such scant film careers, though Eminem was a movie natural, and why someone like Bruce Springsteen never tried.

Jolson figures come in skirts as well, as *Variety* noted when it termed Judy Garland's last film, *I Could Go On Singing*, a "femme *Jolson Story*." Seldom, in any case, were the Garland films the solo exhibits of a Jolson or Crosby or Elvis, or for that matter Betty Hutton or Streisand. She was, like Astaire, an expert collaborator, which makes it fitting that the two of them paired well together in *Easter Parade* despite working styles—planned rigor versus intuitive chaos—that were eons apart. Whether through personal neediness or professional generosity, Garland was always connecting in her films, be it with Mickey Rooney or Gene Kelly or the Munchkins. In *The Wizard of Oz*, she's both the necessary center and part of an ensemble, and the same might be said for *Meet Me in St. Louis* and *The Harvey Girls*. Even in *A Star Is Born*, wherein she holds every single musical card, she works with—not past or at—James Mason, to the benefit of both. One of Garland's greatest gifts was especially evident during her MGM days: as both soloist and partner, she could rein in the trademarked emotion and tremulousness and thus avoid stridency.[5] Amid the wrenching irony of "Have Yourself a Merry Little Christmas," she keeps things in check and leaves the hysteria to Margaret O'Brien. Of course, Garland is not the sort of performer to draw anything like a tempered response. The idolators are still around, as are those put off by virtuosity that can occasionally don a form that might seem fraught or neurasthenic; too, there remain a few crabby dinosaurs who resent, for lack of another way to put it, all the gay stuff. She's not a Jolson, whose art has moved past the recall point for so many; nor is she as crisp as Astaire or laid back like Crosby, screwy à la Danny Kaye or uncomplicated like Betty Grable, nor composed as Julie Andrews or take-charge like Streisand. Insofar as it is possible to look at Judy Garland without the encrustations of her mythology, she can be seen, as much as anything, as one of the warmest of professionals, willing to share and always aware that self-aggrandizement makes for a unproductive route to the top of one's profession.

There are those who prefer Betty Grable and the 20th Century-Fox musicals to Garland at MGM and, setting aside a certain incredulity, this can

---

[5] Originally, in *The Wizard of Oz*, Garland reprised "Over the Rainbow," with different lyrics, in the Witch's castle. While the footage is lost, the soundtrack reveals a sobby, undisciplined performance. Removing it was the right call, enhancing the ensemble spirit and swerving Garland—and the audience—safely away from *Singing Fool* excesses.

indeed be a comprehensible opinion. In her sweet-brash likability, Grable had the clear-eyed and direct appeal audiences needed during the war years—the same time, it might be noted, that Abbott and Costello were the biggest names in screen comedy. Her major stardom arrived when she replaced Alice Faye in *Down Argentine Way*, a title that pretty much said everything that needed to be said. Grable was similarly open and evident, nearly everything on the surface— the great legs, the color-friendly looks, the dancing that trumped Faye's, and the singing that outdid Keeler's. It was easy to set all this into those formula scripts, with their two basic plot arcs and their unchanging spots for love scenes, indignation, and mistaken identity. This was cinema of the lightest sort—a scene of Grable having a miscarriage in *My Blue Heaven* was as a rat-tlesnake at a garden party—and the sameness of both the material and the star was immensely assuring to many millions. Grable was the performer as tau-tology: she was what she was and usually had the savvy to stay within her comfort zone. This made for big profits but oddly unresonant work, and at-tempts to alter her formula usually met with disaster. Exhibit A of the latter was a Continental operetta fantasy called *That Lady in Ermine*. Started by Ernst Lubitsch and finished off by Otto Preminger, it was a unique collision of mutually exclusive parts that made Grable come off as the one thing she usu-ally was not: clueless. Her movie career was over before she was forty—not uncommon with musical women—and it is significant that she is recalled less for any of her films than for that single pinup photo. Work of its time tends to stay there.

The Jolsons and Astaires and Garlands and Grables all found their moment on film, just as Eleanor Powell did and Gene Kelly and the Beatles and Prince. Even, briefly, Ethel Merman. All are object lessons in regard to suitability, timing, adaptability, and other clever variables. What, then, of the lessons of a different sort, the ones who didn't work out or couldn't? Or, like George Jessel, succeeded only once. After his *Jazz Singer* debacle, Jessel stumbled into the presciently titled *Lucky Boy*, produced by a small company to cash in on the Jolson mania hitting the world late in 1928. Instead of "Sonny Boy" it gave him multiple choruses of "My Mother's Eyes," and though he was still a dowdy presence onscreen, both song and the film were hits. Then the time window slammed shut, never again to allow Jessel to star in a successful film. This was around the same time that Fanny Brice starred for Warner Bros. in *My Man*. If her range and talent far exceeded those of Jessel, her appeal was more special-ized, and urban and ethnic, than that of Jolson. The high grosses of *My Man* did not prevent it from being a one-time stunt, and Brice's subsequent film career told the tale: a second vehicle, *Be Yourself,* which fared indifferently, and later a supporting role and a couple of guest spots. Film's loss.

Brice and Jessel's successes came in the musical's catch-all frontier days; in a later and more orderly time they would not have been called on to front an entire film. One against-the-grain attempt in this same area, *Hello, Everybody!,* is an odd film for more reasons than the simple fact that it stars Kate Smith, the radio singer with a voice and frame of generous size. In 1932, musical film was poised to make a comeback, and Smith was such a comfy visitor to millions of American homes that a film appearance was not inconceivable. It came with a guest stint in Paramount's *The Big Broadcast*, after which there followed the erroneous judgment that more would be more. The problem was obviously not about vocal ability, nor even about weight or costuming, though neither was handled especially tactfully. Mainly, it lay in her inflexibility regarding her image, and the resultant, oddly negative, way she read on-camera. At no point in *Hello, Everybody!* did she permit the filmmakers to make her funny or endearing, let alone self-deprecating or raucous; without her singing—or, in one memorable scene, dancing—there seemed to be virtually nothing. Her film's failure soon became a show business legend, and most observers predictably hung the blame on her size. The more pertinent cause became clear many years later, when Smith was constantly on television. By then she was relaxed and warm and outgoing—everything missing from her one try at movie stardom.

From Kate Smith to Mariah Carey in one straight line. While Carey possessed the kind of Madonna-like exhibitionist confidence that would make Kate Smith blanch, the end results were pretty comparable. Like *Hello, Everybody!*, *Glitter* was launched in a time of very few musicals, its production attributable solely to the perceived draw of one wildly successful singer. It too was a thinly plotted Cinderella story centered around a huge-voiced young woman, and once again there was the notion that someone of untested ability could float some questionable dramatics. Even the timing for both films was unhappy: *Hello, Everybody!* opened during one of the most hopeless moments of the Depression, while *Glitter* was one of the first movies to come out after September 11, 2001.[6] Obviously, there had not been the aim to make either

---

[6] It did not help matters that the twin towers of the World Trade Center were prominently featured in *Glitter*, and usually they drew far more applause in movie theaters than did Ms. Carey's high-powered vocals.

woman look ridiculous, but it is fair to question the producers' intentions: were these films designed as one-shot tries, or were there thoughts that their success would spawn more Kate Smith or Mariah Carey vehicles? Either way, the results were worse than necessary, and like Smith, Carey made no more forays into musical drama. At least she was later able to redeem herself on film in a nonsinging supporting role in *Precious*.

Other popular singers offered more misses than hits. Rudy Vallee's *The Vagabond Lover* was a film that many saw and few liked, in this case specifically because Vallee was such a blank on film. Only later would he work well in film, mainly as a character comedian under the direction of Preston Sturges. A few years after him, Bing Crosby's popularity prompted other singers to try film, generally to little effect. One, Russ Columbo, did indeed come over well, which made it doubly sad that he was the victim in a shooting accident that, even in 1934, was deemed highly suspicious and possibly gay-inflected. Later on, there would be Sinatra, with his frustrating roster of musical films. The best of them, *On the Town*, owed little to him, and except for his fine performance in *The Joker Is Wild* there remains little of the later work worth recall. The vocals were stunning, the presence smooth, and *Guys and Dolls, High Society, Pal Joey, Can-Can*, and *Robin and the Seven Hoods* were the work of someone who ultimately did not seem to care. Dean Martin, while he pretended otherwise, did care a little more than Sinatra, but after Jerry Lewis he had few opportunities to prove it.

Doris Day was a singer too, though unlike most others, her entry into film was in the nature of an accident, after Judy Garland was unavailable and Betty Hutton became pregnant. No acting experience at all in the conventional sense, but, like Garland, she possessed some sharp instincts about how acting, in speech and movement, might be an extension of musical phrasing. *Romance on the High Seas* was her first film, and enjoyably typical of many second-rate musicals of its era in that it didn't really need its songs and could have functioned as a straight screwball comedy. Still, those songs (Jule Styne and Sammy Cahn) were excellent, and so was Day, albeit with hepcat slang and big forties hair and makeup that now seem alien to her. If Betty Hutton was extroverted to the point of exhaustion, Day is more soulful and welcoming, at ease showing emotion through song more than through dialogue. The centerpiece of *Romance on the High Seas* was the opulent ballad "It's Magic," its distinctive downward-slanted melodic lines delivered by Day with a kind of contained ecstasy that makes it less about plot pretext than how a fine singer can find the exact means to communicate. The Day star was promptly launched even as the persona took a while to coalesce.

Day was too original, in fact, to jibe very well with her foremothers; she had neither Garland's overt emotionalism nor Hutton's roughhouse, nor the slightly crass cheer of Grable. Her unblinking sincerity made her a little more like Alice Faye, without the street-smart air or that oddly glum cloud that could hang over Faye even at her happiest. On the surface, Day appeared to be sunshine in a woman's body—it's hard to imagine her, in those early Warner Bros. films, not smiling—yet she had darker currents that few of her musicals would make apparent. Doubtless, it would have helped her to be at a studio less capable of outright bilge like *April in Paris*, or less obsessed with the dêja-vu of constant remakes and knockoffs.[7] Unimaginative scripts and direction were the problem here, never Day, and oddly enough her best opportunity came in one of the most blatant imitations: if *Calamity Jane* isn't *Annie Get Your Gun,* nothing is, even to the same leading man, Howard Keel. Day pounced on it as surely as Betty Hutton did with *Annie,* her liberated ferocity making it appear that it was being done for the first time. This time, unfortunately, a hit song ("Secret Love") did not bring financial success, and though there was one more personal and popular triumph in a musical, *Love Me or Leave Me,* she was clearly being led elsewhere. As fine—superb, really—as she was in *The Pajama Game,* it too was a box-office disappointment, and her only further try was *Billy Rose's Jumbo* (so goes its official copyrighted title), which had the singular distinction of being the biggest money-losing musical in MGM history. Day's work has endured past the sex comedies and virgin jokes and dull sitcom and retirement, and she was so wonderful at what she did that sometimes it's hard not to feel ungrateful that she couldn't have been given better, or more.

While timing was only part of the issue with Doris Day, it would be a key reason why, from the mid-1950s onward, good people were unable to appear in good musicals. An original like *Never Steal Anything Small* was unsuccessful

[7] Warners was so addicted to the notion of do-overs that it even copied its old musical sequences. Day's *Lullaby of Broadway* begins the title song exactly the same as in its premiere outing in *Gold Diggers of 1935*: a singer's face coming at the audience through a sea of darkness. Then, it had been the hypnotic start of Busby Berkeley's greatest achievement; now, it's a cheap way to launch a generic number. Day did have the savvy to say no to one remake: *Painting the Clouds with Sunshine,* the old *Gold Diggers* plot brushed off for what seemed the 712th time.

on every level—and heinous in its waste of Jimmy Cagney's talent—while skill-ful adaptations like *Silk Stockings* and *Bells Are Ringing* flopped resoundingly. As fewer opportunities arose, they were sometimes attended by the question-able notion that dubbing solves all problems. This is why Rossano Brazzi and Sidney Poitier could look great, in *South Pacific* and *Porgy and Bess*, and sound ostensibly like the opera singers who were doing the actual vocalizing. While dubbing had been present from the very beginning, it achieved some kind of pinnacle from the mid-fifties to the late sixties. Hiring nonsinging names like Deborah Kerr and Rosalind Russell and Natalie Wood and Audrey Hepburn, even nonsinging non-names like Richard Beymer, was viewed as a form of insurance, conviction be damned.[8]

Casting for name recognition instead of experience has long been part of the film equation, and it cuts both ways. It may, for example, have seemed more astute than desperate to put Lee Marvin and Clint Eastwood into *Paint Your Wagon*, despite the equivocal results. Nicole Kidman in *Moulin Rouge!* was far less a musical player than a photogenic, aurally enhanced artifact, and many people left *Mamma Mia!* wondering if Pierce Brosnan's execrable singing was intended as a deliberate joke. In contrast with these are the film people who take the plunge with surprising ease. Back in the dinosaur days, audiences were surprised to learn that two big silent stars, Gloria Swanson and Bebe Daniels, could sing as well as talk, with Swanson's florid turn as a diva deluxe in *Music in the Air* remaining an ace example of Hollywood casting in a Broadway transfer. Later, there was Marilyn Monroe, consolidating her stardom in *Gentlemen Prefer Blondes*, and Jean Simmons, so winning in *Guys and Dolls* that she showed up the falseness of most of what surrounded her. In *Oklahoma!*, Gloria Grahame's vocals had to be pieced together from tiny shards—effort fully justi-fied by the final result—and for Renee Zellweger in *Chicago*, a lack of musical aptitude was actually a help in depicting the shallow ambitions of a stage-struck amateur. *Evita*, as has already been noted, offered a right/wrong primer for

---

[8] Let it be stated: Deborah Kerr is so great in *The King and I*, and Marni Nixon's voice matches her so well, that the joint performance can serve as Exhibit A on the pro side of the dubbing controversy, along with Jamie Foxx as Ray Charles and Marion Cotillard as Edith Piaf. It might also be mentioned that Natalie Wood did sing for herself, quite adequately, in *Gypsy*; ditto Audrey Hepburn in *Funny Face* and *Breakfast at Tiffany's*. There is also Ava Gardner, whose *Show Boat* vocals should not have been overdubbed. Not that there aren't the converses to these as well, embodied by the experience of hearing a fine actor, Joaquin Phoenix, tone-lessly rechanneling Johnny Cash.

name-driven casting, Antonio Banderas's unexpected fluency versus the steel
monolith they call Madonna. Although Banderas scored in a Broadway revival
of *Nine* and Simmons did *A Little Night Music* in London and on tour, most of
these actors would exist strictly as on-film musical performers, cosseted by flat-
tering recording and helpful editing; the point was brought home specifically
when Zellweger declined to sing a nominated *Chicago* song live at the Academy
Awards and was replaced by her song-savvy costar Queen Latifah.

Sometimes it is less about the performer than the fit. Many years after the
fact, some buffs continue to decry Barbra Streisand in *Hello, Dolly!*—too
young by half, more Levi than Gallagher, a shtick grab-bag ranging from Mae
West to Groucho. While the umbrage is valid, it's fair to ask what else Fox
might have done right at that point. Carol Channing was way eccentric on film,
Julie Andrews was wrong, Doris Day was out of musicals and nearly out of film,
Judy Garland was unreliable and soon dead. Who else—Anne Bancroft? Eliza-
beth Taylor? Mae West herself? While Streisand was cast before the public
had seen so much as a minute of her on film, she had the name, the draw, the
magic. Perhaps the question should be less "Should she have done it?" than
"Why did they make it so damn big?" Not dissimilarly if more abrasively, there
was Diana Ross in *The Wiz*—an age question once again, compounded by a
character rewrite so drastic and unappealing that Pauline Kael titled her review
"Saint Dorothy." On a not-unrelated subject: putting Jennifer Hudson into
Dreamgirls also qualified as a stunt, since she was known only as a worthy
also-ran on the new millenium's Amateur Hour, *American Idol*. The revelation,
then, came with the power and scorch of her acting, so honest that it tended
to expose the superficiality of the rest of that glitzy enterprise. Unlike Hudson,
Anne Hathaway and Hugh Jackman were known as actors who could also sing,
and their casting in *Les Misérables* rated exclamations of "Finally they get to be
in a musical." While the circumstances may have been trying to those not
enamored of the show, their commitment—Hathaway's riveting sincerity in
particular—was as unquestionable as it was fervent. As shows and films,
Dreamgirls and *Les Miz* divided audiences as few others do, and so does *Sweeney Todd*, especially in its highly reimagined film version. Here, as in *Evita*,
stunt casting cut both ways—Johnny Depp with predictably skilled acting and
quite viable vocalism, and Helena Bonham-Carter with a wee-mouse singing
voice that only a director-husband would judge sufficient.

For genuine musical performers, the cinematic terrain after the 1960s was
especially uninviting. What was not killed off by television was rendered, by

rock music, largely obsolete; it was small wonder that so many movie veterans—people like Howard Keel and Mitzi Gaynor and Gordon MacRae—were
compelled to remake their careers in live theater or nightclubs or television.
Astaire, still an astonishment in his sixties, began to work as a dramatic actor
while still occasionally showing TV audiences how it was done, and the two
dancing Genes—Kelly and Nelson—both found work as directors. For many,
there would also be that two-decade phenomenon of middlebrow American
culture, the dinner theater circuit; if it was not always rewarding artistically,
where else could Dorothy Lamour be seen playing in Noël Coward? These
performers, at least, had been around for some of the glory, unlike those who
never had much of an opportunity. Robert Goulet, for example, scored heavily
on Broadway in *Camelot*, after which there were no film roles. Even Julie
Andrews, for all the splendor of her work, could not sustain a viable film career
after the back-to-back disasters of *Star!* and *Darling Lili*. If Streisand was a
great exception, it's also true that she cut way back on musicals and, worse,
made one of them be *A Star Is Born*.

So many right people, such a wrong time. If things had been different, Liza
Minnelli and Bette Midler would have been able to alternate live performance
with one grand musical after another, along with the occasional dramatic role to
show what versatility's about. But what chances were there? After *Cabaret*, Minnelli never again found a true connection with movie audiences; her one subsequent big musical, Scorsese's *New York, New York*, cast so analytic and relentless
an eye on the genre that it seemed to be self-sabotage. Midler, too, had few
chances after the initial breakthrough. At some other time she might have followed the triumph of *The Rose* with any manner of musicals, from rock to classic
Broadway. Instead, her movie stardom was confined mainly to comedy and but
one full-fledged musical, the vaguely off-putting *For the Boys*. Only on stage and
with the televised *Gypsy* could she let audiences know the kind of talent that was
being neglected in a time without musicals. There was also John Travolta, with
the back-to-back smashes of *Saturday Night Fever* and *Grease* and no chance for
a follow-up, and others who might have soared but were given even less. The cult
hit *The Rocky Horror Picture Show* gave Barry Bostwick less opportunity to make
a musical impression than to look nice in skivvies, and *Pennies from Heaven*, intriguing as it was, compelled the über-gifted Bernadette Peters to sing with voices
other than her own. Neither Patti LuPone nor Mandy Patinkin was given any
chance, really, at all, and most subsequent Broadway people know better than to
even make much of an effort. Revivals and *Glee* pay better.

In the twenty-first century, with its perpetual conflation of the permanent with the fleeting, the notion of musical performance carries unsettled currency. A pop performer like Justin Timberlake or Katy Perry will intimate some intriguing aptitude for the genre, then get no venue save for one of those concert films that come and go even faster than some stars' careers. They bring in the fans, make the quick cash, then disappear as fast as if it were on Pay-Per-View. No extraordinary effort need be expended, and it takes less creativity, after all, than even a *Vagabond Lover* or one of the later Elvis efforts. If a Justin Bieber offers a somewhat slim frame upon which to hang a cult of personality, he will still seem far less ridiculous if he plays himself on and offstage rather than attempting to enact a role. Nor will the narrow format be a deterrent to the multimillions of young girls who will turn out and scream lustily, especially when he's in 3-D. Could any of these people function in a more conventional musical-film environment? The potential some of them may have will doubtless not be realized, and not just because of *Glitter*: musical film stardom now functions as an ancillary marketing device, more like a photo-op or YouTube promo than an end in itself. When a Beyoncé makes the effort, the results are as ambiguous as they could be way back in the days of someone like Dick Haymes. The ones who are capable of more seldom get the breaks, the famous ones don't need to stretch themselves, and the movies cost too much to allow chance-taking. It's a tough world out there.

If a contemplation on musical performers must perforce be inconclusive, it can at least be appended by a demonstration of how a film might soar or sink based on the rightness of its cast. The work in question is *Guys and Dolls*, which made a zillion dollars at a time when most musicals were dying. On Broadway, it had been one of those rare shows that really captivated—sharp and immediate, funny and romantic, its songs so masterfully integrated into the whole that one person appeared to be writing the whole thing. (For the record: Frank Loesser wrote the music and lyrics, while Abe Burrows and Jo Swerling wrote the script.) Movie producer Sam Goldwyn, who was known for making meaningful dramas and meaningless musicals, paid a then-record amount of money for the rights, and proceeded from the ironclad philosophy that more cash buys more talent. This included a choreographer, Michael Kidd, of abundant talent, and a major director, Joseph L. Mankiewicz, with no film musical experience whatever, which the lumbering and erratically stylized final result made highly apparent. There was also, in the casting of the four leads, an approach that either covered all the bases (for those who liked the outcome) or was maddening (for those who didn't). Straight from Broadway, there was Vivian Blaine as Miss Adelaide, selected over Marilyn Monroe and proving that a camera requires a stage performance to be freshened and modulated if it is to be anything other than big and forced. She didn't and it wasn't. Opposite her, in one of the most Hollywood of all miscastings, was Frank Sinatra. Look up Sam Levene, the superlative original Nathan Detroit, sometime— he made many films—and see if there can be detected any infinitesimal connection between him, with his Jewish urban gravel, and Frankie, with the golden tones and still-youthful(ish) aura. Sinatra wanted to be cast as Sky Masterson, Goldwyn wanted Brando, and the crooner's runner-up resentment is as apparent as the awkwardness of his Damon Runyon locutions. As Sky, Brando did not exactly phone in his performance—not in the way he alleviated his boredom with a film like *Desirée* by coming up with some ridiculous inflections—yet he didn't totally commit. His singing sounds like Brando singing, for better or worse, and otherwise here is an actor out of synch with his role. Then, at last, is one of those small miracles where the gambles paid off. When Goldwyn couldn't get Grace Kelly, he hired one of the few other film names capable of playing a buttoned-up girl with banked fires. Actually, Jean Simmons was capable of playing just about anything, and the fact that she could sing adequately meant that the dubbers were kept at bay. Alone among the four leads, she *meant* her performance—just as Bebe Daniels meant Rio Rita or Doris Day meant Calamity Jane or Johnny Depp, razor and all, meant Sweeney Todd, the Demon Barber of Fleet Street. When stunt casting works, it ceases to be a stunt. Blaine was the safe one, more or less, Sinatra sang and seethed, and Brando stayed himself, paddling warily through unfriendly waters. Simmons became Sister Sarah. If one out of four isn't a great average, at least it delivers some magic.

Whither musical performers? It's probably too much to ask for another Astaire or Garland, but could there be more Depps or Hudsons? A Sinatra with commitment, maybe, or a latter-day Elvis with more imaginative handlers, or an Andrews or Midler with better luck. Or, more feasibly, a Jackman with opportunities. There *should* always be possibilities, even as the prospects sometimes sink into oblivion and technology makes it possible for any boob to fake his way through a part with the aid of digital enhancement. That part, the fakery, should be declared illegal. Film can either expose limitations or enhance potential, and a musical can do both. As one Broadway star after another has learned, the able ones won't always get the roles, and the lesser talents might end up, in the crazy

Phoning it in: On the screen and in the photo studio, the four leads in *Guys and Dolls* frequently seemed like they had all been compartmentalized in some fashion. Brando seems a tad offhand, Simmons gorgeous and radiant, Sinatra disjunct, Blaine working it. So they are seen here, and so they are through the whole film.

logic of film, working out better. Sometimes a singer can act—here's to you once again, Jennifer Hudson—and sometimes a close-up camera needs someone who can work intimately, which is one of the differences between *Gentlemen Prefer Blondes* on stage and on film. On rare occasions like *Chicago* it can all come together well, though more often, from *Guys and Dolls* to *Evita* and beyond, one has to be grateful for any success at all. Faking it is easy, meaning it is hard, and a well-cast musical should be ever mindful of the difference. So should a bright and deserving audience.

Chapter 5

The Art of the Possible

....

F or game viewers willing to embrace their inner lunatic, there has loomed, since 1930, the presence of an exceedingly odd piece of cinema. Even as it comprises the standard accoutrements of actors and plot and dialogue and songs and dances, it derides any normal categorization. It's been labeled musical, operetta, comedy, romance, and disaster film . . . also, simply, disaster. It is all of those and none, and even in its very title implies the outré: *Madam Satan.* Its maid singing romantic advice has already been saluted here, and the musical program also includes a romantic waltz, something called "The Girl Auction," and a ballet depicting an internal combustion engine. The plot, a wife-husband-showgirl triangle, is set partly on a dirigible where chorus girls prowl the catwalks dressed as cats. Other chorines, dressed as clocks, sound the time by striking themselves in the head. When lightning strikes the blimp, people parachute out wearing masquerade costumes, and the showgirl crashes into a men's Turkish bath. The first half of *Madam Satan* drags interminably, then when it reaches the blimp it blazes from one outrage to the next. It could never rationally be called a work of quality, but it is certainly conspicuous, outlandish, and uniquely diverting. All this places it firmly into the oeuvre of the one director capable of concocting such a thing: Cecil B. DeMille.

Although some of DeMille's spectacles play rather like operas without arias, *Madam Satan* was his one musical, and a costly flop. Later, he had little good to say about it, and in making it must have felt as unmoored as his blimp when it came to setting up song cues, shooting dances, imparting lyrical flow.

Indeed, in no conventional sense does *Madam Satan* flow; it lurches, careens, and finally bails along with all those dressed-up actors. This is a film to watch less with a rapturous gaze than with gawks, all the way through to the final scene, when the heroine calmly reprises the score's non-hit songs to remind everyone that this is a musical. That this is way nutty for DeMille, let alone anyone else, is the point, in a way: as collaborative, even impersonal an art as musicals generally are, the best or most extreme of them usually bear a particular or peculiar creator's stamp. In many instances it's a director, at ease or at sea; it can also be a choreographer or producer or star or songwriter or even costume designer. Even with the well-oiled interactive machinery of musical production, one empowered creator can carry an immense amount of authorial weight, and not consistently to the good.

Around the time DeMille was wrestling with his Madam early in 1930, film studios were beginning to set the basic regimen for making musicals. There were the people who wrote and played music, the singing and dancing choruses, the designers, and the crew. Also the directors, and a Michael Curtiz or a Lloyd Bacon prided himself on one-size-fits-all workmanship. Others were faceless, competent workhorses, and the likes of Ford and Capra would not stray into musicals, just as Billy Wilder found them uncomfortable. Fortunately, there could be the occasional figure who embraced the notion of a musical as a personal statement. Look at any other musical from 1929, then look at *The Love Parade*.[1] Even as the technology seems as antique as some of the sexual politics, a governing aesthetic is always present, and its name is Lubitsch. He had the clout, the wit, and the imagination, and at Paramount he had the accommodation; while no less industrial than other studios, it could on occasion cater to a higher directorial profile. (Its revue, *Paramount on Parade*, was unlike the others in that it had eleven directors, including Lubitsch. This is the way revue films might be done if they still existed.) *The Love Parade* could have happened only at Paramount, only with Lubitsch directing Maurice Chevalier and the debuting Jeanette MacDonald. For Lubitsch, an operetta format was less *Desert Song* seriousness than genial mockery, with slyness and innuendo to subvert the usual pomposity—"meta" in-jokes that are standard now were

---

[1] Conventional musicals, that is, not dramas with atmospheric/incidental songs. Otherwise, there would be a worthy triumvirate—Lubitsch with *Love Parade*, King Vidor with *Hallelujah!*, and Rouben Mamoulian with *Applause*. The latter two have been called musicals but aren't, not in the conventional sense of a *Broadway Melody* or *Rio Rita*.

unimaginably chichi in 1929. Sex was prominent too: the lovelorn queen sings of her "Dream Lover" while bathing, and Chevalier announces his sexual frustration with "Nobody's Using It Now." While the script and songs are the work of others, everything ties to the director's vision, thus making a putative collaboration seem intensely personal.[2]

Another Paramount director was given carte blanche on a film even more expensive than *The Love Parade*, and shot so soon after it that Jeanette MacDonald barely had a day off between roles. This time, unfortunately, the sense of humor was well concealed in both the material and the man in charge. Ludwig Berger had done several imaginative works in his native Germany, so why not a prestigious Paramount operetta? *The Vagabond King* had been big box-office on Broadway, an ornate pageant recounting the fanciful legend of Louis XI raising the activist poet François Villon to the position of king for one day. There were processions and battles and rabble and gorgeous Rudolf Friml music, and the studio felt the project to be so sure-fire that it bestowed a million-plus budget, often sumptuous early Technicolor, a director untested in English-language film, and a Broadway star (Dennis King) unknown to movie audiences. It looked and sounded beautiful, and it weighed a ton. While not an instant museum piece like *The Desert Song*, *The Vagabond King* on film was ponderous and Teutonically unyielding, a non-*Love Parade*, impressive but unmoving. Berger had indeed made a statement as personal and individual as Lubitsch, one saturated with the special pomposity that can summon forth that useful and nearly obsolete word *fustian*.

Lubitsch and Berger produced work that vividly pointed up the disparity of their gifts. Many decades later, there was the case of Rob Marshall, whose talent seemed to diverge from itself. In spite of the objections some had to *Chicago*, it was clear that Marshall would or might assume a place as the musical film director of the new century, even as a follow-up took a long seven years. Like *Chicago*, *Nine* was a "concept" show difficult to adapt, with a non-musical star cast, period stylishness, and potential for a directorial statement. Less conspicuous and ultimately victorious were the differences from *Chicago*:

---

[2] Two signs of Lubitsch's success with musicals: one was that he made only five of them—one co-directed—yet prompted scores of imitators in America and Europe. (One, *Love Me Tonight*, even exceeded the master.) And, the sexual candor of *The Love Parade* was enough to spawn one of those wretchedly "religious" save-our-children campaigns still seen today, usually in protest of things far less classic and tasteful than *The Love Parade*.

the original source, Fellini's 8½, cast a far more ominous and competitive shadow than did *Roxy Hart*; a movie director's creative crisis was not as gripping as a tabloid murder case; and the score often seemed to be dutiful aural wallpaper. On Broadway, in the 1970s and again in the '90s, *Nine* was a *Dreamgirls* kind of show, the presentation carrying more validity than the substance. Marshall, seeming to intuit this, pushed the look of his film even past *Chicago* regions, photographing the many beautiful women in a way to make frames of his film look like scans from early '60s issues of *Vogue*. There were the jumpy edits again as well, which with these songs seemed like anxious quality-enhancement instead of valid technique. Whether or not one liked *Chicago*, it had a unity; *Nine* was a crowded shelf of pieces, and Marshall's high-pressure style simply exposed the work's essential emptiness. As with *The Vagabond King*, looking terrific is not enough.[3]

Nine was depressing because of talent given over to insufficient material. Another kind of misapplication occurs when a director's ability resides outside the realm in question. There have been many such, both at the dawn of time and in the roadshow days of high budgets and desperate credentials. Besides that arresting case of DeMille and *Madam Satan*, there was the prestigious Frank Borzage, the first director to win an Academy Award. His work tended toward the emotional and sentimental, so possibly he could handle a tale of lost love filled with beautiful melody. Unfortunately, the preeminence in *Song O'My Heart* came with a tenor, not a director. John McCormack sang and sang, then sang some more, with little room for much else. Except for pretty shots of shamrock vistas, all Borzage needed to do was have his camera record one man in concert. It was not only that a major director was not given the chance to do what he did best—in this case he was not given the chance to do at all. Since Fox had paid McCormack a dumbfounding salary, the event warranted a big name, not necessarily a suitable one. Comparable circumstances prevailed twenty-five years later on *Guys and Dolls*, for which the nature of Joseph L. Mankiewicz's talent mattered less than his name and quartet of Oscars. As his special gift was for writing and staging wittily observed skirmishes between intelligent adults, a world of sharpies and Damon Runyon dialogue and

---

[3] It probably, too, could have benefited from a different leading man. It was hard, in *Nine,* not to bemoan the sight of Daniel Day-Lewis, an actor of astounding gifts, performing so ably to so little effect. Good casting matters, a director can supply only so much smoke-and-mirrors, and some actors are better off playing Lincoln.

Goldwyn Girls would play to his verbose weaknesses far more than to his flash-
ing strengths. While his input was more evident than Borzage's had been, this
was not, under the enervated circumstances, an especially good thing. When
the governing aesthetic is one of incongruity, the choices proceed like a house
of cards.

The directorial highlights of *Guys and Dolls*, such as they were, were ceded
by Mankiewicz to choreographer Michael Kidd, and in a less inert carnival
Kidd might have been adjudged the show's defining force (along with song-
writer Frank Loesser, and possibly whoever cast Jean Simmons). At that point,
Kidd was coming off a triumph of far more indisputable merit. *Seven Brides for
Seven Brothers* was not precisely what would be called a sleeper hit, since
sleepers are low-budget things that sneak in and do better than expected.
Seven Brides was a healthy-budget MGM "A" picture, more expensive than *Kiss
Me, Kate* and nearly as costly as *The Band Wagon,* and unlike them both in that
it was a massive profit-earner. The hit owed comparatively little to the songs or
the draw of the cast, as perfectly nice as all that was, but to one small and one
very large factor. The minor one was a sort of randy luster, uncommon in big
song-and-dance shows, surrounding the subject matter and shotgun-wedding
conclusion; far more important, this was a movie about dance. In this case,
credit needs to go to both Kidd and the director, Stanley Donen, a former
dancer himself and the veteran of masterly co-directing stints with Gene Kelly.
The dances of *Seven Brides* were presented not as dream ballets—as good as
those could be in *An American in Paris* and elsewhere—but storytelling, live
and vivid and upfront. Kidd provided most of the moves, Donen shot and set it
off, and if the collaboration had its uneasy moments on the soundstage, it
made large parts of the movie brilliant. *Seven Brides* isn't a star vehicle and it's
not a Donen film in the manner of *Funny Face.* If Kidd was but a collaborator,
it's his work that sends the movie soaring.[4]

The particular, not to say peculiar, talent of Busby Berkeley was such that
his "dance creations" tended to take over other directors' work. While *42nd
Street* and *Gold Diggers of 1933* are not in a sense Berkeley films, it is he who
spawns the most recall. Even before Warner Bros., Berkeley was one of the

---

[4] Kidd directed only one entire film, *Merry Andrew,* whose defining stamp, if any, came from
its star, Danny Kaye. With choreographers as with everyone in film, when it comes to directing,
it's hard to know who will work out (Charles Walters, Busby Berkeley, Herbert Ross) and who
won't (Kidd, Robert Alton, Gower Champion).

first dance directors—"choreographer" was an unknown term then—allowed to work separately, in charge, beholden to no one. In his first film, *Whoopee!*, his presence was virtually equal to that of the high-pressure star, Eddie Cantor, carrying infinitely more weight than the putative director.[5] Directors on Berkeley films shot the script while he, who sipped martinis in the bathtub while coming up with ideas, barely even knew what the scripts were about. In *Whoopee!*, following the credits and establishing shots, there are a couple of lines of writ-large exposition and then BANG. A young woman (really young— the thirteen-year-old Betty Grable) begins to sing about cowboys not being wild enough, and suddenly it takes off with chorus groupings and camera angles completely unlike normal 1930 arrangements, finally with an overhead shot of Grable atop a spinning human pinwheel. None of it enhances Eddie Cantor, who hasn't appeared yet, or has anything to do with the plot; nor is the cheeky Grable presented in such a way as to be the number's center. Here and in the later group numbers, it's more about the one impudent and not-always-stable man from Broadway who cared far less about how dancers moved than how they looked to his camera. Berkeley's work in *Whoopee!*, like most of his later films at Warner Bros. and elsewhere, makes for uniquely off-kilter delight that borders on guilty pleasure. His fantasies are the antithesis of traditional musical flow, defying even more logic than usual, and who would be without them? Even when not just about Berkeley—when there's a great Warren-Dubin song or the beatific klutziness of Ruby Keeler or the untoward joy felt when neon violins move in waltz time—one personality clearly dominates. Nor is it a contradiction to add that the best Berkeley films hold components that balance his creations: the forward propulsion in *42nd Street*, Jimmy Cagney's energy in *Footlight Parade*, the amoral audacity of *Wonder Bar*, the wisecracks of *Gold Diggers*, the sheer talent of Rooney and Garland, the wonder of Miranda. Otherwise, in something like the inane *Dames*, it's Berkeley and his art on the one hand and emptiness on the other, an imbalance to breed ingratitude.

Berkeley's move from autonomous musical numbers to full features was, given his profile and the grosses of his early films, most predictable. His first solo credit, *Gold Diggers of 1935*, contains little that any Warner director would not also have done, yet adds kinetic little bits here and there to impart the offhand

---

[5] Let that director's name be, literally as well as historically and figuratively, a footnote. Thornton Freeland. And it happened to him again on his one other well-known film, *Flying Down to Rio*. Astaire (and Rogers), anybody?

cohesion that a *Dames* could not possess. In the manner of *42nd Street* and *Footlight Parade*, the giant musical sequences are rear loaded, and since the second and last is "Lullaby of Broadway," this seems eminently fair—save for a fleeting wrap-up of plot threads, what could possibly come after this number? With its long shadows and odd angles and joyless hedonism and relentlessly pounding taps, "Lullaby" doesn't even try to connect with anything else, and its central figure, the good-time girl sung and embodied by Wini Shaw, is somehow more real and compelling than anyone else seen in the film. When she falls from the skyscraper, the shocking abruptness is more pertinent than the "normal" points laid out by the script. No, long and interconnected arcs are not for Berkeley, who asserts his centrality in punchy small paragraphs—here and "Remember My Forgotten Man" and "By a Waterfall"—and during the in-between moments he knows the audience is waiting for his next surprise. He never did it better than in this *Gold Diggers*, not least because his studio would promptly confront him with slashed budgets and decreased leeway. His next studio berth, at MGM, offered bounty without individuality, and the old nerviness only surfaced in sustained fashion in his foray at Fox, *The Gang's All Here*. Not coincidentally, it was the most expensive Fox film to date, and Berkeley's excesses and personal problems ensured that his future work would be sporadic and uneven. Erratic and bizarre offscreen and sometimes on, he was, categorically, his own kind of treasure. Easy to imitate, impossible to equal, inhabiting and informing musicals as few have ever done.

Berkeley was the first major film director tagged specifically as a musical specialist. The second also came from Broadway, this time with a background that began in design. Vincente Minnelli served a brief apprenticeship at MGM, then cast his eye on the genre in a way no one had done previously. Berkeley saw musicals as a chain of self-contained sequences with connective tissue, just as all those utility men who directed musicals saw the films in terms of the plot scenes they would stage, since song and dance required little of them other than to aim the camera. Minnelli saw the potential unity. To him, a musical did not need to be a rambunctious vaudeville of scattered parts. It could have character and detail and texture, be true to whatever world it conjured, observe or evoke things other than show business or romance. Berkeley applied concept to his best musical numbers; Minnelli did so with entire films. The reach might go beyond the grasp, as with *Yolanda and the Thief* or *The Pirate*, but Minnelli's best, in *Meet Me in St. Louis* and *Gigi* and much of *Cabin in the Sky* and *An American in Paris* and *The Band Wagon*, works out patterns and codes of consistency and reference all but unknown in escapist film. Minnelli is to musicals what John Ford is to westerns: a detectable imprint, consciousness of the big picture, knowledge that a genre often treated as a throwaway can say much and imply more. Look at *Meet Me in St. Louis* alongside an imitator like *On Moonlight Bay*. One, without a conventional plot, makes heartfelt statements about accord, home, belonging. The other pastes together little cells of proto-sitcom shtick. Its period songs are jukebox moments, where *St. Louis* uses music to tell a story and expand characters. *Moonlight*'s concept of design is bric-a-brac out of the studio warehouse, where the house in *St. Louis* is so individualized it can be considered a family member. None of this, rest assured, would have occurred without Minnelli.

Not only through comparison with other directors does Minnelli's art loom large; it occurs also with a look at the times when his own current was hindered

An American family: Vincente Minnelli, the year-old (give or take) Liza, and Judy Garland during the long and arduous shoot of *The Pirate*. As if there already isn't enough history on display here, on the right can be seen a part of one of the original, cumbersome Technicolor cameras. Without it—as without Minnelli, Judy, and Liza—musical film would have been much diminished.

or running amok. *Kismet*, on Broadway, was a riot of music and color and decor and dance, dull of script but mesmerizing of effect. Who better than Minnelli to make it pop on the screen? But he didn't like the show much, and he was intent on a project—the Van Gogh biography *Lust for Life*—he deemed far more worthy. MGM pressed, Minnelli resisted, and finally the ultimatum came: no *Kismet*, no *Lust*. He got through it as fast and perfunctorily as he could, and his boredom is there, in wide CinemaScope, for all to see. The characters come on, say or sing lines, and go off. The sets are generic Arabian Nights, the color schemes are bilious, and except for Dolores Gray the actors are on autopilot. This was a film that needed Minnelli, and his disinterest let it down.[6] His interest had been more engaged, a decade earlier, for *Yolanda and the Thief*, but that was a cardinal example of a film being too much and not enough at the same time: a trifle of a story, an anemic score, and much, much production. Its failure, and the subsequent one of *The Pirate*, helped caution Minnelli to pay less heed to the MGM motto (Art for Art's Sake) and more to the notion that what is imposing should also be entertaining. When Minnelli heeded the lessons, he was masterful. *Gigi*, for instance, had the discipline *Yolanda* lacked and the passion missing from *Kismet*, and it marked the first time a director of a musical received an Oscar.

Arthur Freed was in charge of all Minnelli's MGM musicals, and it's easy to imagine that the great titles under his aegis bear his detectable imprint. In truth, he was not quite that kind of hands-on figure. Freed's skill was more political than creative; almost like a matchmaker, he could bring together disparate talents. If he certainly had major say at all points, the profoundly uneven quality of his output points up his limits. As a lyricist, his work had been serviceable, not inspired, vastly dependent upon a good melody to set it off: think of "Singin' in the Rain" with just the words, not the tune or that wonderful raindroppy vamp. The same is true of "Good Morning" and "Broadway Rhythm" and "You Were Meant for Me" and most of his other songs—lyrics facilitating an overall product and not standing alone. So it was also with Freed as a producer. He could insist to the hierarchy that something like *Cabin in the Sky*

---

[6] He also left it before the job was done—with the remainder shot, according to costar Ann Blyth, by the uninspired Richard Thorpe. *Kismet*, had Minnelli cared more, might have fared better financially as well as creatively. As it was, it ranked with *The Pirate* as one of MGM's biggest money losers up to then. The worst flop on the books was also a musical. For anyone who has seen Frank Sinatra as *The Kissing Bandit*, no explanation is needed.

demands real artistry...but what then can be made of *Cabin's* immediate predecessor, *Panama Hattie?* The material is less worthy, to be sure, and so is the potential as a piece of cinema—but really, now.

There are other odd juxtapositions in Freed's output as well, two films in production at the same time, over which he exercised similar control, and only one turns out fine: *The Harvey Girls* versus *Yolanda and the Thief, Singin' in the Rain* versus the engaging but flimsy *The Belle of New York. Yolanda* was additionally hampered by charting too well the intersecting points of Freed's personal and professional lives: besides producing it, he supplied the undistinguished lyrics and saw that the role of Yolanda was filled, inadequately, by his protégée, Lucille Bremer. And *Ziegfeld Follies*, which truly could have been a Freed monument, was instead a jumble of all sorts of things. It seemed to recall, not in a good way, those *Hollywood Revue* house parties made before the movie musical knew exactly what it could do.[7] Astaire is fine in his numbers (as are his partners, Bremer and Gene Kelly), and there are grand moments with Lena Horne and Garland and others, but the *Traviata* excerpt and the "Beauty" soap bubbles are ludicrous, and the Lucille Ball cat-whipping bit so camp that it's no wonder she parodied it on *I Love Lucy.*

Freed, then, fared better as an organizer than a judge of material. Fortunately for him, the blessing of hindsight induces recollections of *Gigi* more than *Pagan Love Song*, as well as reminding posterity that it was he who provided the basis for *Singin' in the Rain.* "*Easter Parade* was all Berlin and *American in Paris* was the Gershwins. What about those songs I wrote?" While he may not have said it in quite those words, that was the spark, after which Betty Comden and Adolph Green were able to appropriate Freed's own history—*Broadway Melody* and the rest of it—along with his songs. Then, once again, there was that stunning ability to put things together—Gene Kelly and Stanley Donen to direct, Kelly to star, down the line to Walter Plunkett as costumer (and source for some of the early-sound-disaster bits) and to one of the single best pieces of casting in *any* film, Jean Hagen as the lethal-voiced Lina Lamont. The glory of *Singin' in the Rain*, of course, is that the collaboration works so well that no one truly dominates, not Freed and not even Kelly. Let Freed get

---

[7] Another similarity to the early revues: far more *Follies* material was shot than made the final edit. Some of it sounds tempting, like Astaire in a song he wrote and Fanny Brice as Baby Snooks. Not all the blame can be aimed at Freed, but if you're going to hire Jimmy Durante, see that he does something good enough to stay in the movie.

the applause for the moment, though—on good days, he knew how it should fit together.

Call it a curiosity, but it's a fact: Arthur Freed's main rival at MGM played far more of a defining role in his own musicals. That's not to say that "The Pasternak Unit" is ever discussed in hushed tones. Joseph Pasternak produced scores of musicals at MGM, a few of which resound with some familiarity: *Anchors Aweigh, Summer Stock, The Great Caruso, A Date with Judy*. He had access to much of the same talent pool as Freed, and he may bear as much credit as Freed for Gene Kelly's promotion to star stature. First and last, Pasternak's films reflected his own tastes and preferences far more consistently than did those of Freed or other producers of musicals. A Hungarian émigré with experience in the German film industry, Pasternak had found his way to Universal just when new management was taking over and his ideas about musicals fell on fresh ears. At a time when both Shirley Temple and Jeanette MacDonald were big, he put them together, more or less, and came up with Deanna Durbin, whose onscreen personality was as engaging as her soprano. Her films rescued the studio from financial crisis and, one after the other, they varied in their details and not their basic formula. When Pasternak moved to MGM in 1942 he found little need to alter the aesthetic. His sopranos of choice turned into Kathryn Grayson, Jane Powell, and even (in effect) Mario Lanza or Esther Williams. No director working under Pasternak cast a longer shadow than the man himself, which would be one reason (of several) why there were no Pasternak-Minnelli films, and why so much of Pasternak's MGM output was directed by the faceless drudge Richard Thorpe. Thorpe's most affirmative contribution to the history of musicals came when he was fired from *The Wizard of Oz*, and otherwise his films can mostly be watched with an eye toward how much better they might be if directed by Charles Walters or Stanley Donen or, in the case of something like *Fiesta*, anybody. So utter a lack of distinction made him an ideal match with his producer, since the Pasternak aesthetic was pre-etched into stone: genteel escapism with some heart appeal, and otherwise anything short of the kitchen sink. Alongside the daring and enterprise of Freed's best films, Pasternak offered musical comfort food—predictable works with engaging people, pretty colors, and nice songs. It worked quite well for many years, and the consistent success of things like *Thrill of a Romance* and *Because You're Mine* offset the losses of occasional MGM missteps like *The Pirate* and Pasternak's own calamity, *The Kissing Bandit*. He even had a sort-of-cutting-edge hit at a time when television was making most musicals tank, though surely *Love Me or Leave Me* succeeded in large part because it undercut the standard Pasternak nostalgia with nerve-rattling conflict usually taboo in his films. Pasternak endured at MGM several years longer than Freed and, almost always, his stamp is utter and identifiable. Let the man himself offer a neat summation of the way he made musicals: "Never make an audience think."

Before Freed and Pasternak, MGM had generally maintained a lower profile in its producer roster. One early exception was David O. Selznick, whose tenure at MGM came after his stint as production head at RKO and before the time of *Gone With the Wind* and *Rebecca*. One of the many reasons Selznick preferred to function as an independent producer was autonomy in general and choice of material in particular. Literary adaptations were his meat, classics and bestsellers, and he knew quite well which genres worked for him and which did not. In the latter category, most definitely, were musicals, of which he did several at MGM. *Dancing Lady* and *Reckless* are big and star-driven, and include work by Rodgers and Hart and Jerome Kern. They also have, supervising them, a man who seems to lack the first notion of how a musical operates and, moreover, does not wish to know. A reluctant musical makes for a disheartening spectacle, and neither of these movies is comfortable with the music or the genre. *Dancing Lady* is much more at ease as another Joan Crawford-up-from-the-slums story, while *Reckless* exists mainly to give audiences a peep at the scandal engulfing torch singer Libby Holman. The songs and production numbers are fragmented, the people—Astaire excepted—are uncomfortable, and Jean Harlow's dance double in *Reckless* is so obvious that she should get onscreen billing. Both films are as detectably of Selznick as *GWTW* or any of the other hits, and not in a positive sense. Everywhere can be felt his aversion, discomfort, and confusion.

After *Reckless*, David Selznick knew to stay away from musicals. But what of Joshua Logan? A rich reputation as one of Broadway's finest directors, a résumé loaded with seminal musicals as well as major drama and comedy—and, from 1955, high-profile film work that includes adaptations of four musicals, two of which had been his on Broadway. Stage directors have been coming to film since, even before, the dawn of sound, often with spectacular results—Bergman, Cukor, Kazan, on and on. Logan had the name and experience and prestige, and some of his films won fine reviews and major profits. Then, as time passed and some fog cleared, it became apparent that he had virtually no concept of how film worked. He could be good with some actors, like Marilyn Monroe in *Bus Stop* or Charles Boyer in *Fanny*, who already knew how to play to a camera, but much else is leaden and inert. This is apart from the color filters in *South Pacific*, which deserve every particle of ridicule heaped upon them for over half a century; all that need be added is the shock of considering that he had directed the show on Broadway and then, with a huge budget and stunning Pacific locations, made such a blob of a movie. *Fanny*, the best of his musical adaptations, is not a musical, having had its songs removed and used only as background scoring; still, it's good because the material has flavor and the actors are sincere, even when the Logan hand begins to feel heavy. As for *Camelot* and *Paint Your Wagon*: money, desperation, strange vocalism, and still more money, spent and lost. Tonnage, it's called, and even when Logan didn't make some of the bad choices himself, his is the ultimate imprimatur.[8]

The weightiness of the Logan touch was not confined to him: stolidity was a frequent hallmark of roadshow films. Musicals had been committee-made from the very beginning, yet roadshows' corporate nature seemed especially averse to a cult of authorial personality. George Cukor, who won his Oscar for *My Fair Lady*, would grow testy and defensive when asked what he brought to such a preconceived property. The truth, had he replied with it, might have scanned as "Much less than I imparted to *David Copperfield* or *A Star Is Born* or several dozen others." The more defining forces on *Fair Lady* were the Julie/Audrey controversy, designer Cecil Beaton, and the eight-figure cost. On *West Side Story,* the objective for an efficient technician like Robert Wise was less to do anything personal than to make sure the location work blended with the studio footage, and letting co-director Jerome Robbins stage and shoot his dances with maximum effect and few overruns.[9] Wise was similarly circumspect with *The Sound of Music*—keep it moving, make sure that Julie Andrews is center screen at all times, don't stint on the shots of cute kids and cute nuns. As for the august William Wyler on *Funny Girl*, his brand was so subservient to Streisand's that it was easy to forget that he had anything to do with it. The single best sequence, "Don't Rain on My Parade," was the work of Herbert Ross.

---

[8] A sad equivalent to Logan came later with another revered Broadway pro, Harold Prince. That *A Little Night Music* lacked the sparkle it had on Broadway goes without saying, but to *this* extent?

[9] Wise ultimately failed in those efforts, at least on the fiscal end—which was why Robbins was fired from *West Side Story* midway through filming. There could be no better demonstration of the roadshow mentality than in the placing of a massively gifted and famously temperamental artist into a collaborative setting that would not grant him sufficient leeway. Robbins, in any case, had the last laugh: what is *West Side Story* about, if not his art?

The impersonality of the roadshows seemed especially rearguard in a time when movie ads now said "A Film By [director's name here]." *Cabaret*, when it came along, succeeded for precisely that reason: Bob Fosse's force was so overwhelming that more conventional work seemed all the dimmer. Yet Fosse did not stay with musicals, nor much with film, and few major directors of the 1970s cared to confront a dying genre. There were, however, three men at the top of the field who each made an intriguing attempt to reconcile the personal nature of their craft with the collaborative aura of the musical. In *At Long Last Love*, Peter Bogdanovich set out to blend Lubitsch with Astaire/Rogers, using a screwball plot, monochrome decor, and even sung-live-on-the-set Cole Porter songs. Unfortunately, the tribute being paid by Bogdanovich seemed mainly addressed to himself and to Cybill Shepherd, setting up a result that would not appeal to audiences, nor to cinéastes. The alienation with Martin Scorsese's *New York, New York* was more deliberate, if equally personal and capricious. If Bogdanovich was seeking to recreate old forms, Scorsese seemed to be deconstructing, even destroying them. He would later do good musical work in documentaries like *The Last Waltz* and in Michael Jackson's *Bad*, but *New York, New York*'s stunning look and fine moments were counterbalanced by so much fraught negativity that jokes were made about how hard it was to sit through. Between the ironic distancing, the overlength, the creepy attempts to turn Liza Minnelli into her mother, and the most abrasive musical hero of all time, his film could only be a troubling, honorable failure. Another faux-old-Hollywood product, *One from the Heart*, took a different route. Francis Ford Coppola had done a musical early in his career and late in the roadshow age—the flawed but not disgraceful *Finian's Rainbow*—and later declined *Mame* in favor of a move to quite different material. *One from the Heart* was a hard right turn after *Apocalypse Now*, an attempt at larky escapism that went jarringly awry. Like Scorsese, Coppola deployed tons of production concept to come up with a "new" version of big-studio artifice—in this case all gilt and no lily, with a hint of a plot and, replacing a traditional score, wall-to-wall (meaning way too many) Tom Waits songs. Intensely personal projects need not be, in any way, successful ones.[10]

[10] Coppola also came somewhat a cropper with the not-quite-a-musical/nor-quite-not-a-musical *The Cotton Club*. Another talented if erratic director, James L. Brooks, also had a musical oddity in his small body of work. *I'll Do Anything* was shot as a full musical, with eight songs written by Prince, but when preview audiences turned thumbs down Brooks removed the entire score and filled the gaps with outtakes. (A fate not unlike that of a number of films late in 1930.) Alas, the hostility did not abate—*Anything* then became known as the huge flop that had all its songs cut out.

Coppola and Scorsese failed with effortful, deeply felt statements. What of the big directors used only as hired guns? Earlier there had been Wyler with *Funny Girl*, popular if dramatically rickety, and soon there would not even be the financial success. Motown's decision to engage Sidney Lumet to direct *The Wiz* was on a par with the notion to reconfigure it to suit Diana Ross. Seldom have so much potential and so much imaginative design counted for so little, especially given Lumet's inability to shoot even simple musical numbers. This, from a director of this much talent, was shocking, as well as a stark reminder of how difficult musicals can be. John Huston was a little less unlucky with *Annie*, in part because of his cast and because of all 1980s musicals this one was the most reminiscent of the earlier roadshows: a personal touch would be out of place, and Huston, like Wyler, was content to be an old pro and take the paycheck. Richard Attenborough, fresh (as it were) from *Gandhi*, was a similarly odd-fitting choice for *A Chorus Line*, and in this case the result was so exhaustively misconceived that nothing so trivial as a director could have rescued it. With it, as with *The Wiz*, the defining mark is less a signature than it is a crushing interweaving of misapplied talent and bad ideas.

Few signatures are as distinctive and pervasive as Dr. Seuss, whose work comes to the screen often and not always well. Happily, long before the likes of that wretched *Cat in the Hat* movie, Seuss was the writer/lyricist/auteur of a bona fide cult musical. *The 5,000 Fingers of Dr. T* is so strange and Seussian in look and sound that it can only inspire marvel that it was made at all—specifically as one of a group of intelligent, offbeat films produced by Stanley Kramer for Columbia. Few of these were at all successful financially, and with an elaborate Technicolor production *Dr. T.* was the biggest flop of all. The love, most of it, came later, and not only from coteries of Seuss fans and ex-little-boys-forced-to-take-piano-lessons. While some may find the musical sequences impinging on the whimsy, the music (Frederick Hollander) and choreography (Eugene Loring) are good, and Seuss's lyrics are as tart as the occasion warrants. When Dr. T. himself (Hans Conreid) celebrates his day of triumph in an absurdist catalogue of the clothes he wants to wear, it's loony paradise, virtually a Seuss book made real, and beguilingly unreal.

As Busby Berkeley has already demonstrated, a dance director can be a more affirmative force than the director or producer. Michael Kidd occasionally did this as well, and there was also, in the 1940s and '50s, the remarkable Jack Cole. Imaginative, witty, somewhat brutal and quite gay, Cole is best recalled for his work with Marilyn Monroe, and iconography doesn't come more definitive than "Diamonds Are a Girl's Best Friend." More crucial, possibly, are his achievements in films people don't know much, like *Meet Me after the Show*, or don't like much, like *Kismet*. Champagne can indeed come from dreary vineyards, and Cole's mastery may best be grasped away from the glare of a Monroe or a Hayworth. In any number of ways, *The "I Don't Care" Girl* is a film as strange and unpromising as its title. Eva Tanguay was a vaudeville soubrette who parlayed an entire career on the strength, basically, of one song, and surviving film and sound attest that she wasn't much, it can be said, of anything. Even in 1953 most audiences had forgotten her. This would not deter George Jessel, now a producer, from selling his bosses at Fox on the notion of Tanguay's non-story as a vehicle for the studio's own musical soubrette—Mitzi Gaynor. Jessel made it, of all things, a film about his own *Citizen Kane*-like quest for the truth about Eva Tanguay, and Gaynor, as it emerged, was to Tanguay what Hugh Jackman would be to Peter Allen: an improvement of vast measure. With the thing bearing as much relation to facts as *Night and Day* did to Cole Porter, and with old-hand director Lloyd Bacon serving the same function he had with Busby Berkeley, it was a given that any interest would fall on the musical numbers. These, as it happens, were parceled out to wildly disparate hands. Some were the work of Seymour Felix, who had previously shared *Cover Girl* with Gene Kelly; the others were by Cole, who treated them, Berkeley-like, as self-contained pieces without relation to plot or period. The resulting tension between the two styles would have fractured a better film; in a distended and don't-care olio such as this, Cole's work comes as blessed disruption. For Pete's sake, the man stages a vaudeville piece called "The Johnson Rag" as a jokey commedia dell'arte masque, he puts Oscar Levant in drag to play a censorious prude in "I Don't Care," and with the aid of his assistant/muse Gwen Verdon he makes "Beale Street Blues" a near-epic study in lowdown sensuality. Where Felix treats Gaynor like a one-size-fits-all Betty Grable, with routine chorus groupings, Cole's signature moves and design motifs set her off like a droll goddess. Thus is this odd assembly-line movie punctuated by one artist's outbursts of wit and smarts—definitive proof that virtuosity need not occur amid the worthiest climes.

Around the time that Jack Cole was toiling in lesser fields, Gene Kelly was atop his form at MGM. For many, Kelly's work was on a par with Astaire's, but the difference in their approach to musicals was sizable. Astaire was quietly in charge of his films, working with Hermes Pan and Ginger or the other partners and the director, dominating his films subtly by serving his material and setting

Putting the moves on: Jack Cole always worked closely with his stars, especially Marilyn Monroe. Here they're rehearsing "My Heart Belongs to Daddy" for *Let's Make Love*. If only the rest of the film had been one-tenth as good.

off his partners: an unthreatening kind of mastery, quietly driven. Kelly, with his working-class pugnacity and vaguely insincere grin, was more aggressive in both his physicality and his ego. Even now, some are put off by the brashness that seems to propel him—arrogant, sexy, conceivably overbearing. Such a full-bore sense of self was best applied in conjunction with strong colleagues, as when *On the Town* and *An American in Paris* and *Singin' in the Rain* allowed the likes of Stanley Donen and Vincente Minnelli to set off Kelly's good ideas, deflect some of the lesser ones, and tactfully curb his tendency to take over. (One of the joys of *Singin' in the Rain* is to see his own excesses conflated with that of his character, who is then occasionally brought low.) His ambition would not be stilled, however, and following a string of successes and a shelf of Oscars for *An American in Paris*, Kelly convinced Arthur Freed and MGM to stake him to a long-cherished project. It would be a film to expand the boundaries of musical cinema by focusing, simply and solely, on dance. Originally, he had not planned to appear in the work finally called *Invitation to the Dance*, but MGM insisted that a risky project required a major star. So Kelly choreographed, directed, and danced in what he felt would be his defining work—the term "vanity project" had not yet come into common usage—and then the fearful studio shelved it. As shot, there were three segments; by release time, nearly four years after shooting had commenced, one of those had been replaced by a live/animated amalgam that deliberately recalled Kelly's early triumph in *Anchors Aweigh*. If the pretentiousness of *Invitation to the Dance* was as predictable as the disastrous popular response, more regrettable was the fact that it was so boring, less a festival of dance than an insufficient jumble of choreography and mime. Nor has posterity been kind: later in Kelly's life, when his art was being celebrated, his big dance film was mentioned, if at all, as a footnote, just ahead of *Xanadu*.

If *Invitation to the Dance* was an Icarus-like attempt at self-definition, Gene Kelly was as a meek piker alongside Al Jolson. While he left the creation of his films and shows mainly to others, Jolson was not happy as anything other than the all-devouring central force of his films. This is star domination writ cosmic, whereas someone like Chevalier had the balance of collaborators like Lubitsch and Mamoulian and MacDonald; in his lesser films, without the august cohorts, the persona could become grating. Dominance played a different and somewhat ambiguous role in the stardom of Betty Grable, whose iconography was less about commitment than competence. Jack Cole, one of the few to successfully extend Grable's range past its preset limits, summed up both her appeal and her work ethic with acid brevity: "She could do all those pictures forward and backward...while thinking about what horse was going to win that day." An equivalence of a kind can be seen in Elvis, whose films were also never about anything other than him. He would show up and go through whatever script pages the Colonel laid out, and the rare times he was challenged, as in *King Creole* or *Viva Las Vegas*, showed what else might have been possible. How different it was for the Beatles, with their game and inquisitive willingness to allow director Richard Lester to make them more than simply themselves on camera. Or, in another time, Björk, with her endemic idiosyncracy, in Lars von Trier's *Dancer in the Dark*.

When a star doubles as a director, there may be both benefits and, as Gene Kelly learned, pitfalls. By the late 1960s, "creative control" could be a euphemism for "lunatics running the asylum," and so it was with the case of actor-director-writer-composer Anthony Newley. His X-rated *Can Hieronymous Merkin Ever Forget Mercy Humppe and Find True Happiness?* was every bit as elegant as its title, a boorish psychodrama wherein Newley attempted to offer way too much information about his sexual prowess while playing musical-comedy Fellini. Even during a notably crass time in film history, Newley's all-devouring exhibitionism was, if nothing else, quite remarkable. On a far more elevated plane, there was Barbra Streisand, whose perfectionism has traditionally been treated with far less respect than if her name been, say, Frank. Her reputation had preceded her to the set of *Funny Girl*, and it was only natural that all the jokes would be made time and again. "Give her a chance," someone is alleged to have said to a beleaguered William Wyler, "this is the first movie she's ever directed." If that distinction would not technically occur until *Yentl*, *A Star Is Born* still qualifies as one of the largest self-erected temples in the history of film. Streisand co-produced, co-wrote the insistently popular "Evergreen," and saw to it that the credits mentioned that her costumes came from her closet. *Yentl*, conversely, was far less unendurable; in fact, exquisitely directed, and confident enough to qualify as far more than a one-woman show. Even if one might not have liked Streisand or the songs, or not cared for the story or treatment, it was hard not to argue that *Yentl* fully realized its director-star's intentions in an entirely worthy fashion.

Ask people "What, exactly, does *Moulin Rouge!* realize?" See how many answers come back.[11] Producer-director-writer Baz Luhrmann took care to present his phantasmagoric pageant as a musical—"a story told by song," he called it—but with so much designer chaos going on it seemed less an evocation of a genre than a depiction of a state of mind. There was a little plot, sort of a *Camille* thing; any number of songs; and more visual tricks and effects and set pieces than could be tracked by millions of intent eyes. Audiences could be captivated by its audacity, mesmerized by its dazzle, amused by the range of stylistic references, and/or nerve-wracked and exhausted by its hyperactivity and artifice. More than anything else, it was a statement: an utter Luhrmann spree, his attempt to personalize musicals much as he had done with *Romeo + Juliet* by setting it in Miami and giving it a rock soundtrack. There, Shakespeare won the match: poetry can still rule even when spoken by drag queens while a song by Garbage tries to drown it out. Here, Luhrmann's task was both easier and harder: in 2001, the scarcity of musical films gave him, as it were, a wide-open field, an entire body of film to sample, evoke, mock. Not many feet of film had unspooled when there were jokey references to *The Sound of Music*, quickly followed by Nicole Kidman daring to court Marilyn comparisons with "Diamonds Are a Girl's Best Friend." The songs were as fragmented as the editing, the whole of it a barrage of overload to make Bollywood seem austere.

[11] Indeed, see how many answers can come back from just one respondent.

It was fascinating and unnerving, and ultimately it was debatable. What, exactly, was Luhrmann trying to say? That love matters more than anything? That "Lady Marmalade" can fit into a fin-de-siècle plot? That Kidman and Ewan McGregor were figures in an elbow-poking puppet show? Everyone who saw it had a different takeaway. What was clear, eventually, was that *Moulin Rouge!* was neither an epitaph for musicals nor a signpost for a new style, with too much of a muchness to be imitated and too self-conscious in its stylishness to sum up its genre. This did not stop millions from swooning at its spectacle and sound and even that tattered little romance. Excepting its financial success, Luhrmann's spree had an obvious ancestor in the 1930 revue *King of Jazz*. That too had been an ornate riot of color and music, an intense statement (by theater director John Murray Anderson) with more effect than point—mind-boggling, captivating even, ultimately an artifact without a glass case. Effort and artistry produced, in that case, a financial disaster, while Luhrmann's stylistic affirmation raked in grosses like there was no tomorrow. Even so, the bottom-line verity remains: a dead end, no matter how much money it makes, remains a dead end.

The high-decibel glitter and look-at-me pushiness of *Moulin Rouge!* diverted most of the attention from an even more personal work released about the same time. It too was a musical with quirks, ostensibly a stage adaptation made into a mockumentary on the order of *This Is Spinal Tap*, with a breathtakingly eccentric protagonist—a German-born rock diva with issues and the remnant of a botched sex-change operation. John Cameron Mitchell was the star of *Hedwig and the Angry Inch*, and as co-writer and director he centered the project off-screen as well as on. There was a great deal to dominate: between the rock performances, acidic flashbacks, dream sequences, animated segments, and wigs, *Hedwig* toted almost as much luggage as *Moulin Rouge!* It also sported, of all things, a rigorously austere integrity. Even with the noise and ingrained strangeness, Mitchell was the rare director/star to be meticulous and generous with the other actors and the audience. Hedwig (né Hansel) was not a garish caricature out of John Waters, nor were the musical sequences simply post-MTV overkill without reference to character and situation. While Luhrmann worked feverishly to give the people everything plus the kitchen sink, Mitchell made his heroine and his musical controlled and fully realized. How odd that something this peculiar could emerge so thoughtful, and how inspiring that the low-budget shrimp could make a more commanding statement than the pricey splurge.

That "splurge" monicker could also apply to *Love Me Tonight*, for a million-dollar budget was a huge outlay in the Depression days of mid-1932. Like *King of Jazz* (which cost even more), it was a work out of its time, its love-letter reviews counterbalanced by a red sea on the studio ledger. In later years, it acquired a further ignominy when some dense Production Code hacks forced Paramount to make several cuts (including an entire song) for a reissue, after which a masterpiece became permanently scarred. For masterpiece it is, to some the pinnacle of film musicals, and with a master most definitely in charge. Film history is not always kind to Rouben Mamoulian, the stage director from Russian Georgia who moved back and forth between Hollywood and Broadway. Some find his work calculated or even cold, self-conscious in its art and pretentious in its intent. *Becky Sharp* and *Blood and Sand* are sometimes felt to be triumphs of Technicolor over drama, laurels for *Queen Christina* are often given to Garbo instead of her director, and his career's later stages were pocked with financial failure (*Summer Holiday*, *Silk Stockings*) and firings (*Laura*, *Porgy and Bess*, *Cleopatra*). Not even the achievement of *Love Me Tonight* is immune, being once referred to as "Imitation Lubitsch with too many camera angles."

Well, now. *Love Me Tonight* does feature the stars of the Lubitsch musicals, Maurice Chevalier and Jeanette MacDonald, along with some of the same ingredients—the wit, the sly camera moves, and sauciness and innuendo and Paramount elegance. The difference lies in a score, by Richard Rodgers and Lorenz Hart, that can best be described as heavenly, and in a director with the skill of Lubitsch plus a willingness to countenance poetry and romance. The Lubitsch films mock love; *Love Me Tonight* believes that it is a treasure. Long before they meet, Chevalier and MacDonald are linked by a song—the eternal "Isn't It Romantic?"—that starts when he sings it in Paris and is then carried by train passengers and soldiers and peasants all the way out to MacDonald on the balcony of her faraway castle. This is Mamoulian, along with the music of Rodgers and the words of Hart, and it is one of the great sequences in all of film. The joy and surprises continue all the way to the end, where Mamoulian goes so far as to replay silent serials and have MacDonald ride out on horseback to rescue her lover off a speeding train. For those who fault the lack of traditional dance, let it be noted that the camera dances, the editing dances, and so does the soundtrack. And never is the dancing master not in charge, balancing and judging and restraining and allowing. Plus, when appropriate, overdoing.

Love Me Tonight is a work genuinely for the ages, everlasting proof that an art rooting itself in collaboration can also, clearly, be ascribed to, or at least governed by, one overwhelming force. When that force laughs at sanity, a *Madam Satan* emerges; when it's astute, it can produce anything from a *Love Parade* to a *Chicago*. If it knows what it likes, it might be a Pasternak; if it is driven by nerve, a Berkeley or a Cole. When ego comes to or goes beyond the fore, the results can be as varied as *The Singing Fool, Invitation to the Dance*, or *Moulin Rouge!* There are, obviously, lots of ways—far more than there seem, nowadays, to be opportunities. The kicker, fortunately, comes with permanence, the way the best of these creators' most personal works can endure and warm and surprise and renew. *Love Me Tonight*, after all, is nothing if not permanent, and more than simply that. When that great song asks its musical question, the answer can only come back, emphatically, in the affirmative. Yes: it *is* romantic.

Chapter 6

Music Makes Me

....

I
t is in the nature of history's what-ifs to be odd and sometimes discon-
certing. Take, for instance, the case of a song millions believe to be the best
ever written. What has come to be a legend does indeed seem to be fact:
"Over the Rainbow" narrowly escaped being removed from *The Wizard of Oz*.
Slows down the action, some MGM brass said, too grand with that opening
octave arch, not suited to a little girl, not suited to someone from Kansas. Evidently, for at least one of the *Oz* preview screenings, it was taken out on the
orders of people later described by producer Mervyn LeRoy as "Six MGM
executives [who] asked why we had to have Judy sing in the farmyard." Both
LeRoy and his associate Arthur Freed took credit for saving the song, though
seldom is such a decision the action of only one person. What counts is that
"Over the Rainbow" stayed, centered the film, won an Oscar, made Judy Garland's career, and continues without cease to be sung and loved. On the other
hand, another *Oz* song, "The Jitterbug," was cut permanently—fittingly, since a
bouncy song-and-dance fits in poorly at a point when beloved characters are in
danger.[1] Both songs had been written by Harold Arlen and Yip Harburg in the
good faith that they belonged in, were necessary to, the film. While the same

[1] The film of "The Jitterbug" has long been considered lost, while the recording remains.
Garland did perform it with Ray Bolger, plus Jane Powell, on her TV series. It's fun, and it
clearly didn't belong in *The Wizard of Oz*. .

applies to the stage, movies are more involved and prone to interference, with final decisions that can come from the crassest quarters. A few years after the near-loss of "Over the Rainbow," Harold Arlen implied the worst when he told a reporter, "When you're doing a show, everyone's in there pitching. It's your show and everyone else's. But it's never your picture. You're just getting paid."[2]

In the oft-waged war between movies and Broadway, songwriting has been responsible for a great deal of the hostility. Start with the widely held view that film producers tend to be the scum of the earth, which is a large part of why some composers shudder when recalling films of their work. Then recall the case of Rodgers and Hammerstein and *State Fair*, in which Hammerstein was so fed up with the Hollywood bull that his contract specified that he not be required to leave the East Coast. There was also the (likely fact-based) tale of Cole Porter, contracted by MGM to work on the musical spectacle *Rosalie*. After Louis B. Mayer rejected several of his attempts at a title song, Porter is said to have written one so deliberately bad that it ended up in the film. *Rosalie*, it can be added, is a lousy film with a stolid title song, yet it also contains Porter's sublime "In the Still of the Night." Movie songs are like that—the unevenness of the work can be confounding, and an awful amount of crud lies under that cream at the top. Many traditionally hold that film songs are less worthy than those made for the stage, which is neither an incomprehensible nor a totally disputable opinion. That said, it is then fair to ask: "OK, so what stage song is better than 'Over the Rainbow' or 'The Way You Look Tonight'?"

Back when musical film production was a common occurrence, songwriting functioned much as anything else in a studio. Much of it was workaday, and sometimes there were the more painstaking or costly projects. *The Wizard of Oz* falls into that latter category. It was, by a good margin, the most expensive musical made up to that time, and the care it received extended as much to its music as to design and casting. That the deletion of "Over the Rainbow" was even considered seems as vile a Hollywood sacrilege as the truncation of *Greed* or *The Magnificent Ambersons*—though, at least in this case, it remained. Hiring Arlen and Harburg in the first place was a great and wonderful decision, just as Jerome Kern

---

[2] Arlen knew as well as anyone how film operates. In 1935, when he and Harburg wrote the gorgeous "Last Night When We Were Young" for *Metropolitan*, a lovely rendition by Lawrence Tibbett wound up in the discard pile. Thirteen years later, Judy Garland sang it in *In the Good Old Summertime*, and again it was deleted, allegedly for being too sad for a light-ish film. Garland, bless her, knew better: it remained her favorite song, and Arlen's too.

and Dorothy Fields were supremely well suited to *Swing Time*, and Lerner and Loewe would have been perfect for *Gigi* even if they weren't coming off *My Fair Lady*. Such work, the elite sector of film songwriting, is usually *but not always* done by the finest artists. For some reason, and not just seventy-plus years ago, the maw of musical film does not necessarily induce the best people to produce the best work. The lesser lights sometimes go a farther distance.

When MGM commissioned Nacio Herb Brown and Arthur Freed to provide the first cohesive (give or take) song score for a film, *Show Boat* had been running on Broadway for nearly a year. The songs created by Jerome Kern and Oscar Hammerstein were the vanguard of popular music, mature, meticulously crafted, able to stand alone yet integrated into the story in a way rare to musicals. Most songs in most shows were pure Tin Pan Alley, only vaguely connected with plot; in 1928, the Ziegfeld musical comedy *Whoopee!* essentially stopped dead to allow Ruth Etting to saunter on and sing "Love Me or Leave Me"—a fine song so disconnected with everything else in the show (as was the putative character Etting was playing) that even at the time the makeshift was noted. This was the revue-like fashion in which most shows other than *Show Boat* functioned, even when they possessed something like a linear plot. Songs could be added or dropped at any time to suit a star or producer, and seldom was any show's score the work of simply one songwriting team. Musical productions were loose constructs, open to tinkering and change; even *Show Boat* could drop or add scenes and songs on a constant basis.

Movies, it was immediately, obviously clear, would not be so flexible. Except for the ones cut while in release due to overlength or censorship, a finished film was a binding proposition, fixed and permanent. Songs might be moved or removed during editing, or never used in the first place, but a film's release was an iron door, and the dynamic of its music completely different. Even apart from radio and phonograph records and sheet music, these songs would be heard and disseminated immediately and widely by many times more people than would see a show during its entire run. They needed to grab and appeal and sell tickets, and once again *The Broadway Melody* furnished the template. Brown and Freed were based on the West Coast, and most of their work reflected the distance away from Times Square. Freed's words, especially, could border on the elementary—uncomplicated, repetitive, easy to absorb, hard not to remember. His artlessness may have recalled the Irving Berlin of "What'll I Do?" and "Always"—but where Berlin's words were only, shall we say, superficially shallow,

Freed's really were that basic.[3] By accident or design, the Brown-Freed songs for *Broadway Melody* became the precise model for movie songs: efficiently crafted melodies paired with straightforward lyrics, suited to an audience far wider than just the United States. These films and songs traveled the globe, and since the songs were not always translated they might be phonetic hits in far-flung locales. Many hits from the earliest musicals, then, are models of effective simplicity: "Happy Days Are Here Again" (Yellen/Ager, from *Chasing Rainbows*); "Three Little Words" (Kalmar/Ruby, from *Check and Double Check*); "Should I?" (Brown/Freed, from *Lord Byron of Broadway*). All follow the standard by-the-numbers configuration: an AABA form, with words most often of one or two syllables, digestible to anyone.

For many, songs chart the difference between theater and film, seldom to the latter's advantage. Why, people ask, do they spend so much to acquire these shows, then cut most of the songs or, worse, substitute lesser pieces from others? Much of it, as already noted, has to do with the studios buying into music publishers and finding the profit potential of even inferior new work. This was the notion guiding such decisions as replacing nearly all the Cole Porter songs for *Paris* by pieces from the workshop of First National studio employees Al Bryan and Ed Ward. Surely an overeducated flea could realize that "Let's Do It (Let's Fall in Love)" would outdazzle a replacement on the order of "I'm a Little Negative (Looking for a Positive)." Even a mammoth success like *No, No Nanette* would be treated in that fashion, at that studio. In the coming attractions trailer for the now-lost 1930 version, it's specifically mentioned that only the show's two big hits—"Tea for Two" and "I Want to Be Happy"—were judged sufficient to make the cut, and the rest of the score would be brand-new hits. Neither "King of the Air" nor "Dance of the Wooden Shoes" bore out the idea that newer was better, and the same could be said for the dreary, non-Jerome Kern "If I'm Dreaming" stuck into *Sally*. Later, there would be all those new non-Porter things Paramount twice put into *Anything Goes*. Even a show's original composer could buy into this, which accounts for Irving Berlin's "When My Dreams Come True" in the film

---

[3] Generally, as few would dispute, Brown's skill as a composer often needed to propel, even upgrade, his partner's less interesting text. Later on, Freed could get more adventurous with his lyrics, never more than in the great "Temptation" from *Going Hollywood*. While the rhyme scheme adheres to the simple Freed norm, the slant of the song and the tone of the words are pretty racy—quite fitting for a song about, please note, sex and self-abasement.

of *The Cocoanuts*—an example of a Berlin ballad being onerously, not decep-
tively, simple.[4]

Important as publishing was, the situation was not simply fiscal. There were
also considerations of length, since films were—at least until the roadshow
years—going to be significantly shorter than anything onstage. Rarely did they
go over two hours, and a plot, inane as it might be, would be given precedence
over songs. In 1931, the eternally non-musical David Selznick announced that
he was going to film the Gershwins' *Girl Crazy* as a straight, no-songs comedy;
since this was one of the ultimate examples of a great score married to a this-is-
a-plot? book, it was just as well that the final result did use some of the songs,
even adding a new one by the Gershwins themselves.[5] In 1950, *Annie Get Your
Gun* was more faithful to its source than most filmed shows had been in a long
time—yet it was still more than half-an-hour shorter, which accounted for the
loss of an unnecessary romantic subplot with two songs and, far more regret-
tably, "I Got Lost in His Arms." Songs might also be lost due to censorship. "But
in the Morning, No" was never going to be in a *DuBarry Was a Lady* film, not in
1943, so hands other than Cole Porter's crafted what passed for a double-
entendre-flavored substitute called "Madame, I Love Your Crêpes Suzettes."[6]

While considerations of length and censorship are at least comprehensible,
some of the choices made are so counterintuitive as to be downright boorish.
Paramount's film of *Lady in the Dark* is famous for accomplishing the considerable feat of being both wildly overdone and frightfully insufficient, and some
bad judgments involving songs number among its most heinous sins. Several

[4] Back to Arlen and Harburg: they were responsible for the rare movie song written by
someone else that improved a stage score. It helped, too, that they had Ethel Waters to sing
it—"Happiness Is Just a Thing Called Joe," in *Cabin in the Sky.* Jerome Kern, for his part,
avenged that *Sally* business by writing "Lovely to Look At" for the *Roberta* movie, which turned
out so well that it's become an essential part of the show. Similar things have happened, on
occasion, with songs from *The Sound of Music* and *Cabaret.* Even, for those who track these
things, *Evita.*

[5] Sort of new, anyway. "You've Got What Gets Me" was an old, unused melody fitted out with
new lyrics. Film songs often involve recycling of some kind. Brown and Freed, for example,
wrote "Singin' in the Rain" for a West Coast show, where it made little impact. Then they put
it into *The Hollywood Revue,* and the rest is history. Much later, "Say a Prayer for Me Tonight"
was written for and cut out of *My Fair Lady,* then happily rescued for *Gigi.*

[6] Another moderately steamy new *DuBarry* song points out the nature of the film, the show,
and, truly, this strain of musical comedy. "Salome," performed by Virginia O'Brien, has nothing
to do with plot or character, and O'Brien is playing a hat check girl, not a chanteuse—none of
which stops her from coming out and doing it, divinely.

Weill-Gershwin songs were minimized and truncated, a new piece called "Suddenly It's Spring" was not an acceptable substitute for "This Is New," and a particularly dire fate befell "My Ship." The fact that Paramount's head of production, Buddy DeSylva, was a former songwriter—co-creator of *Sunny Side Up* and *Good News* and many others—did not translate into an appreciation for Kurt Weill. According to *Lady*'s director, Mitchell Leisen, DeSylva nursed an active dislike of Weill's music and of "My Ship" in particular. Never mind that much of the plot hinged on that song haunting Liza Elliott, nor the fact that when she finally remembers and sings it, the conflicts are resolved. Nor even that DeSylva's studio was spending more money on this film than it had ever spent before. One song, he deemed, did not make a show, and the scene of Ginger Rogers singing "My Ship" was cut out. Leisen was so annoyed that he made sure the completed film made the deletion quite apparent.

In the case of *On the Town*, Louis B. Mayer decided that he didn't care for Leonard Bernstein's music and had most of it replaced by lesser new pieces. In this case, unlike *Lady in the Dark*, it was quite a good film despite the cuts and the unfortunate need to dumb down work judged a shade urbane for ticket-buying millions. Other decisions are simply incomprehensible. The film of Kern and Hammerstein's *Music in the Air* is quite good in most ways, but glaringly not so in the decision to film and then delete the rhapsodic "The Song Is You." In *Can-Can, not* a good film, "I Love Paris" was relegated to a vocal chorus under the credits, and other Cole Porter shows went west with next to nothing of their scores, even when the censors passed the lyrics. There is also the case of that ghastly Warner Bros. film of *On Your Toes*, a non-musical except for the "Slaughter" ballet, and the decisions that removed all songs from *Fanny* and *Irma la Douce*. With *Chicago*, "Class" was filmed and, when it didn't tally with the "daydream" format, relegated to the lowly status of a DVD extra. It used to happen, and it still happens.

There was also, in the earlier days, the question of how much a song could be played until it was passé. Unless it was as exhaustively ingrained as, say, "Tea for Two," there was not yet quite the concept of established standards, at least as that would be comprehended later on. Newer songs tended, in the public mind, to replace most of the older ones. So they hawked new songs as a way of keeping the show "fresh," just as Broadway hits like the 1902 *Wizard of Oz* constantly had their songs replaced or interpolated. Movies, in fact, were largely responsible, along with radio and records, for establishing the notion of a song's perennial status being, in fact, a good thing. It goes without saying that this occurred mainly through a studio exercising its right to reuse a song it owned in features, short subjects, and cartoons. Paramount's music department would seemingly have been lost without "Isn't It Romantic?," which was still turning up in background scores more than half a century after its creation. At MGM, "Singin' in the Rain" was reused so often that *That's Entertainment!* did a montage of it. There was also the silly ditty that tweaked it in Warner Bros.' *The Show of Shows*, "Singin' in the Bathtub." In this case, it could be argued that the entire art of the Warner cartoon would have been diminished if this song had not existed. Cartoons can, in fact, go far to keep a song alive, given the later TV runs: more people know "Did You Ever See a Dream Walking?" from that Popeye cartoon (*A Dream Walking*) than the feature that introduced it, *Sitting Pretty*.[7]

The later missteps, particularly the deletions and replacements, still seem unforgivable. At least, in the early time, there is the excuse of trial-and-error, when so much was happening even as no one knew exactly how a musical or its songs would function. *The Broadway Melody* had barely begun to run in theaters when the exodus started—scores of tunesmiths traveling west to peddle their wares and talents to the studios. The aggression of these men (no women just then) soon made the entire concept of "Tin Pan Alley West" quite a joke, but the production schedules of 1929 were so filled with musicals that most of them were contracted. These were, for the most part, the second-raters, and if their work had not been attached to the permanence of film they would have vanished from history. This applies even to two names as intrinsically memorable as Paul Titsworth and King Zany, whose mediocre work turned up in an outlandish combination of melodrama and revue called *The Great Gabbo*. *Gabbo* was what would now be termed a quirky indie, so Titsworth and Zany were mere one-timers. At large studios, music departments beckoned with long-term contracts, snaring the efficient, the expeditious, and on occasion the gifted. Harry Akst, who signed with Warner Bros., is remembered far less for his name than his songs—"Dinah," "Baby Face," and, for *On with the Show!*, "Am I Blue?" At Paramount, Richard Whiting was the studio workhorse,

---

[7] There is also the related case of "Good Mornin'." Not the Brown/Freed song (sans apostrophe) but a Sam Coslow ditty performed by Martha Raye in a negligible Paramount epic called *Mountain Music*. Both song and film vanished for decades, then a cereal manufacturer bought the rights, changed some words, and made "A Kellogg's Good Mornin'" an inescapable part of the 1960s television-watching experience.

though the music of *The Love Parade* was the work of Victor Schertzinger, whose day job was director, not composer. Brown and Freed anchored the music wing at MGM, which broke ground by briefly having an African American songwriter under contract: Jo Trent, a former colleague of Duke Ellington, co-wrote the song Joan Crawford performed in *The Hollywood Revue*. Fox aimed high by approaching George Gershwin, who took quite a while to warm up to the idea, and Broadway's DeSylva, Brown, and Henderson, who signed on in far less time—the same DeSylva, let it be said, who later did so wrong by *Lady in the Dark*. At this point he was part of a high-profile, high-output team whose catchy and unthreatening songs for shows like *Good News* suited movies to a T. DeSylva, Brown, and Henderson's score for *Sunny Side Up* was one of the best of those early years: "Sunny Side Up," "I'm a Dreamer (Aren't We All?)," and "If I Had a Talking Picture of You" were major hits that, in retrospect, sum up that age as well as anything. They were also more connected than usual with script and character—a move both wise, in that case, and necessary, as Janet Gaynor's acting was skillful and her singing was make-do-and-smile.

In 1929 and later, *Sunny Side Up* was exceptional; for many films, especially those set backstage, the only connection a song had with a plot might be that it gets performed by a character the audience cares about. Not even that, sometimes. The smash hit *Gold Diggers of Broadway* began life as a straight comedy and was retrofitted with songs in a way that could not be called a true musicalization. This did not stop two of them from being monster hits: "Painting the Clouds with Sunshine" and "Tip Toe through the Tulips with Me" were both efficiently crafted pieces by Al Dubin and Joseph Burke, one a wistful ballad and the other a blissfully dumb novelty. In both cases, the melodist's skill outstripped the lyricist's craft—those famously kindergartenesque words Dubin imparted to "Tulips" had nothing in them so adventurous as that near-octave plunge Burke put in at the break to illustrate "Knee deep." These were the furthest possible thing from character songs, so generic that they could have been performed by anyone in virtually anything. In *Gold Diggers* they (and others) were sung by the pop balladeer Nick Lucas, whose sole duty in the film was to sing while strumming a guitar, and the sole function they served was to provide a musical with music and show off the Technicolor. *Gold Diggers of Broadway* was, then, something like a revue with a plot: an excuse, rather than a reason, for songs to exist and be performed. This very looseness of form has continued, in one form or another, throughout the musical's existence.

Crooners in the early '30s, swing later on, pop and rock, and ultimately hip-hop—it all continues just as it did when Nick Lucas was up there singing "Painting the Clouds with Sunshine" in front of a living palette of chorus girls with different-colored wigs. When the setup is loose and genial and the tunes are well constructed, as here, it works; if the song does not suffice or the setting is chaotic, it quickly turns asinine.

The 1929 boom was also a healthy lesson in the law of diminishing returns. The early films, the ones that often had the least resonant songs, did so well that the studios were able to offer more money to the bigger composers and lyricists. Irving Berlin, George and Ira Gershwin, Rodgers and Hart, Rudolf Friml, Jerome Kern, Oscar Hammerstein, Sigmund Romberg—they were Broadway's best, and unfortunately most of them were signed right before musicals began to take an early dive. Berlin was mortified when all but one of his songs for *Reaching for the Moon* were completely removed, and Friml so hated his experience on *The Lottery Bride* that he disowned the project and went back to New York. Kern saw his work virtually thrown away, Romberg and Hammerstein had two major failures, and the Gershwins did their best to get through *Delicious* in the fastest take-the-money-and-run fashion possible. Only Rodgers and Hart fared better, at least once. Their scores for *The Hot Heiress* and *The Phantom President* and *Hallelujah, I'm a Bum* were all mangled or truncated in one form or another, but in the midst of them there was *Love Me Tonight*—one of the earliest films to show the benefit of a full (and fully excellent) score, integrated yet with stand-alone hits.[8]

Love Me Tonight also helped to bring in a more golden age for film songs, one fully realized as musicals resumed their hold in 1933. The studios rebuilt their music departments—Brown and Freed again at MGM, Harry Warren and Al Dubin at Warner Bros., Leo Robin, Ralph Rainger, Mack Gordon, and Harry Revel at Paramount and Fox, joined later by Frank Loesser, Jule Styne, Johnny Mercer, Sammy Cahn, and more. House talents were supplemented by the occasional guest like Berlin, Gershwin, Kern, Porter, and Arlen. The Astaire-Rogers songs and Harry Warren's best efforts for the Busby Berkeley

---

[8] Two standards from *Love Me Tonight* show the difference between pop generality and film specificity. "Isn't It Romantic" and "Lover" had lyrics so tailored to the plot and characters that they were meaningless out of context. So Larry Hart wrote the more generic words that went out with the sheet music and the recordings and have been used ever since. For the uninitiated, hearing their original version in the film can be something of a jolt.

films were every bit the equal of Broadway's best, and often they were better—
a clear sign of how high the bar had been raised since the days of *The Great
Gabbo*. Formal recognition of a sort came in 1935, when the contributions of
the studio music departments were recognized by Academy Awards for scoring
and song. Here, as in every single category from 1929 to the present, the most
deserving are not always the chosen. "Lullaby of Broadway" and "The Way You
Look Tonight" and "Over the Rainbow" were among the early winners...as was
"Sweet Leilani," and even in 1938 many Academy members were shocked that
this was judged superior to the Gershwins' "They Can't Take That Away from
Me." More recently, the Best Song competition has been something of a joke,
both for the paucity of the choices and the hilarious staging given them on the
awards show. Nothing, in any case, will ever touch Isaac Hayes doing "Shaft"
at the Oscars in 1972.

Even apart from a mediocre pop hit trumping a dark and intricate Gershwin classic, it is an ongoing peculiarity of film that the lights of lesser wattage
may fit the occasion most suitably. If Gordon and Revel, for example, are not
the best remembered of names, their work truly earned them the right to own
many of their films; in a light diversion like *Wake Up and Live*, theirs is the
most emphatic stamp, especially with a stunning ballad such as "There's a
Lull in My Life." In a more important work like *Mary Poppins*, a near-perfect
score by the brotherly team of Richard B. and Robert M. Sherman functions,
deliberately, like a live-action continuation of Disney's cartoon features:
direct, straight-line songs that avoid harmonic clutter or lyrical excess. Since
the Shermans' first work for Disney was writing pop ditties for Annette Funicello, *Poppins* was a major upgrade for them. Even more than usual in the
hyper-controlled Disney environment, its score was discussed and calibrated
endlessly before reaching an artless form so impeccably suited to chimney
sweeps and cartoon holidays and feeding birds and Julie Andrews's crystalline
tones. These songs do exactly what Disney and the Shermans had intended.
Now look at them alongside the score for *The Wizard of Oz*: two works of immense professionalism, ostensibly for children, with vastly divergent approaches
to their music. The *Poppins* songs charm and propel and, with "Supercalifra-
gilisticexpialidocious," surprise. *Oz*'s songs are musically and emotionally
complex, even in their lighter "Merry Old Land" moments. The wordplay is
trickier (Harburg, pure and simple) and Arlen's melodies are more sophisticated. Both scores succeed, yes, but is it unfair to the Shermans and their
lovely work to acclaim the *Oz* men for their richer achievement?

In the dream factory days, when the assembly line operated as efficiently for music as for décor or casting, the songs could blur together. A catch-all like *The Big Broadcast of 1938*, Paramount's fourth and last effort under the umbrella that would now be called a franchise, was a work more of moments than of cohesion. There were comedy bits and slots for guest stars, and Leo Robin and Ralph Rainger would be told who was performing and, if needed, where the songs were spotted. Such work tended more toward the competent than the memorable—a languorous ballad for Dorothy Lamour ("You Took the Words Right Out of My Heart"), something raucous for the high-decibel Martha Raye ("Mama, That Moon Is Here Again"), and little to outlast the time the film was on the screen. The dustpan of this particular *Big Broadcast*, however, contained the diamond of a first-rate song that mattered and endured. According to the script, Bob Hope (in his first feature film) and Shirley Ross were an on/off-again couple who wind up together at the fadeout. Ross was a singer and Hope had starred in Broadway musicals, there was a slot for a song, and Robin and Rainger ran with it. Originally, "Thanks for the Memory" was jokey and bouncy, a remembrance of daffy things past. Then someone (director Mitchell Leisen claimed the credit) saw that the song had deeper possibilities if the tempo were brought down. Rainger's melody opened with a downward-moving swoop, followed by small, halting chromatic steps back up the scale, while Robin's lyrics moved from a wisecrack patina to the genuine feeling beneath, banal recollections like pajamas and canned hash giving way to musings on how a great love can go wrong. To set it further apart from the workaday, it was decided, in a time when nearly all songs were prerecorded, to let Ross and Hope sing it live. Not yet camera savvy, Hope directed his gaze oddly upward during much of the song, callow yet reflective in a way he would never be again, and in the final stretch he was compelled to comfort Ross on camera when she began to break down completely. A silly movie whose main conflict involved ocean liners in a race, and here was this striking, poignant song about life and loss. No wonder it became Hope's theme.[9]

In contrast with the songs-for-order technique, a major figure like Irving Berlin would receive special treatment in pageant-like celebrations of his work: from *Alexander's Ragtime Band* to *Easter Parade* and beyond, a procession of

---

[9] A second *Broadcast* number for the ages is by Wagner, not Robin and Rainger: Kirsten Flagstad in Brünnhilde's "Ho-jo-to-ho." No dramatic connection at all, but thrilling. Repeating: *The Big Broadcast of 1938* is a "catch-all."

Thank you so much: The leads in *The Big Broadcast of 1938*—Ben Blue, Dorothy Lamour, W. C. Fields, Shirley Ross, Bob Hope, Martha Raye—displaying that film's potpourri spirit rather than the poignancy of its best song. Was Fields ever again this genial? Was Hope ever this young?

Berlin carnivals rolled out his old hits and supplemented them with newer ones. These tended to be so much more about Berlin than anything else that his name was placed before the title in the possessive case: Irving Berlin's *Blue Skies* or *White Christmas*. Even for musical fluff, the level of script inspiration was woeful, the writers so subservient to Berlin that they could or would not balance the music with something interesting. Instead, there would be some kind of triangle that compelled Alice Faye or Bing Crosby to moon over Tyrone Power or Joan Caulfield, with interference from a Merman or Astaire or even Marilyn Monroe. *Blue Skies* is especially sad in this regard, and then there is the spectacle of the strangest pop crooner of the 1950s, Johnny Ray, in *There's No Business Like Show Business*. So much wrong is at play here—Ray's acting, his playing Ethel Merman's son, his playing a priest, his twitchy way with otherwise normal Berlin songs. Not that sense and decorum are needed in a film that also has Merman as a tattooed sailor and Monroe and Jack Cole treating "Heat Wave" like part of the Kinsey Report. *Holiday Inn* is probably the best of the Berlin pageants for the simple reason that it really is about the songs. Bing

Crosby opens a Connecticut club only on red-letter days, and Berlin goes from "Abraham" [Lincoln] to "White Christmas." Nearly all new songs, in this case much to the film's benefit. And, considering what happened with "White Christmas," quite to Berlin's as well.[10]

The Berlin celebrations prompted easy imitation in the form of the work of a composer or team set into a slender faux-biographical plot requiring no thoughtful integration. It seemed like everyone who ever wrote a song could be celebrated: Victor Herbert, George Gershwin, Cole Porter, Sigmund Romberg, Rodgers and Hart, and everyone else short of Titsworth and Zany. Occasionally a performer too, especially Jolson. In most cases they used the best-known work, though on occasion there would turn up something on the order of "I'm Unlucky at Gambling," as sung amusingly by a French-accented Eve Arden in the uproarious Porter biopic, *Night and Day*. What was truly enthralling about these films was their alternate-universe distortion of every single fact, not just the sexuality of a Porter or Hart. *Yankee Doodle Dandy* was the main success, since (1) George M. Cohan's manic patriotism was supremely suited to a war-time environment, and (2) Jimmy Cagney's magnetism as an actor and dancer made it possible to portray Cohan other than as the rat many knew him to be. It remains, too, that bios are considered viable even when other musicals are sparse or verboten. *The Buddy Holly Story*, *Coal Miner's Daughter*, *Sweet Dreams*, *The Doors*, *Ray*, *Walk the Line*, and *La Vie en Rose* all come from such times, which made it gratifying that their creators were respectful of the artists and their work, and even sometimes a bit accurate. This, certainly, qualified as an upgrade.

The other trend of these bashes originated with Irving Berlin's insistence that his life not be dramatized on film. (When Fox tried this with *Alexander's Ragtime Band*, Berlin put his foot down.) What emerged was a type of tribute, a composer's work centering a production with no biographical pretense. After the success of Berlin's *Easter Parade*, Arthur Freed turned to the Gershwins for *An American in Paris*, then happily celebrated his own collaborations with Nacio Herb Brown in *Singin' in the Rain*. No one would say that Freed's lyrics were up to those of Berlin or Ira Gershwin, yet one of the many joys of *Singin'*

---

[10] Everyone knows that Crosby introduced "White Christmas" in *Holiday Inn*; few recall that he had help. While it was Marjorie Reynolds moving her lips, the creamy vocalism was by the busiest of all the Hollywood dubbers. If the name Martha Mears is not familiar, rest assured that the voice is. Montez to Hayworth, Lake to Ball—Mears covered 'em all.

in the Rain is the way it presented Brown and Freed's catalogue in its proper context. They had been there at the dawn of sound, they had contributed to many of the biggest early musicals, and their songs, innately simple lyrics and all, fit in better than anything else could. This had not been the case with *American in Paris*, with "By Strauss" thrust oddly into a Parisian setting and Oscar Levant's dreary ego-dream of playing all the instruments in the Concerto in F. But "Good Morning" and "Fit as a Fiddle" and "Would You?" are perfectly attenuated, and no argument need be made for the rightness of the title song. In a new century, this type of retroactive tribute had its equivalent in *Across the Universe* and *I'm Not There*. One was an occasionally schmaltzy reimagining of the songs of John Lennon and Paul McCartney, the other an intriguingly splintered look at the life and work of Bob Dylan, as played by five actors of varying age, race, and gender. They were as different from each other as their source material, and neither was content to simply replay comforting nostalgia. *Across the Universe* reaped not-unwarranted criticism for some of the facile choices made by director Julie Taymor, yet both of these were pointedly about music, and in a non-catalogue sense: the legacy and what the music continues to mean. Just, in a way, as with Nacio Herb Brown.

These films, biopic and otherwise, began to have a fascinating equivalent in the 1990s on Broadway and then on film. With a nod toward hindsight, they have been dubbed jukebox shows, a designation that duly conveys the cohesiveness most of them possess. The logic behind them is irrefutable: pop and rock have displaced show music, and people who loved ABBA in the 1970s or hair rock in the 1980s will tear down the turnstiles to hear these songs once again. Who performs them is as unimportant as their non-context and the fact that the plots make *White Christmas* look like Lorca. As much as, more than, the biopics, this kind of preset diversion is the reducto ad trivium of musicals, escapism boiled down to its least relevant essence. On Broadway, *Mamma Mia!* served the same function as a Betty Grable movie, with the September 11 attacks taking the place of World War II and sugary ABBA tropes replacing Technicolored displays of million-dollar legs. As a perfect respite from talk of anthrax attacks or Al Qaeda, it ran so long that a movie version was both inevitable and, ultimately, successful. For the millions intrigued with the notion of a Meryl Streep musical, *Mamma Mia!* was an eye-opener. There was indeed a slew of those ABBA hits that everyone had heard on car radios all those years earlier, and there was Streep, gallantly working at having a lark along with the rest of the game cast. Most striking, since this was not a concert or revue, there was, amid all the ABBA, an insistent little plot. It was based on an old Gina Lollobrigida farce, and it was connected with the songs in a way to make one long for the radical dramatics of the "How about a song, Nick?" days of *Gold Diggers of Broadway*. There might possibly have been ways to lead logically into "Dancing Queen" or "The Winner Takes It All" or any of the others, but not with a script this oblivious, nor a director so unaware of the nature or needs of film. No wonder that the number everyone loved most was over the final credits. With a *Mamma Mia!* a musical truly does become the insipid smiley-face montage of songs and shtick that the naysayers have always decried, a brazen example of what happens to a musical when it ceases to matter.

With their force-welded links between songs and character and story, jukebox shows are the shadowy underbelly of the "integrated" musicals of the Rodgers and Hammerstein era, and it could be noted moreover that the whole notion of musicals on film began to change with the rise of rock music in the 1950s. Pop-rock did not necessarily lend itself well to the scripted form, which gives the Elvis and *Beach Party* movies their amusingly camp sense of displacement: the beat might be early '60s, but the mechanics and affect are 1929. The Beatles films—the Richard Lester live-action pair plus the animated *Yellow Submarine*—tried for more unity and often achieved it, as in *Submarine*'s pop apotheosis "All You Need Is Love." The more self-serious likes of *The Who's Tommy* and *Pink Floyd The Wall* also could achieve a kind of music-text symbiosis, albeit in a more unctuous, less illuminating fashion than in a superior concert documentary like Martin Scorsese's *The Last Waltz*.

Amid the rock films of the 1970s, it was a country-western musical that demonstrated how it all could best be laid out. Robert Altman's *Nashville* was chaotic yet planned, improvised yet controlled, and so idiosyncratic a part of the Altman canon that some neglect to see it as a musical. Of course it is, specifically of the backstage variety, though like much of Altman's work a film like *Nashville* laughs at the notion of one binding genre. Here was the *Broadway Melody* aesthetic with twangs and cowboy shirts, somehow fitting seamlessly into an epic look at the state of America circa 1975, with songs (done entirely in performances of one type or another) that expanded on the characters singing them. The cohesion was a major achievement for a canvas this crowded, and the secret lay in the nature of the score. Instead of hiring C&W tunesmiths or using preexisting pieces, Altman encouraged his actors to write their own songs, in character—less spontaneous than improvised dialogue, albeit with the same purpose. This gave dimension to even the most perfunctory of the characters, and for those in the forefront, like Keith Carradine and Ronee Blakley and Henry Gibson, the effect was dynamite. Many country stars write their own songs anyway—not to be condescending, but it doesn't take a Mozart—and with an intelligent, enterprising actor like Carradine a song like "I'm Easy" underscored and delineated things already glimpsed, and revealed things not seen. Even the more formulaic and generic songs in *Nashville* did exactly what they needed to do, and not one seemed superfluous.

Nashville is proof that a great musical need not necessarily contain great songs. The Astaire-Rogers films—specifically, the first eight, from *Flying Down to Rio* to *Carefree*—are proof of how great songs can make a good musical better. These are generally recalled in terms of dance and movement: Astaire as master and god, Ginger's contribution variously praised or minimized, the dynamics of their partnership, mention sometimes given to the often-under-rated assistance of Hermes Pan. Then with the films' look—the big white sets, the pervasive aura of Déco, the cinematography that Astaire insisted upon to capture his dances in full-figure long takes. The sound, it seems, is rarely mentioned first. It comes up—how could it not—mainly as an additive to Astaire's genius, as if he could have built those magnificent sequences from castoffs from *The Great Gabbo*. The best Astaire-Rogers songs—still among the finest ever composed for American film or theater—are almost chronically disserved. Yes, people smile when they hear "Cheek to Cheek" or that unfortunate Oscar-loser (to "Sweet Leilani"!) "They Can't Take That Away from Me." And "You Say 'Either'....," more formally "Let's Call the Whole Thing Off," is still used as a tool for satire and comedy. How curious, then, that such work is so taken for granted, as are the men and woman who created it. Even as the songs are known and appreciated, some of them loved, their craft is slighted, their contribution to the films woefully understated. From "Music Makes Me" through "Change Partners," they form the cornerstone of the films and the foundation of Astaire's art, both the new songs and also some of the preexisting pieces like "Night and Day" and the *Roberta* songs. The only exceptions are a few throwaways, like "Let's K-nock K-nees," that actually seem to be more a part of other, lesser films. Not all of them form the basis of dance sequences, and "Orchids in the Moonlight" is sung by Raul Roulien, not Fred or Ginger, yet they are all as much a part of the texture and richness of these films as the dances, far more so than the scripts.

"Cheek to Cheek" is frequently thought of as the archetypal Fred/Ginger sequence for any number of reasons: not merely the sheer swooping romance of its dance but also the pristine elegance of its setting—an apt depiction of the "heaven" the lyrics mention so memorably—and the black-white interplay of its visual contrasts, plus the fabulous unreality of Rogers's feather dress. At the core of it all is the work of Irving Berlin, working well past his normal excellence. "Cheek to Cheek" is a truly unconventional song for Berlin, or for anyone else in 1935, in both length and form. It runs two, nearly three times as long as most pop tunes, with an arresting and imaginative structure of A A B B C A. That "Dance with me!" C-section seems to come out of nowhere, practically, its thrusting minor key vehemence a subtle and astute reminder that all the great romantic duets of this pair, from "Night and Day" onward, were coded depictions of carnality. The up-then-down path of the "A" melody works in a similar fashion, as well as being responsible for the fact that, with its octave-and-a-half range, this is not an easy song to sing. A trained vocalist like Nelson Eddy would have taken it all in polished stride, treating it almost as an aria. With Astaire, great instinctive singer that he was, some of these notes take some effort, as when he can be felt to reach for the highs of "hardly speak." Instead of making it more arduous, a stretch like this gives the song and the film a greater sincerity than are found in its brittle plot turns. And after Astaire has finished singing and the couple go into their dance, the melody provides an infinite palette of opportunities: insouciance, pleading and hesitation, carefree soft-shoe, and that immense final surge that, in music and movement, briefly freezes after Rogers's acquiescent backbend on, once again, those "hardly speak" high notes. Astaire created the movement with Hermes Pan and with Rogers executed it brilliantly, as did music director Max Steiner. And none of it could have been without Berlin and that song. Which, it should be dazedly pointed out, he wrote, words and music, in one day.

Along with *Top Hat*, *Swing Time* is generally felt to be the apex of Astaire-Rogers.[11] The script is less consistent and possibly more ragged than that of *Top Hat*, yet it's more intricate, somehow more sincere, with people who seem more real even when not all of their actions or motives are convincing. Once again, the score provides much of the foundation, in this case the music of Jerome Kern and the lyrics of Dorothy Fields. Unlike *Top Hat*, the greatest song does not support a dance, at least at first. In some ways, "The Way You

[11] Based on the music alone, *Follow the Fleet* would make it a trio. Berlin's terrific songs include the daringly lovely minor-to-major-key "Let's Face the Music and Dance," and that awful script wasn't his fault.

"Heaven," under construction: Magic in the making, as Fred Astaire sings (or synchs) "Cheek to Cheek" to Ginger Rogers while the crew takes it all in. The Venice-via-RKO set looked far more substantial in the final cut.

Look Tonight" is a little like "Cheek to Cheek": longer than the pop norm, an arresting key change in a contrasting section at the two-thirds point, and an intimately conversational start with that opening "Some-day." Nor, again, is it a particularly easy song to sing, as this time Astaire has to grab for the climactic high "of," followed by the octave drop to "you." If there's a potential peril of such a gorgeous song making things too romantic too early in the film, the staging removes it by having Astaire and Rogers in different rooms, him singing at the piano with her in the bathroom washing her hair. It may have been intended for Rogers's headful-of-suds look to undercut the point of the song, but actually she looks glorious that way.

For viewers disappointed that there's no dance with "The Way You Look Tonight," the amends come later as part of the "Never Gonna Dance" number. Unlike "Way," "Never Gonna Dance" is no eternal ballad, but rather tied in so specifically to its *Swing Time* context—Fred and Ginger's sad parting—that it makes no sense otherwise. He (Astaire/Lucky Garnett) vows never to dance again if she (Rogers/Penny Carrol) goes off to marry another man, and the references to "my Penny" and "la perfectly swell romance" belong here and here alone. Even the music seems less a melody than a rather agitated component of an unhappy conversation—and then, as with "Cheek to Cheek," it becomes supremely well suited to a dance. What sets "Never Gonna Dance" apart, and even above "Cheek to Cheek," is that the dance reiterates the couple's entire relationship, with both the music and movement including recollections of "The Way You Look Tonight" and "Waltz in Swing Time." At the end—following that relentless series of pirouettes that caused Rogers's feet to bleed during shooting—she runs out the door, leaving him standing there alone—never to dance again, at least until the plot is set aright. It's a heartbreaking moment, and without that idiosyncratic, can't-stand-alone song it wouldn't have been anywhere near as effective. Quirky as it is, the right song has served the right moment.

A movie that produces great songs must be a cause for gratitude, just as humble thanks are due those who had the insight to not take "Over the Rainbow" out of *The Wizard of Oz*. In that case, as with "Isn't It Romantic" and *Love Me Tonight*, a marvelous song has been joined to a superior film. As Berlin and Kern and Fields and the Gershwins proved with their work for Astaire and Rogers, there need not be a binding formula necessary to make the right impact. With "Thanks for the Memory," and a number of others too, well into the rock age, the song is so much better than the film that it's a marvel that the two could be connected. Similarly, it makes for an arresting thought that a script such as that of *Mamma Mia!* could have been judged sturdy enough to support any songs at all—good, bad, indifferent, or ABBA. There and elsewhere, the songs need not have been created especially for the film, which is where "Singin' in the Rain" becomes a part of history, and so does Cole Porter's brilliant "From This Moment On," cut out of one show and then rescued for the *Kiss Me Kate* movie. It's grand when the film and the song fit together, and other times it's just as well if the song transcends and outlasts the movie. There are no set paths, simply all the worthy composers and lyricists and singers and arrangers and directors and musicians and technicians who get it there. When they're on the best track, the song and the film and the audience form the most delighted triangle imaginable. It all works, and it's heaven. We're in heaven.

Chapter 7

With Plenty of Money

....

I want quality, but I don't want to spend too much money.

MGM's Irving Thalberg was probably not the only producer to utter these words, but it is recorded that he did say them when he began to plan the first movie musical. A film is a work of commerce, not altruism, and MGM's "Art for Art's Sake" motto was more a way of sounding nice than being honest. In 1928, when Thalberg conceived what would eventually be *The Broadway Melody*, he knew the importance of the bottom line. His successors knew it when *The Wizard of Oz* became one of the most costly films, and the second biggest money-loser, in MGM's first two decades.[1] It was also known if not heeded forty years later, when 20th Century-Fox went through all its *Sound of Music* profits to create *Doctor Dolittle* and *Star!* and *Hello, Dolly!* The numbers stayed relevant in 1978 when *Grease* became the highest-grossing musical of all time, and in 2009 when *Nine* was as big a let-down financially as artistically. Nor, as central as they are, do figures have the obligation to send predictable or desirable messages. Take the occasions when

---

[1] The worst loser: the Garbo cataclysm known as *Conquest*. There was, however, a back-to-Kansas happy ending for *Oz*: it entered the plus column even before television, by way of theatrical reissues in 1949 and 1955. Since then, it's been a gusher, and that is not counting the millions a pair of Ruby Slippers will bring at auction.

the MGM ledger runs jarringly against the grain: who might have divined that *The Band Wagon*, that bountiful Astaire-Minnelli collaboration, was one of the company's major financial disasters? History's doors, it seems, are always open for revision.

Numbers, either in cost or profit, do not necessarily decide what makes a musical either great or immaterial: look at financial failures like *Love Me Tonight*, or successes like *Hannah Montana: The Movie*. Where the figures do become pertinent is in supplying a valid guide to tastes and trends, which determine how musicals function and whether more will be made. They are inherently more costly than most films, they will not occur in a deliberately noncommercial guise, and one profit-earner ensures that more are attempted. Just as the staggering success of *The Singing Fool* meant that other faux-Jolson films would be made, the smashes of *The Broadway Melody* and later *42nd Street* ensured a large number of backstage stories. Such logical progressions could play out during the golden age of studio cost-control and, television be damned, into the twilight of the 1960s. More recently, the dynamic is such that a $200 + million Marvel Comic film will be greenlighted when a $50 million adaptation of a Broadway hit is not. In one year only was a musical a sure thing: 1929, when novelty reigned. Even as there have been flush periods since then, the potential for failure has soared along with the costs. The figures, when they are available, lay all this out in an especially pointed way.[2]

Back to *The Wizard of Oz*: cost-and-gross figures have always been in the nature of that man behind the curtain, exposing such corruption and fallibility and bad judgment that the public is seldom meant to know them fully. Nor is it meant to grasp the bookkeeping that can, on occasion, maneuver the numbers into untoward areas; as the *Coming to America* lawsuit in 1995 proved, some of the greatest creativity in film does not show up onscreen. Even though many of the older numbers are lost, those that survive tell their own history, seldom more so than with Warner Bros. Until its figures were made public in the late twentieth century, did anyone truly comprehend how dizzyingly fast that studio skyrocketed, then plunged? Titles like *The Desert Song* and *On with the Show!* pulled in amazing grosses, after which the bad news kicked in so fast

---

[2] *Very* roughly, a film costing a million dollars in 1930 would be equivalent to a $200 million production today. The dyamics, needless to say, change drastically through the years. During the studio-monopoly time, a film could break even before earning back twice its cost, and back then the phrase "opening weekend" was in no one's vocabulary.

that the figures for late 1930 and 1931 make for truly miserable reading. At MGM, the vast wartime profits were followed by a period when budgets rose and viewership tumbled faster than you can say "television" and "divestiture." By the mid- to late-1960s, the financial figures for musicals were made far more public out of a kind of necessity: they were being carved onto the tombstones of the big studios.

The equation, naturally enough, begins with cost. For about one year, at their very beginning, musicals seemed to take their cue from Irving Thalberg's cautious directive and stayed within reasonable budgets—1929 equivalents of a midrange "A" film that, in the present day, would cost around $50 to $75 million. *The Singing Fool, The Broadway Melody, The Desert Song, On with the Show!, Rio Rita, Gold Diggers of Broadway, The Hollywood Revue* were all configured in this way—the average price for this septet was well under half a million—and returned multiple times their cost in gross receipts. Then, when laying out their coming year (approximately September 1929 to August 1930), the studios ramped up both the number of musicals and the budgets. It was at this point that the matrix became set for musicals to cost more and pose a greater risk, and while a few of those newer projects were viable, many more were not. Two constituents of that late-1929 onslaught resound to this day. One had to do with the nature of the market, as applied to musicals: how many is enough? The answer becomes clear when there are too many, as in the backup in 1930, another of sorts in the mid-1950s, a big one around 1968, and possibly another circa 2005. The market cannot load up the way it can with a staple like comedy, suitable at any time in nearly any quantity. The other factor concerns what can blithely be termed the zeitgeist, the prevailing national or world mood that draws or repels a spectator. In the middle of 1930, the financial crisis essentially canceled out musicals, since giddy optimism and heedless song and dance were not set up to serve as a palliative for anxiety and dread. It remained so until a new president and an upturn in optimism made for a newly welcoming environment. Then, in a time of Vietnam and assassinations, what could seem less germane than a high-budget, song-filled biography of a star, Gertrude Lawrence, whom few people remembered? In less than a decade, there followed an immense shift in which the escapism of a *Star Wars* displaced the niche formerly occupied by musicals: a new dynamic for a different kind of moviegoer. Merchandising power and sequel potential became essential to film, and both are basically alien to a musical, which must stand or fall on its own cost and merit.

The corporate world has changed as much as the output. At the beginning of the sound era, the major studios possessed resources sufficient for producing feature films on an average of one per week, without considerations of unions, reasonable hours, or five-day workweeks. The factory system enabled most films to stay reasonably on budget, just as it ensured that few Hollywood films before the 1950s would be shot away from a controlled studio environment. On the profit side, many of the theaters, until the late 1940s, fell under the same corporate umbrella as the studios. Loews, Inc., MGM's parent company, owned a large chain of movie houses, and since other large studios had similar arrangements, the product was essentially presold. The better the product, the greater the profit, and the converse was equally true: a theater might be contractually required to book a film an audience might not come out to see.

In expressing his concern about expenses, Irving Thalberg was fully aware that *The Broadway Melody* would be as much of a test drive in production as in possible audience reaction. One way to minimize the cost was to buy local. While leading man Charles King was imported from Broadway, the rest of the personnel, including musicians and dancers and the songwriting team of Brown and Freed, were already in the Los Angeles area.[3] The final negative cost of *The Broadway Melody*, $379,000 (actual film cost exclusive of promotion, distribution, etc.), was average to high for an MGM "A" feature of the time, comparable to a late silent like *Rose-Marie* or an early talkie such as *Anna Christie*. The receipts, in contrast, were many times above the norm: a domestic gross of $2,808,000, a foreign gross of $1,558,000, a net profit of $1,604,000. Only two of the studio's previous films had grossed more—*The Big Parade*, plus the immense *Ben-Hur*, which actually lost money. Save for *The Big Parade*, *The Broadway Melody* remained MGM's biggest profit-earner until a pair of later colossi, *San Francisco* and *Boys Town*.

Blatant commerciality was something MGM could do very well, and one slightly later musical was so emblematic of this that its cost-to-profit ratio was its main distinction. Indeed, apart from its being Fred Astaire's first film and an early sampling of the art of the Three Stooges, the importance of *Dancing Lady*

---

[3] The vocal quartet that sings in *Broadway Melody* and other early musicals was based at the Biltmore Hotel in downtown Los Angeles and was known as the Biltmore Quartet. (Trio, when one member was absent.) When Joan Crawford stomps through her Charleston in *The Hollywood Revue*, there they are, soldiering on gallantly.

lies wholly in the domain of the monetary. As produced by the musical-averse David O. Selznick, it was in effect a glamorous potboiler fitted out with a maze of inducements: Joan Crawford romancing Clark Gable, gowns by Adrian, a gleaming production, the promise (not the reality) of musical bounty, and a hit song, "Everything I Have Is Yours."[4] It worked so well that for years *Dancing Lady* was held up to be the model of how to make and sell one of MGM's commercial hits. Even so, it reversed Thalberg's *Broadway Melody* dictate, being expensively made and of indifferent quality. At $923,000, it was one of the most expensive films of 1933, nearly twice the studio average for the time, and not all of the money showed onscreen. There were some below-par production numbers that could not be used, and Gable held up shooting with illnesses that may not all have been real. (MGM's punishment was to farm him out to tiny Columbia Pictures—a penalty with a happy ending titled *It Happened One Night*.) All this mattered less than the final figures: domestic gross was $1.49 million, foreign returns were equal to the cost, and profit for MGM was $744,000. Although it did not earn the studio's biggest profit of that year (that would be *Tugboat Annie*), its cost versus gross proportion was felt to be the ideal toward which a Metro production might aspire. Aesthetics had taken a back seat, and this too would remain a kind of model for the future. A product that returns as healthy a profit as *Dancing Lady* would always be judged a success, even when the lady in question doesn't prove to be much of a dancer.

The Singing Fool, on the other hand, did not produce financial figures that could be held as a model for anything. Instead of a carnival of MGM gloss, it was a modest production whose cost reached $388,000 only because of Vitaphone and Jolson's salary. The returns, it can be conservatively stated, blew the roof off the early sound era. In the United States it took in $3.8 million and overseas just under $2.1 million. Legend holds it to be the highest earner prior to *Gone with the Wind*; not so, for, from the standpoint of gross, there were *The Big Parade* and *Ben-Hur*, as well as *The Birth of a Nation*, whose astronomical financial figures will never be fully known. At any rate, and far more than *The Jazz Singer*, *The Singing Fool* essentially bankrolled the enormous expansion

---

[4] It's a very attractive song, with its chromatic Burton Lane melody, but so tricky to sing that while it was written for Crawford, she wasn't up to it. This created a marketing problem, since sheet music sold better if emblazoned with the legend "SUNG by Joan Crawford." The ingenious (if sniveling) solution: singer Art Jarrett did the song from a bandstand as Crawford danced by with Franchot Tone and hummed the little "da dum" motif punctuating the melody. Thus was the tag "Sung by Art Jarrett and Joan Crawford" *sort* of justified. At least it billed him first.

that Warners undertook in 1929, including moving its plant from Hollywood to Burbank. One parallel it does share with *Dancing Lady*, however unintended: the stark difference between work created to endure and work made for the moment and the cash.

The Jolson films found an odd equivalence in a group of star vehicles that began in 1944, when MGM was producing more costly musicals than any other company. Some had imagination, more followed the model of *Dancing Lady*, and among the most successful were the ones that got wet. Everyone who knows old movies knows Esther Williams and usually, even with a wry chuckle, likes her. She was a big and pretty and amiable young woman, healthy as all get-out, and it was always fun to see exactly what excuses they could come up with to get her into the water. Her roles, tailored to her talent, seldom traveled more than one narrow path, and in a Betty Grable age this was judged sufficient. If people didn't go to her movies simply to see her swim, seldom has a star this big scoped out a more circumscribed area. (The closest, Sonja Henie, was virtually nothing without her skates.) The leading men and supporting comics and songs mattered only an iota's worth next to Esther and, since she was so likable and could wear clothes and sing pleasantly, she was even OK on dry land. Her films, meanwhile, were of a popularity so absurd that their financial figures deliver a necessary corrective about the nature of spectatorship.

In her autobiography, Williams made a few disputable claims (look up Jeff Chandler in the index), and one statement that seemed especially...the right word might be *augmented*. Regarding her first starring film, she noted that *Bathing Beauty* began as a showcase for Red Skelton called *Mr. Coed* until the title and emphasis shifted, lucratively, to her. "MGM made a monster profit," she wrote, then added a specific: "In its era *Bathing Beauty* earned more money internationally than any picture except *Gone With the Wind*." Now, even in the canon of Esther Williams films—not that high a bar—*Bathing Beauty* ranks well below *Million Dollar Mermaid* and some of the others. It has Skelton's slapstick, specialties by pop organist Ethel Smith and the inevitable Xavier Cugat, and finally an aqua ballet that only hints at the waterlogged majesty of Esther at her apex. As a musical, it's less cohesive entertainment than Technicolor playlist—a pop artifact people liked, not loved, certainly not the way they did another 1944 MGM musical, *Meet Me in St. Louis*. Could her statement about the numbers have any accuracy? One guess.

Bathing Beauty cost $2.361 million, more than *The Gang's All Here*, which had recently become the most expensive production to date at 20th Century-Fox.

It was, in fact, the most any musical had cost except for *The Wizard of Oz* and *Lady in the Dark*. Much of it was directly attributable to Williams's specialty—a new pool with hydraulic lifts and fountains and camera windows, plus ten weeks of swimming rehearsal—and to a long ninety-two-day shooting schedule.[5] To say it was worth the investment is an understatement; the US gross was $3.284 million, and, per its star's claim, Latin and South America, the source for wartime foreign profits, obviously doted on beautiful athletes who swam. The foreign tally, $3.6 million, was the highest of any in-house MGM film—which *GWTW* was not—since the silent *Ben-Hur*. The final posted profit was well over $2 million—a major return even during the World War II time of record attendance. Nor was Esther Williams a one- or two-hit wonder. Quick: what was the name of her second starring film? *Thrill of a Romance*, anyone? Neither a good film nor a cogent musical, with a drowsy plot, songs and arias from the avuncular Wagnerian Lauritz Melchior, and little swimming. And, at the end of it, a domestic gross such as few films of the time achieved—well over $4 million, plus a profit far greater than *Bathing Beauty*. And so it went, to the extent that even the notorious *Fiesta*—universally decried, then and now, as stupid and incoherent—scored a giant profit that was, assuredly, due far more to the presence of Esther Williams than to Aaron Copland's "El Salon Mexico." *The Duchess of Idaho, Texas Carnival, Skirts Ahoy!*—forgotten films, all of them, and the kind of money-spinning bread and butter that financed more inventive and risky items that earned far less. A studio's films buoyed each other then; they don't anymore.

Between *Dancing Lady* and Esther Williams, as well as the Joe Pasternak films and Mario Lanza and many others, MGM had a virtually infallible way of channeling musical routine into financially astute realms. This showmanship had been forged, years earlier, through a drastic trial by fire. Before *The March of Time* was the title of a series of preachy short subjects, it was the grim tag attached to one of the great disasters in all of film, the movie musical as black hole. The saga began in that lush, black-ink autumn of 1929, when MGM had gotten the jump on all the other studios by releasing its plotless,

[5] This was more time than MGM would spend on any of its musicals except for *The Wizard of Oz* (understandable) and *Anchors Aweigh* (really?), with the Lubitsch *Merry Widow* a close fourth. Even so, other MGM budget-busters of 1944 took longer: *Dragon Seed, Kismet, Thirty Seconds over Tokyo*. Later, there would be the epic waste of 145 days and $4 million on *Desire Me*—a fiasco of such lunatic magnitude that no director would put his name on it.

No more *Mr. Co-Ed*: Red Skelton still rated top billing by the time *Bathing Beauty* reached its public, but the posters left no doubt about the real star, and the real draw.

star-filled *Hollywood Revue*, which quickly made hand-over-fist profits. It had been supervised by Harry Rapf, a studio stalwart who specialized in money-making schmaltz, and as a reward for this smash, Rapf's bosses indulged his idea for a kind of sequel. Having retained a special fondness for the kind of turn-of-the-century vaudeville that everyone else had forgotten, Rapf filmed a bunch of ancient variety stars in some unusually tired songs and sketches. Then, moving from the then to the now, he shot production numbers notable for their size, irrelevance, and lack of stars. Even for a revue, by definition a kind of catch-all, *The March of Time* had little cohesion and, worse, scant reason for existing. If the same might be said of many musicals, this one took trivia to its farthest extremes and, at $800,000, to nearly twice the cost of *The Hollywood Revue*. Instead of quickly releasing it, MGM tinkered with it while, in the outside world, musicals and the economy took a nosedive. Some footage was put into short subjects and some into a German-language comedy, and the rest was kept on a well-hidden shelf. In 1933, a few *March of Time* minutes turned up in a feature called *Broadway to Hollywood*, after which the accountants were allowed to write it off as one of MGM's biggest losses to that time.

The March of Time affair could only have been possible at MGM and at the dawn of the musical, yet it reverberates over the decades to a similarly hubristic, out-of-control production whose creators misconstrued what audiences wanted. *The Wiz*, in 1978, should have worked. When Motown purchased the film rights to the Broadway hit, there were huge hopes and a cornucopia of possibilities. The jivey reworking of *The Wizard of Oz* was configured to make it more urban—in fact, a valentine to a '70s-ravaged New York City—with Tony Walton designs that turned the World Trade Center into the Emerald City and put yellow cabs onto the Yellow Brick Road. The Cowardly Lion would be one of the guardians of the Public Library, Dorothy was from Harlem, and the Wicked Witch would be flushed down a toilet. Plus Quincy Jones doing the musical arrangements and Michael Jackson as the Scarecrow and Lena Horne as Glinda. The decision to shoot it in New York was intriguing and also expensive, since it required the refurbishment of the former Paramount studio in Astoria, Queens. All this heralded an exciting, old-as-new show, memories of the beloved 1939 film mixing with the most engaging and accessible modernity.

Enter Diana Ross. With two successful films under her belt, the Queen of Motown resolved that, age and logic be damned, she must be Dorothy. Tone down the vivacity (hers and the role's) and reconfigure Dorothy from a scrappy adolescent to a repressed, weepy schoolteacher. Give her more ballads. Give her Sidney Lumet, after John Badham was fired because he wouldn't go along with the casting; never mind that someone known for intense drama had no notion of how a musical might operate or how to photograph dance. Amid rumors of mismanagement, the money flowed without cease, the final $24 million cost making it the equal of *Hello, Dolly!* as the most expensive musical up to that time. Still, it might have been a breakthrough, a crossover hit to revive the entire genre—until it opened. There was Ross, there was grimness where there should have been joy, and there was lighting so dim that the production's one economy seemed to have been to use fewer bulbs. After the potential, the money, and the bad decisions, Motown and Universal posted a significant loss.

A pre-sold title can generally be felt to justify a large expenditure. So it was with the huge sum ($250,000) MGM spent on the film rights to *Good News*— which went on, in 1930, to make a slight profit. Light years later, only a small handful of early-1960s films cost more than the $5.5 million Jack Warner paid simply for the rights to *My Fair Lady*. Betting on a star could be more problematic. In 1929, Marilyn Miller's very name seemed to conjure up the magic of musicals, and acquiring her services for *Sally* was so literally a big deal that her studio advertised it as "$1,000 an hour for 100 hours of work!"—a claim less accurate than catchy, and it worked.[6] Unfortunately, her increased fee on a second film (*Sunny*) made a profit impossible. Also in the realm of impossible: Al Jolson, an even bigger headliner than Miller. Between the talent, the popularity, the ego, and the gambling problem, Jolson's salary discussions were more exciting than his films. Following his first three Warner features, he demanded a half-million dollars per picture, fully the equal of the eight-figure payouts given in a later era to a Tom Cruise. (At the time, its only equal was what Fox paid that concert-hall Jolson, John McCormack, for *Song O' My Heart*.) Warners could only agree, and the raise coincided, with laser precision, with an immense plummet in Jolson's box-office appeal; the worldwide gross of his second half-million dollar film, *Big Boy*, did not cover his salary. By that time, radio had become more pervasive and convenient than Broadway, and nothing in the very early Depression was more popular than Amos 'n' Andy. Fittingly, it was Radio Pictures (presently RKO) that paid the show's creator-stars an immense sum to star in *Check and Double Check*. Planned as a musical, it ended up as a dowdy comedy with a few songs, and the brand was so magic that an unimportant movie scored the year's biggest audience.[7] Many years later, the first million-dollar salary for a musical was paid to Audrey Hepburn for *My Fair Lady*—a choice well in tune with that film's ethos of success-at-any-price. Generally, however, few mega-budgeted musicals of that time, or later, would count star salaries as the biggest line items. The Jolson days were finished, although it should be mentioned that Fox was compelled to pay Christopher Plummer $300,000 *not* to appear in *Doctor Dolittle*.

A greater contributing factor in the skyrocketing of musical costs came with expenses that can be summed up in the word Production. Ever since the days

---

[6]   Miller's studio, First National, had recently been acquired by Warner Bros., and as Miller was a player (in both senses) of no mean skill, she found a sure way to maintain good standing: *extremely* close relations with management, in the person of the same Jack Warner who much later spent all that money on *My Fair Lady*.

[7]   *Check and Double Check* is an early example of a ballyhooed event film that opens sensationally, then dies once the word of mouth gets out. It's common in these days of lousy *Transformers* sequels; in 1930, it was freakish.

of *The Black Crook*, bigger should be better in some fashion, and any musical more adventurous than *Beach Party* is expected to dazzle. Early works such as *The Hollywood Revue* and *On with the Show!* were sold largely on the basis of a particular kind of spectacle—stars in one, Technicolor in the other—yet managed to keep the overall cost down and earn huge returns. The same, only more so, held true with *Gold Diggers of Broadway*, which lived up to its title. What then followed could have been predicted: the million-dollar mark was approached and then crossed, seldom in sure-fire projects. Few operettas were successful enough to justify the $1.2 million Paramount spent on *The Vagabond King*; nor, at Universal, would bandleader Paul Whiteman's appeal keep *King of Jazz* from losing most of the $1.5 million-plus spent on it.[8]

In 1933, when musicals staged their comeback, Warner Bros. led the way with *42nd Street* and *Gold Diggers of 1933*, both of them in line with Thalberg's dictum of quality on a budget: a negative cost of $439,000 for the first and $433,000 for the second. This was high for this studio at this time—Warners had recently slashed the salaries of all employees save executives—but otherwise both films were models of money efficiently spent, if on occasion under the brutal circumstances of twenty-four-plus-hour work shifts. The profits, at any rate, were far more than the studio had seen since that previous *Gold Diggers* in 1929, and Warners promptly gave Berkeley carte blanche for *Footlight Parade*. The result was "By a Waterfall," an aqua ballet so swooningly spectacular that it swelled the budget up to $700,000, three times the average cost of a standard Warner feature. While *Footlight Parade* scored almost as well as *Gold Diggers of 1933*, Berkeley's costly fantasias promptly began to bring in diminished grosses, to which Warners responded predictably: they cut his budgets and his opportunities.

Warners, undoubtedly a big-league studio, often functioned like one of the more economical companies, Universal and Columbia, or, further down the road, Republic and Monogram. At these, most of the musicals of the 1930s and '40s tended to be modest, even B-grade, far from the arabesques of MGM extravagance. Universal was particularly astute at building a rickety film around a pop song and putting it out as part of a profitable double feature—which explains the likes of *Where Did You Get That Girl?* and *Six Lessons from Madame*

---

[8] These figures need some context. The two highest-cost films up to that time were problem-plagued aberrations—*Ben-Hur* ($4 million) and *Hell's Angels* ($2.85 million). Other than them, *King of Jazz* pretty nearly hit the ceiling.

La Zonga. Swing and Latin American music were particularly well suited to such fare, made cheaply enough to all but guarantee a profit. The bare-bones nature of some of them bordered on the surreal, as with one Republic opus with a title (*Sing, Dance, Plenty Hot*) that sounds more like a capsule Twitter review. These lower-case items tapered off after the wartime era, then resumed around 1955 with the pop sounds of *Rock around the Clock* and the immortal *Bop Girl Goes Calypso*. Still cheap and generic, still with the specialty music and piddling scripts, and still—well into the next decade—making money in neighborhood theaters and drive-ins. The first Elvis films were a shade more high-profile than these, and so was the caviar apex of rock' n'roll musicals, Fox's *The Girl Can't Help It*.

By the time of Elvis and his kind, musicals were in a financial predicament. Divestiture, television, rock music, and other cultural shifts all made for declining grosses, and the average cost of a musical—over $2 million in the mid-1950s—was becoming unsustainable. A blockbuster hit like *Seven Brides for Seven Brothers* (cost $2.5 million, profit $3.2 million) or *White Christmas* (gross over $12 million), was increasingly rare, and MGM, house of musical plenty, was hit particularly hard. Starting, alas, with *The Band Wagon*, the studio had a series of major failures: *Brigadoon*, *It's Always Fair Weather*, *Kismet*, *Silk Stockings*, *Les Girls*, *Ten Thousand Bedrooms*, and the misbegotten arabesque that was *Invitation to the Dance*. All of these posted seven-figure losses, and not even the formerly fail-safe Esther Williams was immune: *Jupiter's Darling* was lavish and silly in all the wrong ways, and when it posted a $2.2 million loss, it marked Williams's last swim at the studio. It was at this same time that musicals, the non-Bop-Girl variety, began their shift into high roadshow gear. *Oklahoma!* and *Guys and Dolls* were first, followed by *South Pacific* and *Gigi*. Were any of these necessarily better, on the whole, than what preceded them? *Gigi* was in the league, and it was the only one created directly for the screen and not transferred from the stage. With the others, pedigree obviously counted for a great deal. Despite the camera filters and deadening Logan touch, *South Pacific* was, at a gross of over $20 million, an astronomical money-spinner. This, if nothing else, seemed to justify the fact that it had been the most expensive musical made up to then.

The smash of *South Pacific* marked the shift, in the musical-financial division, toward the haywire side of the spectrum. Thus, increasingly, out with the more modest works and on with more biggies. *Can-Can* was as expensive as *South Pacific*, *Porgy and Bess* more so, and neither earned back its cost, but then came *West Side Story*. Expensive once again, and this time with big ticket sales and great reviews and Oscars. There was a brief respite with *The Music Man* and *Gypsy* and *Bye, Bye Birdie* and *The Unsinkable Molly Brown*, all of them reasonably budgeted and non-roadshow and successful. Then there arrived the *Cleopatra* of musicals. At $17 million (recall that upfront charge for the rights), *My Fair Lady* was the most expensive film yet shot in the United States, and the ballyhoo and elitism of its roadshow engagements were breathtaking. So were its Oscar haul (8) and worldwide gross (well over $60 million)—which then seemed modest alongside the next one, *The Sound of Music*. This time the cost was a more modest $8.2 million, and the reaction literally unprecedented. Forget about no musical having done this well: no *film* had done numbers like this, not even *Gone With the Wind*. Rarely, if ever, had so many return customers paid high ticket prices again and again to hear Julie and the kids doing "Do Re Mi" and to see how good works and songs could thwart Nazis. The many critics to voice objections were annoyed and bewildered, and the Fox accountants were overjoyed that something was finally able to balance out *Cleopatra*. Most crucially, *The Sound of Music* was the final installment, after *Mary Poppins* and *My Fair Lady*, in a mighty triumvirate: large of budget, filled with music, a more-or-less family-oriented entertainment that seemed to bring comfort in a time of unrest. No one in charge of producing movies missed this point.

There was a short downtime, and then came the parade. One big musical followed another, mostly in roadshow engagements: *Thoroughly Modern Millie, Camelot, Half a Sixpence, The Happiest Millionaire, Doctor Dolittle, Funny Girl, Star!, Finian's Rainbow, Oliver!, Chitty Chitty Bang Bang, Goodbye, Mr. Chips, Paint Your Wagon, Sweet Charity, Hello, Dolly!, On a Clear Day You Can See Forever, Darling Lili, Song of Norway, Fiddler on the Roof*. There were others too, less costly, such as *A Funny Thing Happened on the Way to the Forum* and *How to Succeed in Business without Really Trying*, plus the most blatant of *Sound of Music* knock-offs, *The Singing Nun*. It was the big ones, naturally, that took most of the attention and oxygen. Too many, too relentlessly highspirited, too out-of-touch. Too expensive as well: this group came in at costs ranging from about $4 million, high-but-acceptable in 1967 dollars, to $25 million, insane and indefensible. Several in this group—*Millie, Funny Girl, Oliver!, Fiddler*, and the modestly priced *Finian's Rainbow*—did well or better; most could not begin to cover their costs. Nor were they quiet, skulk-away-in-ignominy failures. Roadshow engagements were by definition *events*, and if they failed, everyone heard the thud.[9] When *The Happiest Millionaire* was pulled after a few weeks, the public knew that Walt Disney's final feature was a bomb. As for *Star!*, it quickly moved into general release with half an hour gone; then, absurdly re-edited and a full hour shorter, it was reissued as *Those Were the Happy Times*. Could irony be any more acrid?

The level of fiscal madness, as prompted by *The Sound of Music*, was made clearest in a baleful piece of reportage by John Gregory Dunne titled *The Studio*. Allowed a year's worth of nearly unlimited access to 20th Century-Fox, Dunne chronicled all he heard and saw, most memorably the strenuous brouhaha over *Doctor Dolittle*. Eighteen million dollars of leaden whimsy, *Dolittle* tried mightily to cover the three roadshow bases of *Mary Poppins* (kid fantasy), *My Fair Lady* (Rex Harrison), and *The Sound of Music* (everything except nuns and Nazis). If the fact that it went horribly over budget—try directing this many animals—might not signify that it was good, it did mean that Fox needed to push hard. At the end of the nonstop promotion, there was a remainder bin of soundtrack albums, a fount of red ink, and a pair of Oscars for subpar special effects and an ordinary song about talking to animals. Most extraordinarily, all this was taking place while Fox was in effect doing *Cleopatra* all over again: spending $40 million on *Star!* and *Hello, Dolly!*, exclamation points and all. These were not the only mistakes Fox made in all that time—this was the age, after all, of *Myra Breckinridge*—but they did seem to point up the excess in especially graphic fashion. It was 1930 redux in some ways, and this time no one had the stock market to blame. At least in *Hello, Dolly!* the money was there on the screen; people wanting substance might have objected to a production resembling a convention of wedding cakes, but this may have been preferable to *Star!*, with its sickly color and oddly tacky sets, or Paramount's *Paint Your Wagon*, with its Gold Rush/hippie aesthetic coming in at an indefensible $20 million. Insufferable as it was, *Paint Your Wagon* did manage a climax both revealing and appropriate. As the plot had it, Lee Marvin and Clint Eastwood build a system of tunnels under a mining town in order to catch gold dust seeping through the floorboards of all the saloons. A bull gets loose in the tunnels, knocks away the supporting beams,

---

[9] The most massive single roadshow disaster came in 1964 with a film few recall, or wish to: a poorly dubbed West German version of *The Threepenny Opera*. Embassy Pictures imported it in the hope that it might compete with *My Fair Lady*. It premiered in Detroit, and in some places lasted, literally, one day.

Bigger, longer: Not all of the massive quantity of the marathon "When the Parade Passes By" sequence in *Hello, Dolly!* lay in its cost. Nor in the number of people, of which only a tiny fraction is seen here. It also came musically, with Barbra Streisand singing (or synching) what the publicity department called "the longest note of any movie musical." Anybody got a stopwatch?

and the entire town-built-on-greed crashes down like a house of cards. Anyone who can't find metaphors in this isn't trying.

Fiddler on the Roof, which opened as a roadshow late in 1971, was less costly and more profitable than its immediate predecessors, better, and in a certain way more apropos. It also brought the age to something of an end. There had already been portents when Paramount announced that both *On a Clear Day You Can See Forever* and the ruinously expensive *Darling Lili* would not run as roadshows, a situation that caused neither film to earn back its high cost. Then, shortly after *Fiddler*, there was *Cabaret*, which played roadshow in some places (adding an unnecessary intermission) but was in essence a popular-run, and profitable, attraction. The change was underlined a few months later with *The Godfather*. Earlier, this kind of must-see epic would have run long and profitably with high-price reserved seats. Now it ran as ordinary films did, and ran and ran until it became the new highest-grossing film. Soon, there were the flops of *Man of La Mancha* and *Lost Horizon* and *Mame*. Musicals, those mainstays of the roadshow experience, now seemed only part of a time officially lost.

There were musicals made between *Cabaret* and *Chicago*—some very successful, like *A Star Is Born* and *Grease*, and some very good, like *Hair* and *Nashville*—so it was not a time of complete silence. It merely seemed that way. *Annie*, in 1982, became for a bit the most expensive American film yet made, its $50 million price tag far in excess of the cost of *Heaven's Gate*, although the money was neither apparent on the screen nor recoupable at the box office. Then there was *A Chorus Line*: so actively, unnervingly bad and such a dire money-loser that a time-warp kind of split began to occur. Home video made older musicals seem greater than ever, and new ones were, obviously, impossible. A 1995 adaptation of *The Fantasticks*, modest in budget and intent, was not deemed worthy of any kind of release for five years, at which point a $10 million film scored a total US gross of about $50,000. For *Evita*, which did turn something approaching a profit, any success was less attributable to the property itself than to a worldwide following that would have turned up to see Madonna play Hedda Gabler. *Moulin Rouge!* was a new musical in a new century, and while it did not earn the insane profits of a *Grease*, it made the kind of look-at-me splash that encouraged producers to consider musicals once again.

A year later, *Chicago* was in some ways the polar opposite of *Hello, Dolly!*, its budget whittled down to the approximate cost ($45 million) of a standard romantic comedy, with energy and ingenuity substituted for lavish trappings. Not since *Grease* had so many people gone to see a musical, then return for repeat viewings. A total worldwide gross of over $300 million was small-ish potatoes next to a *Spider-Man*, yet substantial enough to justify a number of successors. If most managed to keep their costs down to *Chicago* levels, neither *The Phantom of the Opera* nor *Rent* nor *The Producers* recouped those costs, in part because they failed to capture whatever had drawn people to the original shows. *Hairspray* and *Mamma Mia!*, like them or not, did succeed financially, as did the third installment—the first for the big screen—of the phenomenally popular *High School Musical* series. Then, in 2009, *Nine* returned a worldwide gross of $54 million on an outlay well over $80 million. Nor did original projects score well, least of all the financially catastrophic Beatles fantasia *Across the Universe*. Depending on one's point of view, it was either a comfort or a bad thing that this was when inexpensive concert films started to score, and with the same sought-after demographic who had gone to see Elvis in *Jailhouse Rock* all those years before.

In the second decade of the twenty-first century, the outlook for conventional movie musicals—not a concert, not animated, not derived from a video or computer game—seems, at best, ambiguous. Costs can be ruinous, grosses seldom appear promising, the merchandising opportunities are extremely limited, and not enough people seem interested. Why, for example, would paying high theater prices to see a disappointment like *Rock of Ages* be preferable to staying home to see the original hair-bands performing on cable, DVD, or YouTube? Or better, to see gloriously spruced-up DVD or Blu-Ray transfers of *Swing Time* or *Gigi*? Some, too, will prefer to get their kicks from *American Idol* or *Dancing with the Stars*, or whatever else passes at any given time for musical entertainment. That's life, and that's the modern attention span. A *Les Misérables*, when it succeeds, seems an outlier, strangely beside the point, possibly even as nonrepeatable a stunt as *Check and Double Check*.

There is also the unanswerable question: how many more great musical films remain to be made? Maybe, at least, there is room for some water in that glass. Some young Mamoulian might enthrall with a *Love Me Tonight*, or a Von Trier-in-waiting may provoke with a *Dancer in the Dark*. (True to the musical equation, one of these succeeded financially when it was new, and the other did not.) It would be glorious to think, when imagining the possibilities, that money does not need to be a factor. Fat chance; it does and it always will, and the days of an unlimited budget—the kind of thinking that brought forth *King of Jazz* in 1930 and *A Star Is Born* in 1954—are over. Musicals of that dimension may be as obsolete as that *Hello, Dolly!* videotape in *WALL-E*: extinction multiplied by itself. Still, producers inclined to look at historical figures might note that *The Sound of Music* remains at Number Three of the list of highest-earning films (domestic gross, adjusted for inflation). Perhaps, too, there might be room for more *Chicagos*, astutely made at a sensible price. Granted, it's been a long while since that near-inconceivable time when the average movie ticket cost twenty-five cents and a *Top Hat* cost $625,000. Would it be possible to have a modern-day equivalent? Maybe not, but remember it's money and it's movies. Never say never.

Chapter 8

I Get the Neck of the Chicken

....

Did Lucille Ball sync her own singing in Mame, *or did Dick Cavett dub it for her?*

By the time Pauline Kael raised that impudent question, there had been such a piling-on that the venerable and beloved star of *I Love Lucy* would break down and begin to weep during interviews. While Kael's snark had its own distinct pungency—which was why she was Pauline Kael—the objections were not unique to her. No review failed to mention the lens filters that attempted to smudge Ball's face into a semblance of youth, few neglected to note that Beatrice Arthur stole their every scene together, and the words "toneless" and "croak" were frequently invoked. *That's Entertainment!* was running in theaters at the same time, alongside which *Mame*, like its predecessors *Man of La Mancha* and *Lost Horizon*, made it all seem not to be possible anymore. It was also, in its uniquely blurry fashion, a demonstration of how conspicuous musicals are. Their risks are as amplified as their budgets and soundtracks, their fiscal and aesthetic stakes are high, and they stand out as much when they fail as when they succeed. To put it ungallantly, Lucille Ball made herself a sitting duck when she decided to crown her career by becoming a musical diva. The genre offers no light-concealing bushel, and when you're not up for it the whole world knows. And makes jokes about how you can't sing.

If a genuinely bad musical film is a rotten egg—it can be argued that *Mame,* while wrongheaded, is far from the worst of the carton—it can offer many lessons to those willing to pay attention. Teachings tend to hit home the most when attended by monetary calamity, and some of the worst musicals did manage to offend both the financial and commercial bases. *Lost Horizon* became known as *Lost Investment,* and it occurred to more than one person to call the producer's failed revue *Goldwyn's Folly.* Others fail in subtler ways, not always with the thud of public apathy. Through thwarted ambition, arrant misconception, deluded incompetence, and plain grandiose inanity, a select few journeyed the whole route into all-devouring wrongness, into proving that art sometimes teaches the most thorough lessons when it is completely absent.[1]

Surely the lessons of trial and error were expected in the early years, when musicals were finding their bearings and that experimental, archaic *Desert Song* could play to a huge, curious public. Returns such as it amassed will always make for imitators, and there soon followed the bane of the era, ponderous, anti-cinematic operettas. One of these, *Captain of the Guard,* is a virtual textbook on how musical cinema should not function. It was made at the wrong time, at the wrong place—Universal, a studio with no affinity for musical drama—by people ignorant of genre or audience. It opens with a foreword apologizing for its twisted history, after which it gives Rouget de Lisle barely enough time to write "La Marseillaise" before storming the Bastille to save his girlfriend. *Les Miz* is as an airy romp alongside this reimagined French Revolution, in which the music is indifferent and the dramaturgy splintered and erratic. Onstage, even in 1930, it would have played like parody; on film, with massive sets and crowd scenes, it seemed actively unhinged. Nor was its sin simply artistic, as Universal learned when it opened in Canada to a response so hostile as to make clear that the thing could never run in France. This much disaster can instruct the earnest in any number of ways; unfortunately, the slag heap of film is seldom very accessible, and *Captain of the Guard* is so unseen and unknown that it might never have happened.

---

[1] Not everyone agrees with the view of bad work as a necessary caution. A favorable *New York Times* review of *A Song in the Dark: The Birth of the Musical Film* (1st ed.) took exception to what was felt to be excessive attention paid to the worst early musicals. A reply, then, many years after the fact: it was not only the best of these films that served as signposts to their era. The disasters made every bit as significant a contribution to their time and helped to shape the genre, sounding warnings that should have been better heeded—plus some of them are way fun.

If offense to history and the French is bad, violating common decency can be even worse. While *Golden Dawn* is a title unfamiliar to the general public, to lovers of musical arcana it evokes appalling magic. Every bad deed (save boredom) a musical can do it does, with relish. The racial insensitivity alone— the heroine is purportedly an African girl so favored by the gods that she was born white—would put it alongside *The Birth of a Nation* in some inflammatory pantheon, yet its musicality is what sends it over the edge into loony-bin majesty. It was a stage operetta that had fared only middlingly on Broadway (Cary Grant, then Archie Leach, had a supporting role) and was part of a buying spree that Warner Bros. took up in its first flush of early-sound profits. They gave it a high budget, Technicolor, and much misspent care and energy. Plus, bless them, they gave it Noah Beery, an ace villain in silent film who happened to possess a strong bass voice and the capacity for attacking his roles with more relish than practically anybody. Here, effortlessly, he raises many serious questions about exactly what constitutes a bad performance. This is not inferior acting in any conventional way, for Beery is wholly committed to devouring his role as an Emperor Jones–style despot, complete with streaky dark makeup and Amos 'n' Andy dialect. Nor does the rest of *Golden Dawn* shy away from conviction. The singers go all the way with their material, the melodrama is played out to utter extremes, the score includes items like "Africa Smiles No More" and "My Bwana," and some genuine African American extras manage to keep straight faces. After earning some truly catastrophic reviews, *Golden Dawn* died at the 1930 box office, then somehow the fates saw to it that it survived (albeit in black and white) where many of its fellows were lost. For a willing audience, it offers an especially compelling kind of terrible— enthusiastic, assertive, beyond tasteless, and of such immensity that it can fairly be termed epic.

One of the countless errors of *Golden Dawn* concerned the raw, faithful fashion in which it transferred stage conventions to film. Early talkies frequently did this, and much of *Dawn* is the kind of overwrought melodrama meant to be seen from far back in the balcony, not in close-up. Some adaptations take the opposite route, departing from their source so vigorously that they have no cause to call themselves any kind of a version. This is an area where, forty years after *Golden Dawn*, *Paint Your Wagon* became a textbook case of how not to do, in essence, anything. It had not been a major hit on Broadway in 1951 yet lingered in some minds as a pleasantly offbeat title, with good music, coming between *Brigadoon* and *My Fair Lady* in the Lerner and

Loewe canon. In a post–*Sound of Music* age, *Paint Your Wagon* translated as a major possibility, and so it was that Alan Jay Lerner, for the first and only time, was permitted to take up the mantle of movie producer. To direct, Lerner selected that most august and troublesome of Broadway-to-Hollywood figures, Joshua Logan, then coming off the costly and odd film of *Camelot.* Then he turned to the script, the one he originally wrote. It is probably safe to assume that the concept of change is not unwelcome to a man whose marital tally reaches the number eight, and Lerner was nothing if not zealous. He scrapped everything except the setting, a few character names, and half the songs. Judging the original plot—an Anglo prospector's daughter loves a Latino bandit—to be passé, Lerner turned instead to a Swingin'-Sixties ménage-à-trois: an older and younger prospector and an escaped Mormon bride, with the more provocative aspects of the triangle remaining unmentioned. At this point it is fair to quote one of the Broadway songs that did not make it into the film: "What's Goin' On Here?"

Good advice: A patchwork Alan Jay Lerner confers with a pensive Clint Eastwood on the set of *Paint Your Wagon.* Neither the nature nor the outcome of this conversation is known; it might be argued as well that Eastwood's thoughtfulness is not particularly evident in the completed film.

Lerner's other choices for *Paint Your Wagon* marked an odd intersection of the trendy with the quixotic. Lee Marvin and Clint Eastwood, both hot and current, were not singers in any rational sense, and neither was Jean Seberg, cast as the bride after Diana Rigg dropped out. Paddy Chayefsky was hired to add urban intensity to the script, André Previn wrote the music for Lerner's new songs, and *Camelot* production designer John Truscott would take the same retro approach to the Gold Rush that he had to Arthurian England. The final coup came with the selection of location: a completely undeveloped section of rural Oregon prone to heavy rains and mudslides and approximately seven miles from the middle of nowhere. Calamity then followed without cease: bad weather, transportation problems, Seberg's affair with Eastwood, Lerner's escalating megalomania, and marauding hippies, which sounds oxymoronic but is in essence accurate. Around the five-month, $20 million mark, Paramount pulled the plug. Finally, after exhaustive ballyhoo and promotional barbecues (true), there were the inevitable roadshow engagements. The reviews were at best querulous and, more consistently, withering, the public's response one of indifference. Logan never worked in film again, and Lerner's only subsequent foray was the screenplay for another Paramount failure, *On a Clear Day You Can See Forever*.

The ill-starred odyssey of *Paint Your Wagon* is significant on several levels. First, there are the "My God, it's a train wreck" aspects of it, on- and offscreen. (A few buffs cut it slack because of Previn's attractive arrangements.) Most arrestingly, there is its pervasive, intrinsic strangeness. What *is* this thing? How could esteemed professionals create such a Sisyphean anomaly? The blame cannot be placed on bad weather and out-of-control flower children. Lerner's intentions, and Logan's as well, were neither incomprehensible nor unworthy. They had conceived a musical with a fresh and pertinent sheen, an un-*Sound of Music* for the more liberal folk who hated Vietnam and wanted films to dare more and try harder. And, truly, a feisty and coherent reimagining of the show with singing actors could have been intriguing. Francis Ford Coppola had attempted the same thing with *Finian's Rainbow* to mixed if not odious effect. Instead, there were attempts at strenuous transformation. Even without the managerial ineptitude that hobbled everything, there was at the core of it an unbridled fraudulence far beyond the untruths that musicals are prone to tell. *Paint Your Wagon* was a big fat phony, a product of the old dying studios pretending to be a cutting-edge indie, spending millions in an effort to look cheap and current, trying desperately to corral and flatter an *Easy Rider* audience that would never show up under any circumstance. In the process, how could it not undermine itself and betray its roots and ancestors? It contained virtually no dance, and the one trained singer on hand (Harve Presnell) seemed spliced in from another movie. If, in *Camelot*, Logan could camouflage some of the falsity with magical shimmer, such was not possible in a grimy Gold Rush setting. Even the supposed frankness was mainly a matter of some leering jokes, along with the cheap slapstick of that raging bull knocking everything down. The might-have-been can be glimpsed only in a few vagrant moments, and oddly enough one of them is Lee Marvin's much-derided rendition of "Wandrin' Star." Yes, the notion of this actor lofting his cement-truck tones in song is one of the most bizarre notions in a musical film since Noah Beery sang, in *Golden Dawn*, about loving to whip people; next to Marvin, Vanessa Redgrave sounds like Kristin Chenoweth. It is, nevertheless, one of the musical's lead tropes: a fine song, a resourceful actor, and a dramatic point can come together in a meaningful way. Strange, certainly, not inauthentic—a tiny validity amid the desperate fakery of nearly everything that *Paint Your Wagon* attempted or achieved.

The heavy hand of Joshua Logan was even more prominent in an adapted show that adhered too closely in too many wrong ways, under the too-unblinking eyes of Richard Rodgers and Oscar Hammerstein II. It must be noted that both *Oklahoma!* and *South Pacific*, the films Rodgers and Hammerstein produced themselves, are among the most faithful of Broadway adaptations, both making use of stunning open-air locations far away from the usual Hollywood soundstages. *Oklahoma!* was filmed largely in, well, Texas, and *South Pacific* in pre-statehood Hawaii, and the locations ensured an authentic look in both cases as well as a high budget. Some find *Oklahoma!* just right, and *South Pacific* grossed sensational sums; yet the question of slavish devotion does need to be raised, particularly with the latter. While it moves a few things around (some of the restructuring occurred when the roadshow print was cut), the film *is* the show to such an extent that it reinstates a song that had been removed in pre-Broadway tryouts ("My Girl Back Home," and it works reasonably well). Everything in *South Pacific* is, on the surface, as it should be. Except for those moments when Logan's fabled filters make everything go purple, there isn't the insane this-is-so-wrong aura that hangs over *Paint Your Wagon*. Yet something always seems missing. *Oklahoma!* has vibrancy in its dances and quirks in its Ado Annie, *The King and I* has two fine performers enacting that central conflict, and *The Sound of Music* has

Julie Andrews, plus whatever else it is that so many people love about *The Sound of Music*. *South Pacific* should be propelled by that wonderful score and the lush backgrounds and air of romantic tragedy. Instead, even apart from the dubbed voices and some insufficient casting, it's overpowered by a "don't tamper with it" reverence that, paradoxically, makes it seem too slight. Small wonder that in spite of its initial success, it has always seemed beside the point. Where a *Golden Dawn* bestowed more theatricality than could be healthily tracked by a camera, *South Pacific* on film seems wan alongside its best stage incarnations. When people speak of adaptations they love, they mention *The Sound of Music* or *Cabaret* because they love the films that the shows became. If they mention *South Pacific*, it's because of the beloved show that happened to have a film made of it.[2]

The entire dynamic of adapting a successful show has an inherent sticking point that must ever be addressed: comparisons are unavoidable. *Man of La Mancha* was a show many people saw and loved (and a few loathed), even apart from the fact that "The Impossible Dream" rapidly became something like middlebrow America's new national anthem. On the stage it was epic, a modern-day operetta for full-throated singers with personalities to match, with some fiery Jack Cole choreography. The film version was an event to be both anticipated and, in a way, dreaded. There seemed to be several options: big and empty like *Hello, Dolly!* or, like *Fiddler on the Roof*, impassioned and respectful yet cinematic. In the event, it was neither, and dread still took the prize as, once again, a choice of director was followed by a domino procession of bad and weird decisions. By the end of the 1960s, directorial niche was nearly an irrelevant concept, and almost any large-budget film would have a director with either a good track record or connections. With *La Mancha*, it was a case of the hit-maker, and what a hit: *Love Story* made so much money that no one connected with it had to say they were sorry. As the director of so genuinely monstrous a success, Arthur Hiller had his pick of properties, and he chose Don Quixote and Aldonza. With few if any bankable film names able to handle the vocal end of these roles, Hiller took the Logan path with a fine actor needing to be dubbed (Peter O'Toole) and a sensational Aldonza with slight vocal ability

---

[2] Nor did the movie garner more love after the later Glenn Close TV version. There was, however, one passionate adherent who felt moved to post an online excoriation of the rather tempered audio commentary on the DVD. By the end of this fan's screed, "somebody named Richard Barrios" stood accused of nearly everything short of matricide.

(Sophia Loren).³ He then scaled down both the music and the drama to such sketchy and de-energized proportions that it all seemed like Cliff Notes. *Cabaret*, earlier in 1972, had reconfigured its show excitingly; *Man of La Mancha* seemed reductive and parched, with strangely existential musical interludes and underpowered arrangements. This of all shows could not sustain so dispiriting a transformation, and its failure seemed to embody everything that film could no longer achieve.

One more musical after *Man of La Mancha* was given, very briefly, a roadshow run. In 1973, Vietnam was still a war, the Nixon presidency was beginning to wobble, and the price of gasoline was going up. For producer Ross Hunter, who clung desperately to myths about "old Hollywood," such times demanded a Utopian panacea. A musical retread of the Frank Capra classic *Lost Horizon* might indeed have been appealing, and Hunter engaged some promising participants. Unfortunately, he also opted for a post–*Sound of Music* approach, a patchwork of frolicking and kids and nostalgia and pre–New Age platitudes. Peter Finch and Liv Ullmann appeared stranded and, in their dubbed songs, embarrassed, while Charles Jarrott was as ill-suited a director as Arthur Hiller had been and Sidney Lumet would be. The fact that Shangri-La was made out of the redecorated big set from *Camelot* probably did not make for great karma, and Hermes Pan's dances resembled lampoons from *The Carol Burnett Show*.⁴ Worst of all was the unsingable score by Burt Bacharach and Hal David, so irredeemable a brick wall that Hunter later claimed he would have thrown it out and commissioned new songs had there been enough time. If *Paint Your Wagon* was wrong and *Man of La Mancha* was off-putting, *Lost Horizon* was an instant punch line, so outlandish a piece of camp as to almost seem deliberate. Its failure was of a magnitude to encompass more than mere fiscal loss, more than all the jokes that were made, more even than calling a halt to its producer's career. It emphasized, broadcast

³ O'Toole's attempt to sing for himself quickly prompted the enlistment of dubber Simon Gilbert. While O'Toole had done his own Rex Harrison–style talk-singing in *Goodbye, Mr. Chips*, such vocalism was a far cry from "Impossible Dream" sounds. It was the same with Raul Julia in the 1992 Broadway revival: fine with the acting, overtaxed by the music.

⁴ When *Lost Horizon* made its quick move to general release, it lost its most derided scene: Pan's "fertility dance," with men yoked to teapots encircling a twirling Olivia Hussey. (It finally resurfaced nearly forty years later on DVD.) Another much-noted "special" moment did stay in: the Shangri-La library, repository of the finest human endeavor, boasted shelves of *Reader's Digest* Condensed Books so visible they could be spotted on small TV screens.

even, what *Man of La Mancha* had already stated: a traditional musical should not occur, not even as a flossy diversion, when it is unable to make a viable case for its own existence.

Multidimensional disasters on the order of *Paint Your Wagon* and *Lost Horizon* were sad emblems of the end of the traditional studio system, a time when one major project might be a make-or-break proposition. In earlier years, when the factories ran smoothly, the fiascos were more easily absorbed, though no other studio would have taken the drastic step MGM did in 1930 to completely derail *The March of Time*. A more insidious phenomenon, one quite familiar in recent times, involves a film that performs profitably yet poisons the well in some fashion. Here, again, there is Jolson. His stardom had not initially been based on bathos, and he might have done well after *The Jazz Singer* and *The Singing Fool* to move into something looser and funnier. Instead, he revisited the no-rest-for-the-weary division with a numbing concoction titled *Say It with Songs*. It was *The Singing Fool* redux, with the little boy surviving this time, after being hit by a truck. Otherwise, it played like farce: Jolson as a radio star who accidentally kills a man, is arrested over an open mike, spends Christmas in the penitentiary serenading the other inmates, and sings his son back to health with a clone of "Sonny Boy" called "Little Pal." Drawn by both star and title, huge crowds turned out and felt betrayed—an early instance of millions paying to see a film they then actively dislike. Jolson's stardom was so dented that he would not resume true preeminence until 1946, when he was heard and glorified in *The Jolson Story*—not an accurate or great film in most particulars, but one which, this time, people adored.

Stardom at the Jolson level often leads to shoddy goods, and the Elvis vehicles of the 1960s are especially egregious in this regard. With their budgets and premises becoming more and more threadbare as time went on, with interchangeable people and a series of excuses to stand in for a plot, they reduced musical stardom to its most wretched essence. Here a song, there a love scene, now a fight, and Elvis's eyes would glaze over as much with boredom as with whatever excess of substances he was ingesting. While it is easy to marginalize something called *Clambake*, it should be noted that this dynamic was fundamentally a continuation of the trend that had started with Jolson and moved through other stars over the years whose names mattered more than the titles. Gene Autry and Roy Rogers did all their westerns-with-songs, Betty Grable had all those excuses to be indignant and show the legs, and Bing Crosby was laid-back and had that voice. This was filmmaking as the purest commerce, a prefabrication of tested ingredients made for a willing public that knew not to expect anything else—fast-food as cinema. For the most part, it would be as unfair to disparage these films as it would to, say, hold Grable in contempt for not being Judy Garland or Doris Day. They were work of their time and for their audience, as most musicals are, so expendable that it's more of a quirk—due to television, then home video—that they have, in some fashion, endured.

An overbearing or by-rote star vehicle would be a less of a foreseeable event for Fred Astaire. He was meticulous in ways Jolson could not be, he served creators and costars attentively, he cared about the entire work, not just his portion. If the quality of the films could vary, his own contributions were never less than august and committed. It follows, then, that two disasters from the mid-1940s are bad despite, not because of, Astaire. One was a much-noted box office disaster, the other a major popular success, and together they show that neither a bad destination nor an object lesson need have one simple route. With *Yolanda and the Thief*, one culprit was the comprehensible hubris that enfolded Arthur Freed after the success of *Meet Me in St. Louis*. Lightning, after all, might strike twice, even as it is lightning's nature to be highly destructive. No question about it, *Yolanda* is genuinely fascinating, made with audacity and a rarefied kind of imagination. It's also an elegant exercise in futility, a hothouse case study of talent misapplied, of lily-gilding gone haywire. The central, insurmountable problem lay with Freed's choice of material, a fey and insubstantial magazine story about a Latin American heiress and the conman who poses as her guardian angel. Compounding this error, Freed collaborated with Harry Warren on a group of indifferent songs and cast Lucille Bremer as Yolanda. A fine dancer who had already fared well in *Meet Me in St. Louis* and *Ziegfeld Follies*, she was confronted here with a role to stump Garbo—spiritual, carnal, trusting, aware, fairy-tale princess, real woman—and if Astaire was far better cast, there was little in the role that was worth doing, nor enough opportunities for song or dance. Freed's accomplice in all of this was the guiding spirit of *Meet Me in St. Louis*, Vincente Minnelli, who overcompensated for the weaknesses by going madly over the top with décor and design, producing less a cohesive work of cinema than a chic artifact for hard-core cultists. With its mad Technicolor outbursts and rococo surfaces, *Yolanda* is as a magnificent pastry, with meringue and sprinkles and icing piled on beguilingly without cease, while the substance beneath it all is a cracked sliver of melba toast. It came to life exactly twice: a fascinating (if unsatisfying and symbol-clashing) dream ballet and the extraneous, captivating Astaire-Bremer jive dance to

"Coffee Time." Otherwise, it's as conflicted as Yolanda herself, a kamikaze dive into style that is both excessive and deficient.

Where *Yolanda* cost $2.44 million and lost way over half its investment, *Blue Skies* cost $3 million and made a sizable profit. Instead of a closely managed product of the Freed Unit at MGM, *Blue Skies* came from the less meticulous climes of Paramount, where producers and directors seldom had specialties and a musical was an undifferentiated component of the general output. Such an approach rarely created either art or calamity—*Lady in the Dark* was, here as elsewhere, an aberration—and had worked especially nicely in 1942 with *Holiday Inn*. Nothing groundbreaking there, simply a rich bunch of Irving Berlin songs joined to a thin functional plot, Bing Crosby singing "White Christmas" and much else, and some predictably stupendous dancing from Astaire. *Blue Skies* was intended as a return to the same field, this time in Technicolor, with Crosby and Berlin reunited with Mark Sandrich, who had also directed many of the Astaire-Rogers films. The differences lay in the costar—Broadway's Paul Draper was an outstanding dancer who lacked Astaire's presence—and the script, a triangle so vacuous as to be borderline revolting. When Sandrich died before shooting, he was replaced by Stuart Heisler, who knew the ropes of film noir and had never gone near a musical and would not again. Then Draper either—the accounts vary—was discharged because of a stammer or quit because he couldn't stand the female lead, Joan Caulfield.[5] Astaire happened to be available and, as he quickly stepped in, announced that this would be his farewell appearance. The film was a hit and Astaire's retirement lasted all of two years, at which point he was once again called upon as a replacement in an Irving Berlin cavalcade, for Gene Kelly in *Easter Parade*.

Blue Skies has one archival moment, and it's all Astaire, in fact, Astaire multiplied—"Puttin' on the Ritz," featuring a solo song and dance backed by a chorus line composed entirely of more Astaires, done with a photographic virtuosity to almost match the skill of its central, sole performer. This is sheer wonderment, in the vein of such other Astaire trick solos as that dance-around-the-room in *Royal Wedding*, and in *Blue Skies* it's a lonely oasis.

---

[5] There seems to have been a continuation of the Lucille Bremer ethic here, since Ms. Caulfield was reportedly a close friend of Bing Crosby. Perhaps this kind of casting makes for good on-set morale, but a show as big as *Blue Skies* attempts to be needs a central participant who can do things, not simply look great in Technicolor.

Astaire's character, as written for the less winning Draper, is a self-destructive egotist whose alcoholism finishes off his career. It's repellent to see the supreme Astaire treated this way, yet he's a digression from the central conflict between Crosby, who's barely awake, and Caulfield, who seldom registers anything. (In a hardly-worth-recounting nutshell: he buys and flips nightclubs while she keeps after him to settle down and be a husband and father.) Musical cinema has had few bigger stars than Bing Crosby, yet no matter how beautiful and astute the vocalism and likable the presence, relaxation that goes this far can stray into boredom for everyone. Another debit comes with the crypto-gay presence of Billy De Wolfe, who served as comic relief in a great deal of forties fluff without being amusing. Between his specialty piece here, playing an old lady getting plastered, and Crosby versus Caulfield, and Astaire's drunken, crippling fall during "Heat Wave," *Blue Skies* plays out as an exercise in alienation, Brecht by Berlin. One great Astaire dance, plus Berlin sung (too languidly) by Crosby and bubbly support from Olga San Juan—and otherwise this is ghastly.

Yolanda and the Thief, for all its wrongness, was at least trying for the new or novel or different—the better-luck-next-time kind of misadventure that teaches lessons. (*Sweet Charity*, after all, begat *Cabaret*.) *Blue Skies*, in its unctuous overstuffed take-it-and-like-it way, has no such compensation. Worse, its great financial success meant that it served its genre only in a detrimental way. If *Yolanda* might hold the possibility of expanding musicals, a *Blue Skies* will only turn them into temples of mediocrity, bigger in scope while smaller in ambition. *Yolanda* looks forward to the better parts of, say, *An American in Paris* and *The Band Wagon*, while *Blue Skies* portends *White Christmas* and *There's No Business like Show Business* and worse. Possibly even *Mamma Mia!* Given the affection that many hold for *White Christmas*, this might be judged worthy; given what a musical could do and might be, it is, sadly and definitely, not enough. Musicals need not settle for the bland or safely profitable, nor even the repetitive, and it is their eternal tragedy that, so often, they do. Take chances, get out there, wake up—don't just focus the camera on another anesthetized rendition of "White Christmas," which is, needless to say, something else that *Blue Skies* insists on doing.

Sometimes a failure traverses a route that overlaps both *Yolanda* and *Blue Skies*, adventurous yet earthbound. Here can be cited the case of the biggest, most jinxed musical film that almost no one gets to see. In 1959, *Porgy and Bess* became the most expensive musical yet made, a distinction it would hold (at $7 million) until the dawn of *My Fair Lady*. That cost is only a small part of what may be the most cataclysmic saga in musical film history, one that continues unresolved up to the present day. It begins, of course, with the groundbreaking opera created by George and Ira Gershwin and DuBose Heyward, directed on Broadway by Rouben Mamoulian. While its original 1935 run had not been a success, recordings and subsequent productions and an international tour had, by the mid-1950s, made it an American treasure. Producer Samuel Goldwyn was, it is fair to say, obsessed with the idea of making a film of it.[6] Never mind that it was an opera, with some racial aspects that, by 1958, seemed questionable; Goldwyn replaced the recitatives with dialogue, ignored the warnings, sent the NAACP a donation, and hired Mamoulian to direct it. Just before shooting began, a fire of mysterious origin destroyed the entire production. It was quickly rebuilt, after which Goldwyn fired Mamoulian and replaced him with Otto Preminger, who brought all the drama of *Carmen Jones* to the set and not to the film. When Preminger focused his abuse on Dorothy Dandridge—there was quite a history between them—a cast already on edge became nearly mutinous. Finally it came time for the inevitable roadshow opening, a mixed critical response, and returns that made it one of the biggest money-losing films up to that time. Goldwyn retired shortly afterward, *Porgy* had one play on network television, and then it disappeared. In dire need of restoration and with its rights in a longtime, incomprehensible tangle involving the Goldwyn Company and the Gershwin Estates, it has continued, well into the twenty-first century, to be a film in limbo.

Give Goldwyn credit: he was a determined man, and come hell or high water or possible arson, he was not swayed from *Porgy and Bess*. For him, with its incredible music, it was "class," and he thought the objections would be quieted if Catfish Row was made spotlessly clean. That cuts to the most damning aspect of *Porgy and Bess*: Preminger shot it on a huge soundstage set with static tableau blocking and long takes that resemble an early talkie. Worse and nearly unbelievably, he chose to shoot the entire film without a single close-up. Characters who already seem stylized and remote became distanced even further, with the transitions from spoken dialogue to dubbed song made even more

---

[6] He was hardly alone: all the major studios hoped to make a *Porgy* film. Harry Cohn at Columbia had the most arresting idea: Al Jolson as Porgy, Rita Hayworth as Bess, and Fred Astaire as Sportin' Life. In blackface.

"It's Gershwin! It's Glorious!": So said the ads for *Porgy and Bess*—even as this rather stiff and stagy shot of Dorothy Dandridge and Sidney Poitier reveals the other part of the equation. The tin roof and peeling plaster look way calculated, everything's spotless, and the camera isn't willing to get too close.

cumbersome.[7] Except for Sammy Davis Jr.'s nifty Sportin' Life and the sturdy Pearl Bailey, it is airless and stiff, with Dandridge and Sidney Poitier too modern and sophisticated to be convincing in these quaintly elemental situations. Really, could anyone even then totally buy the idea of Poitier moving his lips as Robert McFerrin sings "Bess, You Is My Woman Now"? The music is glorious, as are André Previn's arrangements, and otherwise this is perhaps the ultimate incarnation of the old saw about good intentions paving the road to hell. The most honorable disaster in the history of musical film must remain a disaster nonetheless, one made all the more fascinating by its current taboo status.

[7] *Porgy* does have fierce adherents, and not just among Preminger cultists who like *Skidoo*. It can be stated at very least that what now seems dim and dull on (ssshhh) pirated DVD was doubtless impressive in enormous Todd-AO and fabulous sound. Still, *Carmen Jones*, with its low budget, embraces a dynamism that *Porgy*'s pricey auspices do not. Go back to the original reviews and, after the praise for the music, count the variants on the word "lethargic."

The complete, worthy failure of *Porgy and Bess* is one of truly great things going wrong, and few musicals equal its awful grandeur. The all-but-unreleased film of *The Fantasticks*, for example, was not so much woeful as simply dim and pointless. Whatever it was that Richard Attenborough made of *A Chorus Line* was far more offensive—useless in every way save as a pedagogical exercise in poor adaptation. Its absurdly tacked-on Michael Douglas "back-story" and wan musical interludes could not give its much-liked (if overrated) source any kind of a chance and seems to prove once again that some shows—like *Porgy and Bess* and possibly *Nine*, among others—should be left undisturbed and likely unfilmed. On another hand are the shows whose film versions split the difference between more and less terrible. While *Pal Joey* might have served better had the material not been so insufferably sanitized, *Can-Can* was irredeemable, no matter how well Frank Sinatra sang Cole Porter.[8] As for that London/Broadway/global behemoth *The Phantom of the Opera*, which many people admit to disliking in any form, Joel Schumacher's film might have been made a shade less overstuffed and turgid, and Gerard Butler could have had less detectable trouble with his high notes. This *Phantom* came to life exactly once: a dubbed Minnie Driver showing, with the parodistic "Prima Donna," the zest of a truly good musical. Not dissimilarly, *The Producers* had one authentic moment to offset its anemic and dutiful remainder: Nathan Lane in his big eleven o'clock song "Betrayed," showing how well theatrical flair can read on film and how much better it all might have been.

There is also a hideously exhilarating converse to the dull musical with one redeeming sequence: a film with moments so feral and misconceived as to be transcendent. Even for a 1929 pick-your-genre piece, *The Great Gabbo* is such a work, a series of gauche and overscaled revue sequences grafted onto a plot about a mad ventriloquist (Erich von Stroheim). In all of film, very little can match the madness of its "Web of Love" number, a spider-and-fly pas de deux with insect chorines. Work at this level is too rare and stirring to be called camp, just as Joan Crawford's *Torch Song* zooms far beyond the simple notion of stardom gone berserk. The mere idea of a middle-aged Crawford as an all-devouring Broadway diva is mesmerizing in major baroque ways, and with a

---

[8] As dreary a botch as *Can-Can* is—Sinatra and Shirley MacLaine turning Montmartre into Vegas—its script did have the right idea in reconfiguring the ragged Broadway original. There remain the "what ifs" of better casting and direction; some songs, unfortunately, stay the same, and it's not Cole Porter being spoken about here.

dubbed voice and earnestly granitic dance moves, amid leftover *Band Wagon* trappings, she is at her most Easter Island-implacable. For good reason, *Torch Song*'s coup de grace, "Two-Faced Woman," has passed into legend. Normal-strength Crawford is tensely monolithic, so imagine her as a serenely confident brown temptress, tossed about by male admirers while chorines wince and point. This is foolishness as only musical cinema can deliver, and then only rarely. In that same year, *The French Line* ostensibly seemed a more conventional work; in reality, it was no less than an epic tribute to Howard Hughes's undying obsession with large breasts. "J.R. in 3-D," leered the ads, and so it was—a deliberate trashing of *Gentlemen Prefer Blondes* and of one of its stars, featuring the likably unpretentious Jane Russell ambling through musical numbers shot and lit to maximize top-heaviness. Devotees of breast fetishism—and musical sleaze—would not see its equal for more than four decades, and surely *Showgirls* was worth the wait. With its backstage plot, lurid details, and horrific dance sequences, *Showgirls* was less a conventional genre piece than crossover of an especially demented variety. Seldom, in musical cinema, does the distance between reach and grasp approach this sublime an infinity.

Granted, most unsuccessful or unproductive musicals do not provide fun in the inverted fashion of a *Golden Dawn* or *Torch Song* or *Glitter*. Many are of an irksome myopia—the cluelessness of a *Paint Your Wagon* or the dutiful wrongness of a *South Pacific*—or simply useless, as with works as diverse as *Panama Hattie* and *A Chorus Line*. Too often, they can be simply routine, too dull to be even unintended amusement—surely a *Blue Skies* can act as proof of why some people do not like any musicals. This is why, oddly enough, the special occasions when they veer wildly off-track must be noted and absorbed, these moments of fertility rites, lustful near-geriatric mulattos, prancing insects, and croaking stars. A *Lost Horizon*, so completely erroneous as to be a monument of misunderstood cause and effect, or a *Porgy and Bess*, the epitome of good intentions gone vastly wrong. Amid the pain or boredom or wonderment or hilarity, they offer volumes of information and caution and warning. This is not how it should be done, they relate, and by doing so they provide an education that will always need to be heeded. After all, it is hardly through its greatest moments alone that history will reveal where it may yet go. Or recall all the cuckoo places it's already visited.

Chapter 9

Turn on the Heat

....

*L*ove Me Tonight begins in a mood of odd expectancy. The onscreen credits are plain and generic, the underscoring is made of hesitant little
snatches, and none of it necessarily announces that a musical is about
to unfold. As a bell tolls on the soundtrack, a series of shots show Paris in early
morning, each edit hitting with a striking chime. The camera focuses on a sleepy
district where a laborer strikes the pavement with his pickaxe. Cut to a bum
snoring in an alley, then a charwoman sweeping a front step. Thump, snore,
swish, and as more people rise to begin their day the sounds grow in number
and rhythm, the editing faster and more percussive. A baby cries, cobblers start
to hammer, a car horn beeps, and the city comes to life as the aural and visual
blend in a riot of reckless decorum. More conventional music comes in when a
young woman cues up her phonograph, and as a Parisian morning finds its stride
the sounds grow more frantic. Finally the camera peeps through a window to
discover a straw hat hanging on a wall, above a set of plaster cracks that seem to
describe a certain jaunty head and body. Pan to a head popping up through a
turtleneck—and Maurice Chevalier begins his own day by complaining, "Lovely
morning song of Paris, you are much too loud for me!" He bangs the window
shut, then capitulates by saluting the city with "The Song of Paree." Before
many minutes, he will sing "Isn't It Romantic?," which will travel through Paris
and into the countryside to finally reach a lovelorn princess on the balcony of a

remote castle. Chevalier has wakened to a Parisian song, and his own music will link him with Jeanette MacDonald even before they meet. Thus might the remainder of *Love Me Tonight* be termed a magnificent follow-through.

When it opened in early autumn of 1932, *Love Me Tonight* was not a financial success. The ecstatic reviews, the acclaim for the stars and director Rouben Mamoulian and songwriters Rodgers and Hart, could not float a profit for an essentially intimate musical costing over a million dollars. This was a time when musicals were persona non grata, and when they came back into currency they would do so as brassy backstage stories or even operettas, not elegant fairy tales. *Love Me Tonight* would have influence—there were copies of its "Romantic" song being carried along—but few emulators. It remained unique and singular, in a sense too good, surely too rarefied, for its own time. Such failure comes in opposition to a *Golden Dawn* or *Wiz* that betrays its public, a *Blue Skies* too rich and lazy to serve its audience, or a *Paint Your Wagon* that can't even find the right way to pander. In short, *Love Me Tonight* is a great film, relevant and meaningful in a way few musicals are.[1] Work on this level, and on that of its finest fellows, is simply not reproducible. Counterfeiters will try, with their *At Long Last Love* or forged *42nd Street* or *Meet Me in St. Louis*, and will not succeed. Instead of making copies, they should work to comprehend and appreciate all the things that make a great musical possible. Rare as they are, the masterpieces offer signposts as clear as those given by the worst of the turkeys.

Next to no one is inclined to ascribe masterpiece status to many of the earliest musicals, the ones for which *Love Me Tonight* serves as an elated culmination. Technique has changed, times, tastes, everything. *Singin' in the Rain* happened, and so did *The Sound of Music* and MTV. In the twenty-first century, something on the order of *Sunny Side Up* has been relegated to the same status that, say, the *Twilight* Saga will have in around 2089—a marker of its era, an indicator of what consumers wanted at a specific time, a finite phenomenon to vanish when its instant passes. That connects with a big part of the myth that the first musicals carry, about being briefly sensational in something of a vacuum, with no further repercussions after their brief day was done. This is the kind of thinking that wants everything to start with Fred Astaire—and it's nonsense, as propagated by snobs and those too lazy for homework or context. *The Broadway Melody* is central to all

---

[1] As previously stated, some carp over *Love Me Tonight*'s lack of dance. True, and big deal: if the performers don't dance, Mamoulian sees to it that the photography and editing and soundtrack all do. Often.

this, and it is so faded now, so raw and halting, for the precise reason that it *was* so good, and so inspiring and innovative. By laying out everything that would be expanded and refined later, it made itself obsolete. The furor it caused was far more than that of simple novelty, more than the mere newness of sitting in a movie house and hearing sounds. The response viewers had to this film—it can be read about in the reviews and contemporary reports—was the peculiar kind of rapture occurring when people discover something completely new. Not like the stage, and not like silent film. It even offered, in its climactic scene, a kind of catharsis: Hank, the feisty hoofer, coming apart at her makeup table after giving up the man she loves. If this was basic stuff, Bessie Love played it for keeps: emotion so genuine, poignant, and identifiable that people in theaters wept along with her. When the film was done they bought the sheet music and records and told everyone they knew about this wonderful new kind of movie. Then they returned to see it again. This was attention and esteem different from, greater than, that of the early Jolson films, as important as they were and are. Instead of being about one huge figure and his stardom, *The Broadway Melody* connected with the masses in multiple ways, essentially the same ties that the best of the breed have made ever since.

Two other 1929 films covered the same populist swath as *The Broadway Melody*. (The champagne of *The Love Parade* is a different matter.) One of the most ingenious aspects of *Sunny Side Up* was the way it bridged silence to sound with a kind of triangulation: silent-movie sweethearts (Janet Gaynor and Charles Farrell) put into a universal Cinderella plot, with songs to enhance and expand the drama. This was not filmmaking of *Potemkin/Kane* transcendence: it was as shrewdly commercial a piece of goods as any hit from *The Great Train Robbery* past *Avatar*. Seen and heard now by the unsympathetic, it can seem an exercise in naïveté, too long and technically shaky; and Farrell's voice inspires marvel that someone so tall and handsome could sound so dank and tinny. What sells it is the score and, particularly, Gaynor. Even with her own somewhat daffy-sounding voice, she was a major pro, with that same can't-forge-it air of straightforward wonderment that can also be observed in Garland's Dorothy, and Andrews's Maria, and Ethel Waters's Petunia in *Cabin in the Sky*.[2] It makes

---

[2] Note that the examples given are all women. Few men in musicals exude such agendaless purity—Chevalier was way knowing, Astaire often posed as someone he wasn't, Kelly could never tame that brash edge, Danny Kaye was manic. Perhaps the joyful, underrated Donald O'Connor came closest. Being swell in mostly run-of-the-mill stuff does not make for an inspiring career arc, but a "Make 'Em Laugh" can compensate for a whole lot of sludge.

her too innocent, in fact, to participate in *Sunny Side Up*'s most outrageous sequence, the aptly named "Turn On the Heat." Here, a year before the movie dawn of Busby Berkeley, is a flagrant display of the luscious crassness a production number can deliver: female flesh, phallic images, and even real fire that makes one fear for those underpaid Fox chorines. It's spectacle for its own dumb sake, as extraneous from the plot of *Sunny Side Up* as it is from good taste or simple propriety, a prototype for the loony extremes of escapism that can and should punctuate musical cinema at least once in a blue moon. Were it done too often, this kind of vulgarity would quickly become charmless—but it could be argued that some staid and respectable works do occasionally benefit by turning on a little more heat, or by at least trying to loosen up. Imagine if anything else in the *My Fair Lady* movie had been as nervy as Liza's Ascot hat.

Gold Diggers of Broadway was also seminal, and audacious in its fashion. A smash of *Broadway Melody* caliber, it was so precisely right for its moment that it vanished when that moment was gone. Not just obsolete: physically gone, in the way that most studios failed to take care of and preserve their films. For the longest time it was completely lost except for its on-disc soundtrack, then one reel turned up and then another. While a film's rightness may not be easy to judge on the basis of mere shards, the 20 percent or so of *Gold Diggers* that exists explains a great deal. There was no particular depth or meaning, no all-encompassing star or for-real human insight; this was an audience picture, vivacious entertainment packaged in the brightest two-color Technicolor. There was the imperishably silly "Tip Toe Thru the Tulips with Me," a raucous comedian named Winnie Lightner, and a joyful mid-1929 message of money being fun even if it doesn't buy happiness. Warner Bros. frequently misjudged its audiences and miscalculated its musicals—see *Say It with Songs*—and this one was the exception. The love and grosses were such that when it was remade four years later during the second musical vanguard, the new version was titled to deliberately harken back to the original hit: *Gold Diggers of 1933*, old is new. Even when it was no longer around, *Gold Diggers of Broadway* stood with *The Broadway Melody* in the happy recollections of many people who had gone to see it again and again. The pleasant part of its afterlife is that, as of now, just enough of it survives to make that success and love comprehensible.

Most of *Gold Diggers of Broadway* is likely irretrievable, as are all or most of major early works like *The Rogue Song* and *My Man* and *No, No, Nanette*. Later films that are not seen are less lost than unavailable—*Porgy and Bess*, for example, and for a long time *Annie Get Your Gun*—and, as with anything out of reach, disappointment can come when they finally emerge. This is what makes *Where's Charley?* such a surprise. It also helps that, in 1952, *Charley* was less than a major event. It was simply a piece of mid-level Warner Bros. product, an adaptation of a hit Broadway musical with a star, Ray Bolger, of less than universal appeal. One hit song in "Once in Love with Amy," no other big names or *Singin' in the Rain* spectacle, decent reviews, finally some TV runs. Then near-oblivion, due in this case to its withdrawal by the estate of another composer (and lyricist), Frank Loesser. An easy film, in short, to neglect and forget—and one which, without any single extraordinary component, manages to do everything right. As with *Annie Get Your Gun*, *Charley* was part of the new, less-violent method of adapting stage works—elisions and cuts without wholesale denaturing, theatrical formality maintained while opening the windows to let in just enough cinema, and in this case preserving a pair of first-rate Broadway performances: Bolger and Allyn McLerie. Shot in England by an old-hand Hollywood director (*Sunny Side Up's* David Butler), *Charley* is so reasonable and proportionate that it can even manage a dream ballet ("Pernambuco") that is content to be witty rather than astounding. Very shortly, musicals would forsake this kind of concision for elephantine budgets and crowded canvases and noisy ballyhoo: the roadshow age had precious little room for pieces of wit and non-knockout grace. *Where's Charley?* had good lessons to teach, but few would heed them.[3] As talented as Ray Bolger was—and, in truth, quite too old for his role here—he would never again have such a film opportunity; *Charley*, available or not, offers definitive proof that he should never be thought of simply as the Scarecrow.

Gigi was by no means as diffident as *Where's Charley?*, yet it too was a gorgeous dead end in the realm of '50s musicals, coming in just before the slam-it-home roadshow mentality took over. Then and now, some find its ties to *My Fair Lady* too invidious, its Paris-via-Culver City air too phony, its careful élan fussy and calculated. None of these complaints are fully invalid, and none give *Gigi* the credit and esteem it deserves. Without being quite the finest achievement of the Arthur Freed/MGM musical, it manages to convey a grace that can brusquely be termed captivating. Here are met all the lessons learned by Freed

---

[3] At least Warner Bros. was able, on occasion, to heed the lessons. Director Butler went from *Where's Charley?* to *Calamity Jane*. Later, from co-directors George Abbott and Stanley Donen, there would be *The Pajama Game* and *Damn Yankees*. Works of craft and personality, and none of them did very well. So: on with the blockbusters.

and Vincente Minnelli and their collaborators, and by all those working on Hollywood musicals since the time of *The Love Parade* and *Sunny Side Up*. Minnelli's *Yolanda* bent for baroque décor here finds an ideal Belle Époque environment without being stultifying, and the diffuse sideshows of *The Pirate* are harnessed and made part of the overall tapestry. With Freed, too, *Gigi* was as much a culmination as *Singin' in the Rain*, here with the drive toward integrated storytelling that began with *The Wizard of Oz* and continued through *Cabin in the Sky* and *Meet Me in St. Louis*. Dance, again, is not a prime component, even as movement most assuredly is; Freed and Minnelli had already given dance an apotheosis in *Singin' in the Rain* and *The Band Wagon*, and Leslie Caron needed no dream ballet to chart Gigi's path from schoolgirl to woman.

Very little in *Gigi* seems extraneous. One possible exception is that grace note at the end of Chevalier's "I'm Glad I'm Not Young Anymore," in which the entire film history embodied by this one performer is paid irresistible homage. Beyond that, *Gigi* is a rather different kind of compendium, a retrospective of wisdom learned, technique refined and heightened and buffed. In place of the bogus Made-in-Hollywood U.S.A. Paree that compromised parts of *An American in Paris*, there is much supple location shooting, and the atmosphere seems more authentic than the rather synthetic, if witty, Broadway world of *The Band Wagon*.[4] The traditional crassness of so many musicals, with their choruses and specialties, has been miraculously curbed, the achievement all the more impressive since the subject matter of *Gigi*—how to train an innocent kid to be a mistress—is so questionable and racy. The only moments that seem even remotely vulgar are deliberate, as when Eva Gabor comes onscreen wearing a gown of such blatant colors that she can instantly and accurately be tagged as a vain and insincere piece of work. For the most part, *Gigi* seems effortless, which is one reason that some don't like it—with its little Colette story and wry air, it's not a work of knock 'em dead bravura, no matter how beautiful Cecil Beaton's costumes are or how wittily

---

[4] It was a miracle the location work in *Gigi* turned out so well. With Paris still reeling from the intrusion of another fine musical, *Funny Face*, Minnelli and company were given an icy reception, and the Maxim's shoot was especially tense. Then a money-conscious MGM pulled the plug early, forcing the remainder to be done in California. Maybe the bosses had a point: the negative cost of *Gigi* stayed under $3.5 million, far less than *South Pacific* and *Porgy and Bess*, and the profits were immense. If only "I Remember It Well" could have avoided that soundstage look.

Minnelli paints his pictures. It doesn't have a big final ballet or a breakdown scene, nor is its appeal the straight-to-the-heart kind of *Meet Me in St. Louis*. Its cathartic moment is adult and a little bit jaded, a young roué taking an agitated stroll through Minnelli's nighttime Paris as the music surges and the unavoidable realization dawns that Gigi is not a little girl, nor a cocotte, but a woman to marry. With all its echoes of Lubitsch and René Clair and *My Fair Lady* and *Love Me Tonight*, even its reminiscence of "I've Grown Accustomed to Her Face," it somehow manages to seem fresh and reasonably new. This is the fusion a good or great musical achieves when the material is solid and the director is an on-form Minnelli and there's a possibility that it might add up to something deeper than a sweet song. If there is a culmination of the American musical, *Gigi* surely is not it, not with its winks and bedroom politics and "Thank Heaven for Little Girls." Yet it is such a graceful traversal of its prescribed course that the final effect can only be one of contained elation. Everything has been kept orderly, perhaps without a manic highpoint— and when effected this masterfully, poise and discretion are eminently, even staggeringly, rewarding.

Swing Time is not a perfectly-ordered check-and-balance entertainment as *Gigi* is, or for that matter *Top Hat*. It is the connoisseur's Fred and Ginger film, perfection diluted with a hint of unevenness. A few things in the plot don't quite come together, and George Stevens is a shade less comfortable directing the musical idiom than the über-smooth Mark Sandrich, who could evoke the fantasy Europe of *The Gay Divorcée* and *Top Hat* with such nonchalance. *Swing Time* deals with more reality than its predecessors—it's set in Depression Manhattan, and neither Ginger nor Fred is rich or privileged.[5] He's a hoofer with a gambling problem and she's a dance instructor, and the standard misunderstandings and conflicts of their films here seem to carry a little more depth. So do the songs, alternately wry and jaunty, sarcastic in "A Fine Romance," supremely romantic in "The Way You Look Tonight," and finally, in "Never Gonna Dance," close to tragic. One of the cornerstones of Astaire-Rogers was, of course, that they were the most mortal of gods, real people touched with a divine spark. He wasn't idol-handsome and she could be coarse around the edges, so they were accessible as well as

---

[5] They weren't ritzy, either, in *Swing Time*'s immediate predecessor, *Follow the Fleet*. There, as already noted, only the numbers matter, plus Lucille Ball's few wisecracks. Also, look fast for Betty Grable. Then skip the rest.

complementary, and not just in that old "his class/her sex" trade-off that's gotten cited way too much. Contrast their collusion with Astaire's brilliant dancing with Rita Hayworth and Cyd Charisse, whose goddess perfection could make it all a bit off-putting: they seemed too fabulously unreal for him or maybe for anyone. When Astaire and Rogers recap their romance in "Never Gonna Dance," there isn't simply the platinum-and-feathers luster of "Cheek to Cheek," wondrous as that is. Instead, they distill something deeper and more telling about how people relate and connect and tear apart. The beauty of *Swing Time* is that, for all its gorgeous music and choreography and Moderne sheen, it's about a great deal more than song and dance.

The year for magnificently uneven films with Jerome Kern music was obviously 1936, for *Swing Time* arrived just a few months after the second film version of *Show Boat*. It too is incontestably perfect in some major ways, a tad off at other points. How could it not be, really, with material this epic? "Ol' Man River" was already something of a hymn, and with "Fish gotta swim" and Paul Robeson and Helen Morgan, there was heavy resonance here, even legend. As with *Swing Time*, there is a director from outside the musical pool, and though James Whale was best known for his horror movies, he was also a master of theatrical drama, knew how to handle comedy, and could set off the music without kowtowing to it too eagerly. Except for the Expressionistic vignettes he gives to "Ol' Man River," he shoots and stages the songs with a naturalistic candor that makes them all seem, as much as they possibly can, essential to these people's lives. Things don't stop when Magnolia and Gaylord go into "You Are Love," nor even for Morgan's heartbreaking "Bill." It all keeps moving and connecting, and if it's an idealized past being depicted, there's also a sense of period such as few 1930s films deliver.

The letdowns of *Show Boat* should be cited as well, since they make the high points all the greater. While Irene Dunne is an excellent Magnolia, she was (at around 37) a shade mature in both look and voice, especially alongside the younger and more callow Allan Jones. There is also that problematic final stretch, with a dull production number that doesn't matter and a plot tying itself in coincidental pretzels to bring the lovers back together. *Show Boat* is one of those pieces that starts off better than it ends, in part because it won't do what the original novel does—fade out with Magnolia as valiant and solitary, not reunited with her man. That unhappy an ending, however honest, would have been too far a bridge for even a piece this brave and innovative.[6] It's a measure, then, of Whale's achievement, and that of Dunne and Robeson and Morgan and Jones and Charles Winninger and Helen Westley and Hattie McDaniel, that this ending can be forgiven even as some may still feel a shade shortchanged.

Because of the MGM remake, this *Show Boat* was out of circulation for many years and became, in the 1970s, a grand rediscovery. (The same thing that will happen with *Where's Charley?*) What of the great musical that has never been away, so perennial that for many years its annual television run was a major event? The most quoted of musicals, likely the most loved and internalized, the most seminal cultural influence this side of *Star Wars*, the icon of children and gay men everywhere—really, what is there left to say about *The Wizard of Oz*? Between the tense mythology of Judy Garland and the everlasting wonder that is "Over the Rainbow," the marvel of the MGM production mechanics, the sheer brash timelessness, the Horse of a Different Color and "Toto, too" and everything down to Margaret Hamilton's eternal cackle: can it possibly be approached with any kind of an objective mien? Doing so can be harder, even, than finding someone who hasn't seen it. Of course, there will be those who won't deal with it for one reason or another, so leave them out of it, or have the Flying Monkeys drop them into some chasm, and step back to consider just how it all happened. A great deal of the triumph is based in the sheer Dream Factory skill of it, encompassing the casting, the choice of Arlen and Harburg to write the songs, the clean and direct leadership of Victor Fleming, and such little glories as turning on the Technicolor when Dorothy opens the door to Munchkinland. The engineering is massive, yet it is the brilliance of *Oz* that, as with all the great musicals, the effort doesn't show. How completely fitting this is for a place where outlandish magic is routine, a kingdom erupts in operetta outbursts, a trio of ballerinas is ever at the ready, and people come and go so quickly.

Fleming's achievement is often underrated—really, the man deserves supreme credit if for no other reason than directing this back-to-back with *Gone With the Wind*—and it is his guidance of Garland that truly sums up why it all works and holds up. "Now, darling, this is serious," Fleming would tell her

---

[6] It's a virtue of the 1951 MGM version, so über-splashy in so many other ways, that the quandary of the wrap-up is solved rather neatly, and in a way that allows the audience to see more of the Julie character. And Ava Gardner.

when she'd ruin a take by cracking up at Bert Lahr's Cowardly Lion. And she would stop laughing and play it for real, with that common-sense emotionality that centered everything. Seldom would Garland ever again get so precise a showcase—*Meet Me in St. Louis* is an ensemble piece, and *A Star Is Born* is in some ways too big and too much. *Oz* allows her to be the center from beginning to end, and even when Bolger and Haley and Lahr get their chances to shine, it's all seen through Dorothy's eyes. Had that "Jitterbug" number been retained, *Oz* might have been as disfigured as that last reel of Whale's *Show Boat*, though the excision means that the last third has no songs.[7] There are those who see other flaws as well, and for some a disqualification will come with sentimentality and sheer familiarity. Let the naysayers rant—this film does not have its stature simply because of TV or tradition or repetition. For those of us who love it, *The Wizard of Oz* will remain something beyond conventional film, past being a childhood treasure or a piece of movie magic or the ideal amalgam of fantasy and show-biz. It's home. There's no place like it.

Like most musicals, *The Wizard of Oz* gains a good deal of its credence through a wealth of clever calculation. That is, after all, how a genre should function. Few works, however, do this at the astronomical level of *42nd Street* and *The Sound of Music*. Granted, there's a far, far gap separating those two. One is a product of, and a depiction of, Depression-era desperation, while the other is retrograde optimism from the 1960s, heedless of Vietnam or civil rights (not to mention the underlying causes of World War II). Considering them side by side may perhaps not seem the sanest of pursuits, at least until specifics are passed up in favor of overriding intent. For in all of musical cinema, there has seldom been a pair of works so dumbfoundingly astute, each in its own way gauging and calculating its bull's-eye. In craft and presentation, they each traced a precise trajectory from what the creators wanted to what the public bought. *42nd Street* was done in a kind of blind grope, at a time when the word *musical* was all but verboten, while *The Sound of Music* was colossally self-confident, coming on the heels of *My Fair Lady* and *Mary Poppins* and splitting the difference between them with absurd efficiency.

---

[7] This situation could have been modified but for the decision to cut the choral "Ding, Dong, the Witch Is Dead" as the quartet returns in triumph to the Emerald City. As with "The Jitterbug," only the sound portion remains, along with a tiny snippet visible in the coming-attractions trailer. With its music and transition, it would have worked better than the quick dissolve from the castle to the Wizard's throne room. For once, MGM's wizards cut too much.

42nd Street turned out as it did—tough, punchy, anxious, and desperate—because it was a product of Warner Bros., a studio so attuned to Depression angst that the low production values of most of its films seemed less a result of cost cutting (which it was) than as an accurate reflection of the struggles of average Americans in 1932. While *42nd Street* was a putting-on-the-show story of the sort that had worn people out by the end of 1929, it had a melancholy edge that was startling. The show's genius director (Warner Baxter) is ill and possibly gay, its star (Bebe Daniels) is an alcoholic sellout, and the chorines get their jobs by sleeping around. Not even its songs were immune from a baleful cast, with references to drugs and sex and, in the title number, a phalanx of tap-dancing hookers and a fatal stabbing. Little of this stuff would have been possible after the coming of the newly enforced Motion Picture Production Code, but *42nd Street* was nothing if not immediate. It was also optimistic, with its hopeful newcomer so memorably embodied by the appealing and not terribly gifted Ruby Keeler.

With its star breaking her ankle and the unknown going on to instant acclaim, *42nd Street* has become such a Holy Writ of clichés that it seems a testament to all the lies that musicals wish to tell—yet in the spring of 1933 it sounded notes of hope that audiences needed. Ruby succeeded, and so might they, especially if Busby Berkeley is around to give the production numbers a darting camera and spicy vignettes and overhead formations. Yet even with its final show-within-a-show triumph, *42nd Street* does not let itself end with the audience applauding Ruby; instead, it has the Warner guts to show us the bleary and depleted director standing outside the theater, listening to the audience filing out as they praise the show and belittle his contribution. That's the fade-out![8] So *42nd Street*, tough and captivating and built for speed, even managed some honesty along the way. The quality of the work itself would have been enough to make it successful, possibly even to single-handedly bring back musicals, which it damned near did. Then Warners, which did not always market its product in an imaginative fashion, enhanced it with possibly the most effective movie stunt of all time: it equated the musical world of *42nd*

---

[8] The only musical (until *Cabaret*) to end on a comparably dark note is Warner's quick successor to *42nd Street*, *Gold Diggers of 1933*. It finishes with Berkeley's great "Remember My Forgotten Man," a bleak tribute to the unemployed veterans who participated in the Bonus Army March in early 1933. The original intention was to wrap it up with the randy "Pettin' in the Park"—but nothing could follow the power of "Forgotten Man" save The End.

Street with the fresh America promised by Franklin Roosevelt. As noted earlier, "A New Deal in ENTERTAINMENT" was the slogan, and there was a promotional junket, co-sponsored with General Electric, involving a train (The *42nd Street* Special) full of movie people, including a young Bette Davis, going from city to city hawking the new movie and the newest appliances. Then, since the Warners were the only Democrat moguls, the train rolled in to Washington, DC, on the day of Roosevelt's inauguration—ingeniously giving their film the same winner-aura as the new chief executive. The amazement was that the film then had the substance to back up all the hype. Eighty years and more later, it still does—hokum and cynicism have rarely been so well calculated and combined, nor huge success so well deserved.

"Calculated" is also a word frequently invoked in discussing *The Sound of Music*, most commonly with negative connotations. This has always been a work to divide audiences—some people who often don't like musicals adore it, while many who do like them put their hands over their ears, just like with *Les Miz*. It was far too big and influential for attention not to be paid, and unlike that later smash *Grease*, it was "respectable," not just a merry cartoon. It had Oscar roadshow prestige and Rodgers and Hammerstein pedigree and, heavens, all those people who went to see it again and again and again. If many professed to be astounded (and some repelled) at its level of success, this may be due to their inability to see the reasons laid out in plain sight: *The Sound of Music* was ridiculously well crafted, both in its technical sense (including the enthralling Salzburg locations) and in laying out all its targets, one by one, then picking them off with ineffable dexterity. The can't-get-them-out-of-our-heads rightness of the songs, the irresistibly absurd Cinderella-thwarts-the-Nazis turns of plot, the constant specter of divine intervention, the kids and the puppets and the curtains made into clothes à la *Gone With the Wind*. It was as if they were all parts of an especially ornate watch—and the watchmaker was not the director, Robert Wise (he was surely the maker's apprentice)—but Julie Andrews.

Andrews's dominance was as absolute as it was dumbfounding—a young woman with a beautiful voice who did not tear passions to diva shreds nor hog the camera in any intrusive way, pushing the whole cloying pageant along with a scrubbed efficiency just whimsical enough to be endearing instead of revolting. This was not the slay-'em-all bravura of Garland in *A Star Is Born* or Streisand in *Funny Girl*, but something perhaps even more dexterously sneaky: open, fresh-faced, and so devastatingly in charge that prisoners were not an option. She had been the controlling force in *Mary Poppins* as well, in more tart

Say, or sing, what you will: An informal portrait of *The Sound of Music*'s Von Trapp family, in the persons of Kym Karath, Debbie Turner, Angela Cartwright, Duane Chase, Heather Menzies, Nicholas Hammond, Charmian Carr, and proud sort-of parents Julie Andrews and Christopher Plummer. Yes, it's as relentless as it is cheery—and, for many, resistance will be futile.

fashion, but the stakes here were higher, her appeal a check to keep the excesses from spilling over. None of it would have worked so well a decade earlier or even a few years later, but *The Sound of Music* was a product of the most perfect timing imaginable. Its aura then continued to hold so fast that *Will and Grace* could build an entire episode around a singalong screening where everyone comes in costume. Those really happen, as do Austrian tours based solely on seeing the locations and as did the live TV production of 2013, ostensibly of the show but in reality an homage to the film. This is musical success so unparalleled and irreproducible that it made the later imitators (*Song of Norway* especially) seem notably crummy. It shouldn't happen again, and there are arguments to be made that it shouldn't have happened that one time. Musicals, some feel, should be more than this. *Can* be more, and have been. But give credit to them for firmly conceiving the goals and then accomplishing every single one of them. That too is a kind of perfection.

Cabaret is a Nazi-musical horse of an alarmingly different color. If *The Sound of Music* was a sociological phenomenon, *Cabaret* was the specialists' dream musical, so virtuosic that nothing good could follow in its wake for the longest time. Seldom since *Love Me Tonight* had a director been in such spiky command of everything—the actors, the micro-editing, the look and feel and cynical sheen. On *Sweet Charity*, Bob Fosse had been compromised by the need to pick through the remains of the old studio system—Universal, to be specific, with its glaring made-for-TV patina and dully processed air. Here, in his second film, an independent production gave him free rein to run riot and transform an innovative Broadway show into an even more daring and shocking vaudeville. It was all as deliberate in its crafting as *The Sound of Music* and in unimaginably different ways, with Liza Minnelli and Joel Grey as Fosse's prodigious accomplices and the Kander-Ebb score used entirely as in-performance commentary. Something this sensational could only portend an exciting new era, but no. Few musicals of any intent or import seemed to follow Fosse's lead: Brian De Palma's *Phantom of the Paradise*, the cult smash *The Rocky Horror Picture Show*, Milos Forman's *Hair,* and such fascinatingly off-putting things as *New York, New York* and *Bugsy Malone. Saturday Night Fever* and *Grease* owed far more to John Travolta than they did to Fosse, or indeed their own directors, and otherwise there was neither the incentive nor the interest. With VH1 in the wings, the aesthetics were about to change as well. *Cabaret* could, or perhaps should, have been a gateway; instead, it was a coda.

If Bob Fosse had made another post-*Cabaret* musical besides that lacerating crossover piece *All That Jazz*, it likely would have been *Chicago*. Life and fate and everything else passed that job from Fosse to Rob Marshall and, as has been faithfully noted, the result did not win over everyone. It is fair in any case to wonder if any big musical would, by 2002, have drawn any kind of consensus. (Nor, really, have any since.) Many viewers were in heaven while some grumbled over the cuts and the softened ironies and hyper-cut dance. Like it or not, Marshall had conflated twenty-first-century cinema with the musical-film heritage, his references and sources ranging from Jolson to *42nd Street* to Marilyn Monroe and on past *Cabaret* and MTV. Even the presence of the stunning Catherine Zeta-Jones seemed to bridge the generations, classic Hollywood va-voom with a modern edge, plus dance skills and a fine belt. If those who loved it onstage missed some of Fosse's darker currents, Marshall's sense of control and momentum were impressive and, at points, brilliant: in "We Both Reached for the Gun," it was as if he had compressed the entirety of musical theater *and* film into one succinct package. It lacked the self-indulgence of *Moulin Rouge!* and, with the superb Kander-Ebb score, had a far better focused and performed musical program. Like Zeta-Jones, *Chicago* was old-as-new, a sly *Gigi* for the post-Madonna crowd, completely calculated, invigorating, and, withal, more satisfying than any of its successors (not all that hard) and even many of its predecessors (remarkable).

One antecedent that *Chicago* could not exceed—nor did it try—has crowned the musical Olympus for so many decades that it's instructive to recall its initial reception. Most critics liked *Singin' in the Rain*, and it earned a healthy gross at a time when many musicals were starting to slide or crash. "Like" and "healthy" are guarded and mild words; nowhere, in 1952, was there much of what is now called buzz, let alone the Oscars or stature of its predecessor, *An American in Paris*.[9] Nor was it remotely as big a hit as *The Great Caruso*—believe it or not, the biggest profit-earning musical in MGM history. For a time the more tangible effect of *Singin' in the Rain* seemed to reside with the odd career trajectories of its participants: producer/songwriter Arthur Freed had but one musical success remaining (*Gigi*), which was one more than Gene Kelly, for all his brilliance, would either star in or direct; co-director Stanley Donen would have one smash, *Seven Brides for Seven Brothers*, and the successes d'estime *There's Always Fair Weather, Funny Face* and *The Pajama Game*, then leave the genre; writers Betty Comden and Adolph Green interspersed Broadway glory with only a bit more Hollywood work; Donald O'Connor returned to routine; Jean Hagen went to television and then oblivion; Debbie Reynolds and Rita Moreno worked hard and kept going and survived. Otherwise, with no Oscars or innovations, it was not in the annals.

Why, then, or how was the greatness of *Singin' in the Rain* discovered? Some buffs knew it very early on, and the French discovered it around the time they were starting to deify Jerry Lewis. Then it started being written about, first by the august likes of *Cahiers du Cinema* and then in a pop history called *All Talking! All Singing! All Dancing!*, which flatly declared it the greatest musical ever made. It was clearly up there by the time of *That's Entertainment!*, and a theatrical reissue in 1975 made it official: it was neither dated nor sappy, it was

---

[9] Two nominations for *Singin' in the Rain*, no wins, versus eight nominations for *American in Paris*, with six wins plus a special award to Gene Kelly. *Rain*, however, was one of the rare musicals to garner an acting nomination—and, with due respect to Gloria Grahame, does anyone truly believe that Jean Hagen shouldn't have won?

all highs and no lows, and—hallelujah—the script was on the same heavenly level as the music. It wasn't just about that title number, nor, as with *An American in Paris*, was it completely dominated by its climactic ballet. It was hysterically funny and romantic and just a bit spiteful and, most marvelous of all, it managed to sum up its entire genre—the entirety of film, even—by going back to the very beginning of the sound era. The icing was that it was awash with authenticity. Arthur Freed had been there at the birth of musicals, and so had costume designer Walter Plunkett and sound engineer Douglas Shearer and some of the others. Even the odd-featured geezer in the "talk-ing pic-ture" demonstration, an actor named Julius Tannen, had appeared in an early Vitaphone short, and the vocal coach in "Moses Supposes," Bobby Watson, had starred in one of the first musical features, *Syncopation*.

All musicals, knowingly or not, draw from their predecessors and past; the smarter ones acknowledge this and, like *Chicago*, find ways to refer to and celebrate it. The wonder of *Singin' in the Rain* is that it places itself, consciously and firmly, in the precise center of the musical film experience and then, from 1926 on, traverses the entirety of that history. Where most musicals tend to forget the very first of the species, there is here an active awareness of *The Broadway Melody* and Jolson and *The Hollywood Revue* and the rest, all of it treated with a respect as knowing as it is, at times, malicious. There are echoes, further, of Astaire and Rogers and Berkeley and many others, all the way to *An American in Paris*, quoted during "Good Morning." Naturally it is the subject matter that permits the wealth of reference, yet this is all more than simply an air-quote homage to cute old movies—that would come later, with Ken Russell's *The Boy Friend*. It is, rather, a conscious celebration of how much work goes into making a musical, and artistry too with any luck, and how much a good musical can give its audience. The condescension comes only with a too-simplistic depiction of silent-film production, and by leaning back on that tattered *Jazz Singer* folklore that compresses about three years of event-filled history into a few short months. (Another, slighter glitch, for those who care: *The Dancing Cavalier* should probably not end "within" its period flashback.) Most of the details, however, are spot-on, including an authentic look that contrasts vividly with how the 1920s are depicted in most films. This wasn't just another big MGM musical, as well made as those were. In a particularly inspired and generous way, they cared enough, here, to extend themselves.

More so than with Astaire, Gene Kelly isn't for everyone. Some will take issue with the sandpaper singing or the physicality or overreaching or, most particularly, with the ego that can't dim its glare. There were points in *On the Town* and *An American in Paris* where it was clear he was trying to tone it down, and the humility could seem fake. One of the wisest decisions of *Singin' in the Rain*, then, was to play up the hamminess. Even at his most sincere, or when he hears hard truths from the feisty Kathy, Don Lockwood is still going to be full of himself—not a jerk, nor even the hard-driver Kelly evidently was in real life, but a born performer always prone to dramatizing everything. That configuration isn't only right for this movie, it undercuts nearly all the objections some may have to Kelly the performer. Don *couldn't* be other than completely self-absorbed. Otherwise, he could not have achieved stardom while at the same time suffering the ignominy of constant contact with the lush and dim and venal Lina Lamont. For once, the brash showboating works with the character, and even Kelly's pretentious streak—his pas de deux with Cyd Charisse and the mile-long blowing veil—finds a benevolent niche. The aggression of his dancing, too, finds such an apt setting that it gets a nod in the "Broadway Ballet" when his hoofer rises to the heights by, sequentially, doing less and less.

The ballet itself—apart from Charisse's sublime recreation of Louise Brooks—is, to be sure, a digression within *Singin' in the Rain*, something of an autobiographical self-glorification of Kelly, not Lockwood. It would seem that Kelly and Donen did it mainly because after *An American in Paris* it was expected, and its introduction into the film is tenuous at best, since no 1929 musical would ever have had anything remotely like it. Thus, as fun as it is, as gasp-worthy as Charisse is, its presence could, in the cold light of criticism, be seen as intrusive. The same might be said of O'Connor's wondrous "Make 'Em Laugh" as well—and, in all honesty, who among the millions who adore this movie would want it to be without either of them? The remainder of the film is so direct, so completely self-actualized, that Kelly and O'Connor can be permitted, each in his own way, to go off-script to do something masterfully nonessential.

Like the finest literature and music—like the best politics, even, if such exists—*Singin' in the Rain* understands its roots, respects its ancestors, and by embracing its own history is enabled to soar. For those too willing to brand any musical—even the greatest one—as trivial, let it be considered that diversion taken to this level of craft and awareness may truly become art. For the yeasayers, little more need be said; as for the hostile forces, even they may be willing to make the admission, just as they should with the other masterworks spangling the musical pantheon. In the case of *Singin' in the Rain*, Kelly and

O'Connor and Reynolds and Charisse and Moreno and Millard Mitchell and Kathleen Freeman and the rest of the cast, and Donen and Comden and Green and Freed and Brown and all of its creators, have done far too well to warrant any notion to the contrary. Then, with a special nod to Jean Hagen, let the divine Lina Lamont speak for all those who made this film the astonishment that it is: they have brought a little joy into our humdrum lives, and their hard work ain't been in vain for nothin'. Bless us all.

Chapter 10

Painting the Clouds
Snow White, South Park, *and*
Other Ways to Animate a Musical

....

Fred Astaire was king of musicals in 1936, so it naturally followed that film would turn up any number of faux Astaires. George Murphy, Paul Draper, Lee Dixon, Johnny Downs, and presently the young Bob Hope all had deft moves and nonchalant grins, and never were they quite up to the original. The one that came closest occurred when Walt Disney produced a short called *Through the Mirror*. Mickey Mouse was at that point one of the nerviest characters in American film, and his tribute to the great Fred was magically spot-on. While movie-star parodies were a standard part of cartoons, Mickey goes beyond simple imitation, honoring Astaire in the precise fashion that Astaire honored "Bojangles" Robinson that same year. There was even some prescience here, since *Mirror* foreshadowed the trick numbers Astaire would do later on. If Mickey's effortless coordination with the music was completely in the Astaire manner, it was also what he himself had been doing since the very beginning of sound. This musicality was, indeed, animation's bottom line: where flesh and blood people required a reason to sing and dance, excuses were superfluous for animated characters, or objects, or anything that could be made to move. When Mickey does his Astaire bit in *Through the Mirror*, he doesn't need to scramble for a top hat and cane, nor is he required to be part of a putting-on-a-show plot. It just happens, as things do in cartoons. Disbelief need not be a factor, and song and dance can come out of anywhere for any reason and for no reason at all. Mickey, after all, *should* be a great tap-dancer in a kind of world where anything can be a vocalist and the most graceful ballerina might be a hippopotamus. It's so easy with ink and paint. At least—since these films are musical and many of the genre's rules apply—that's how it's supposed to look.

Animated cartoons—shorts, then features—are so intimately connected with music that it's easy to forget how many of them existed before sound. There was Felix the Cat and *Out of the Inkwell* and Disney's own Alice series, putting a live child into a cartoon world. They bent time and space and logic into the most outlandish contortions—yet, even more than with live-action, the absence of sound could be glaring. This is why *Steamboat Willie* made such a sensation in November of 1928. While it was not, as history likes to recount, the first cartoon made with sound or with music, a look at its immediate predecessor shows exactly why it was so special. That precursor is called *Dinner Time*, a Farmer Al Falfa cartoon directed by Paul Terry that opened about a month before *Willie*, with music and barnyard sound effects and a few words here and there. The country was sound-crazy in that autumn, and it's a measure of *Dinner Time* that it came and went virtually without comment. It had images and it had a soundtrack, and neither was particularly interesting on its own. Nor, when paired, did they fit together in any kind of eloquent way.

Steamboat Willie, on the other hand, was as much about its music as its drawings, from its opening frames of the boat chugging and tooting in time with the music, onward to its climactic, animal-abusing performance of "Turkey in the Straw." Disney and his cohorts had recorded and synched the score with the aid of a metronome, which gave *Willie* an inherently rhythmic character and sophistication far beyond the halting live-action likes of *The Singing Fool*. In a sense, *Willie* was the first truly musical film, and its resounding hit meant that future cartoons would be intimately connected to their music. Disney and company were so aware of the connection that in 1929 they launched a series of shorts based on music instead of continuing characters. They were called, very pointedly, Silly Symphonies, and once again there was an ideal leadoff: *The Skeleton Dance*, with its Carl Stalling score and unforgettable all-bone xylophone. Very quickly, the Silly Symphonies began to resemble brief operettas, often with new songs—most famously with the epochal smash of *The Three Little Pigs* and "Who's Afraid of the Big Bad Wolf?"

The impact of the Silly Symphonies meant that other studios would quickly find their own equivalents. At Warner Bros., there were the Merrie Melodies and Looney Tunes, which drew extensively from the studio's supply of hit tunes composed for live features. The Merrie Melodies in particular were conceived as vehicles for their songs, with titles such as *Shuffle Off to Buffalo* (from *42nd Street*) and *I Love to Singa* (from *The Singing Kid*, a later Jolson vehicle). Songs like "Singin' in the Bathtub" became so familiar from their use in Warner cartoons that they grew to function virtually as mnemonic devices, and many people first knew Harold Arlen's "Get Happy" as the theme song of the early Merrie Melodies. Paramount's Max Fleischer cartoons used both pre-existing songs and new pieces for two distinctive drawn-and-painted vocalists, Betty Boop and Popeye the Sailor. Fleischer also did the Bouncing Ball cartoons, with the likes of Ethel Merman or Rudy Vallee exhorting the audience to lift its collective voice in song. Music was as constant a presence in the titles of the series as in the films: Walter Lantz produced Car-Tunes at Universal, while at Columbia there were Color Rhapsodies. The song performances could be straightforward, or anarchic, or sometimes both, especially in Merrie Melodies, where a nest of cockroaches could sing and dance to "The Lady in Red," or a quartet of coins roll out and have their presidents harmonize with "We Are the Money!" Similarly, Fleischer's work could verge on the surreal—Cab Calloway's shape-shifting performance of "St. James Infirmary" in the Betty Boop short *Snow White*—or the unforgettable, as with Olive Oyl sleepwalking her way through a hazard-strewn construction site to "Did You Ever See a Dream Walking?" The parodies and in-jokes were everywhere: one early Silly Symphony, *Egyptian Melodies*, took a break from dancing hieroglyphs to allow a spider to get down on one Jolsonesque knee and exclaim, "Mummy!" Disney had the best animators, Fleischer came up with the cheekiest gags (frequently the dirtiest), and nearly all these films employed music with a level of creativity and imagination seldom present in live film. Indeed, around 1931, many features were using next to no background scoring—a few bars under the opening and closing credits and that was it. Only the short subjects would offer any kind of musical performances, and only the cartoons did so with wit and inventiveness.

By 1934, Disney was making shorts that were full-blown mini-operettas, and doing so as conscious preparation for the next frontier: a cartoon of feature length, its music fully integrated in a fashion that few live features would dare. Look, then, at *Snow White and the Seven Dwarfs* alongside even the better live musicals of 1937 or thereabouts—Mamoulian's ambitious *High, Wide, and Handsome* at Paramount or Fox's *Alexander's Ragtime Band* or RKO's Astaire-

Rogers *Shall We Dance* or MGM's erratic and at-points-rapturous *The Great Waltz*. If the songs are better in the latter group—not too surprising, considering they're the work of people like Kern and Hammerstein and Berlin and Gershwin and Johann Strauss—they seldom make a consistently graceful merger of drama with music. There are plot scenes and then there are songs, and in the case of *The Great Waltz* in particular, the music so outstrips the script that the two might as well be in separate movies run as a double feature. *Snow White*, in contrast, is completely intertwined with its score, and just about the only time the music recedes is when the Queen is onscreen, since she's too evil for song. Otherwise song and score blend seamlessly with choreographed movement and, occasionally, rhymed dialogue. Certainly "Whistle While You Work" ranks with "Isn't It Romantic" and "Never Gonna Dance" and "Lullaby of Broadway," to name three paragons, as an acme of 1930s musical cinema: storytelling combined with music combined with visuals, unified, vivid, captivating.

At the time of *Snow White*'s devastatingly profitable first release, the Dwarfs, especially Dopey, seemed to get the largest share of the credit. This wasn't surprising, given their enormous share of screen time, their differentiated personalities, and that benign grotesquerie that seems to provide a bridge from shorts to features. Hindsight, a completely different matter, makes it clear that an enormous part of this film's greatness and appeal comes from the unforced musicality that variously propels and underlines the slapstick, romance, tragedy, and triumph. It carries right through the moments when Adriana Caselotti's fluting soprano gets a tad perturbing, or when some of the animation seems stiff or cutesy, all the way through to that ecstatic choral "Some Day My Prince Will Come" at the end. Even without the fearsome marketing titan that is the Disney organization, *Snow White* was built to last—very much of the 1930s yet peculiarly timeless, an irreplaceable cornerstone of musical cinema.

Never does a film succeed the way *Snow White* did and not draw imitators. Most conspicuously, within two years of its release, there were two Technicolor musical fantasies, one live action and one animated, one peerless and the other an also-ran. Truly, *The Wizard of Oz* would have happened without *Snow White*, yet could it have carried the same charge? Would its song and fantasy have rested so blessedly on its "normal" heroine and her odd sidekicks? Would the welcome to Munchkinland have been quite so thorough in its melodic propulsion? And, for that matter, would its Witch have been quite so spectacularly

Wicked? Fortunately, *Oz* is dissimilar enough from *Snow White*, and serene enough in its own identity, to defuse any notion of plagiarism. The first animated feature to follow upon *Snow White*'s bow-festooned heels is quite another story. It's with a somewhat terrible earnestness that Max Fleischer's *Gulliver's Travels* wants to be *Snow White*, but it's more like the *Dancing Lady* to *Snow White*'s *42nd Street*: reasonable and shiny in its externals, all wrong in its soul. While the animation is decent, the production betrays the derivative zeal with which it was put together; it's like being present at out-of-town try-outs for a particularly troubled show and being forced to watch the kinks that haven't been ironed out. Start with the choice of material, which had already served Disney as a Mickey Mouse short: the Fleischer version is a crass diminution of everything Swift's satire stood for. No satire, no edge, just the outlines of the Lilliput story, which here seemed merely an excuse to go Disney several-hundredfold better on the Dwarf vibes. The specific musicalization was especially inauthentic, since it involved waging the war between Lilliput and Blefuscu over which national song will be sung at the wedding of the countries' prince and princess. Though they were given "name" radio vocalists for voices (Jessica Dragonette and Lanny Ross), the young lovers are ciphers to put Snow White's cardboard boyfriend to shame, and their love songs ("Faithful," "Forever," and finally the amalgamated "Faithful Forever") are not remotely exciting. While Gulliver himself gets one good song, "I Hear a Dream," he and the others, the kings and spies and an irksome town crier, are never anything more than drawings that happen to move. In their shorts, Fleischer and his crew had done wondrous things with simple animation and good music; here, they try too hard for rotoscoped grandeur, and very little of it works. Fleischer made another feature in 1941, this time an original story with songs by Hoagy Carmichael and Frank Loesser. The fact that it is now known by three titles— *Mr. Bug Goes to Town* and *Hoppity Goes to Town* and *Bugville*—indicates how well the enterprise succeeded.

When Disney discontinued the Silly Symphonies in 1939, he formally transferred their creative impulses into his features. His trio of successors to *Snow White*—*Pinocchio, Fantasia, Dumbo*—all, in their varied ways, represent something of an apex of animated musical cinema. *Pinocchio* is in many ways less a musical than a drama with music, which in this case is all to the good since the drama is so potent—and in the Pleasure Island scenes so disturbingly creepy—that the songs are less inherent than they are in *Snow White*. "When You Wish upon a Star" is a motto and benediction, and "Hi Diddle Dee Dee" and "I've Got No Strings," the latter with its chorus line and changing scenery, are cheeky shout-outs to the backstage musical. *Dumbo*, too, has roots in the backstager, while playing down the circus hoopla and keeping things unpretentious, as in "When I See an Elephant Fly"—natty and funny and, alas, now incorrect and squirm-inducing. Most inventively, there is the drunken spree of "Pink Elephants on Parade," as funny musically as it is creative visually.

Fantasia is to Disney as *Intolerance* was to Griffith, loved and loathed with a passion imparted to few animated films or musicals. Disney's intent was nothing short of a distillation of music's essence, and seldom does mainstream filmmaking get this ambitious or pretentious, with results that must be both mighty and flawed. For imagination this vast and overreaching this conspicuous, we have to go back to 1930 and *King of Jazz*—another piece of mixed effect.[1] One of the hallmarks of *Fantasia* is the way it takes itself so damned seriously: the jokes and visual/musical puns of the Silly Symphonies are mostly gone, and the rather ponderous host segments with Deems Taylor only add to a feeling of pedagogical duty. This is music that's supposed to be good for you—small wonder that *Fantasia*'s two best-loved segments, "The Sorcerer's Apprentice" and "The Dance of the Hours," are the loosest and funniest. The rest is mesmerizing, often magical, and once in a while profoundly trying. Topless centaurettes prancing to Beethoven, Schubert's "Ave Maria" as the cure for the evils so rivetingly set loose in Mussorgsky's "Night on Bald Mountain," Stravinsky juxtaposed with T-Rex. This is the kind of folly someone can produce after receiving vast amounts of critical approval and box-office love, with a comparable falling-off of self-awareness; echoes of it can be seen later on with Vincente Minnelli (*The Pirate*) and Gene Kelly (*Introduction to the Dance*) and even, arguably, Bob Fosse (*All That Jazz*), plus Samuel Goldwyn with *Porgy and Bess*. Yet—there's always a "yet" where *Fantasia* is concerned—a piece of this scope and risk must, almost inevitably, be great in some fashion. If the failure rate is considerable, so are the rewards and repercussions. If nothing else, without *Fantasia* Warner Bros. would not have given the world Bob Clampett's *Corny Concerto* or Chuck Jones's *Rabbit of Seville* and the triumphant

[1] If it sounds like a stretch to equate apples *Fantasia* with oranges *King of Jazz*, consider that both are huge, plotless, and ostensibly centered around a mainstream musical figure (Whiteman and Stokowski), both using animation and concert-hall pieces. *King of Jazz* director John Murray Anderson designed the "Rhapsody in Blue" sequence with a true *Fantasia* purpose—to evoke a listener's thoughts while listening to the piece. The Rhapsody itself turned up in Disney's *Fantasia 2000*, so uneven a work as to make the original seem a model of consistency.

What's Opera, Doc? Think, too, of how many people now know "Le Sacre de Printemps," because of *Fantasia*, even if they can't hear it without recalling all those blasted dinosaurs.

From the extreme of *Fantasia*, Disney animation settled, over the next thirty years or so, into more orthodox configurations. If the technique was generally of staggering accomplishment, the groundbreaking of *Snow White* and the depth of *Pinocchio* and the gaga bravura of *Fantasia* were flattened, generally, into a highly accomplished level of complacency. *Cinderella* had some truly lovely moments and could be considered a good medium-grade musical—but the virtuosity of "Pink Elephants" surfaced only fleetingly in a moment like "Oh, Sing Sweet Nightingale," with Cinderella's soap-bubble reflections singing back to her in close harmony. Similarly, *Peter Pan* and *Lady and the Tramp* were perfectly fine as far as they went, and rarely was that far enough, apart from the nice notion of Peggy Lee as co-writer of the *Lady* songs plus several of its voices, including both Siamese cats. *Alice in Wonderland* did at least attempt to climb some anarchic peaks, unfortunately with fragmentary song presentation and a forced, enervating level of lunacy. In *Sleeping Beauty*, the visual dimension was effected with such awesome attention to detail that even Tchaikovsky's music was hard-put to compete, especially with vernacular lyrics grafted on. A stunning achievement in some particulars, *Sleeping Beauty* seemed a summary of the ways the Disney people had gone back on the early promises of the Silly Symphonies and *Pinocchio* and the rest, preoccupying itself so much with the externals that there seemed to be little opportunity for the drama and the music to explore and challenge one another, let alone the spectator.

The most frustrating part of what came to be known as Disneyfication was that, for many years, the more daring possibilities were still there, just visible and aural enough to make one regret the prosaic overall picture. In the more extreme moments of *The Three Caballeros* and in the pre-LSD hallucinations of the "Blame It on the Samba" number from *Melody Time*, the Latin American rhythms had obviously encouraged the creative staff to go bolder, less literal, more exhilarating. Even in something more conventional like the "Willie, the Operatic Whale" segment of *Make Mine Music*, there was creativity in such sufficiency that Nelson Eddy, usually so stalwart and stiff onscreen, was inspired to give the most virtuosic performance of his long career.[2] Some notably

---

[2] With Eddy voicing all the characters, this remains one of the great vocal achievements in all of animated film, a true whale of a job. (Sorry.)

edgy moments could also peek through in something like *Toot Whistle Plunk and Boom*, the first cartoon made in CinemaScope and the studio's first conscious attempt at the stylized animation gaining currency at the UPA studio. *Toot* was a capsule history of music—a less affected stepchild of *Fantasia*—and despite its homey pedagogy it made some loose and neat statements about music and movement, as well as some distinct, perhaps unintentional, homages to *Love Me Tonight*. There was also the wholly engaging *101 Dalmatians*, which was less a musical feature than an adventure-comedy with a few incidental musical moments—as well as a worthy tribute in song to the most sublimely louche of Disney villains, Cruella DeVil.

The less representational cartoon work of the 1950s—the pendulum swing away from *Sleeping Beauty* and *Peter Pan*—was in a way a prediction, in its anti-Disney stylization, of the animated onslaught that would shortly engulf television. The endless work, from Hanna-Barbera and other studios, would contain some of the most insipid animation imaginable, canned prefab music, and the same sound effects repeated endlessly. Things like *Yogi Bear* and *Huckleberry Hound* were driven by dialogue, not visuals or music, and so, in truth, was *The Flintstones*, which at least had the saving grace of wit and sometimes a song from a guest star on the order of "Ann-Margrock." Soon, with the likes of *Scooby Doo* and *Fat Albert* and the rest, big-screen animation would seem even more obsolete than was already the case. The decline of animated features fairly paralleled that of live-action musicals, with only an occasional hiccup like the odd *American Pop* and the like-clockwork success of the Disney reissues such as *Snow White* and—now billed as "The Ultimate Trip" yet—*Fantasia*. For the most part, any thought of putting music to animation in a new film seemed as dim a part of the past as *The Skeleton Dance*.

It was out of virtually nowhere that Disney went retro, in 1989, with *The Little Mermaid*: old-style animation, a full score to rival that of *Snow White*, the traditional animal sidekicks, and a return to the great villains with Ursula, the sea witch who looked like Divine and sounded like (and was voiced by) Pat Carroll. Children were enthralled, as were adults who still doted on *Snow White*, and everyone took note of the quality of the songs by Alan Menken and Howard Ashman, until then best known for *Little Shop of Horrors*. "Part of Your World" and "Poor Unfortunate Souls" and "Kiss the Girl" were not only enjoyable on their own terms, they advanced the characters and situations and action more pointedly than the final, rather perfunctory action scenes. While the young lovers were cute and Sebastian the calypso crab a genuine crowd-pleaser, the main charm of *The Little Mermaid* was the pride with which it waved its musical flag. Even with naysayers less than impressed by the animation and old-style storytelling, how long—truthfully—had it been since a musical number of any kind would be greeted, in a movie theater, by cheers and an ovation? It happened, in screening after screening, with the marimba-driven "Under the Sea" and, after more than a half-century, it was like "Whistle While You Work" all over again.

Beauty and the Beast followed less than two years later, with the same song-writing team, even greater assurance, and an outright Broadway vibe such as animated films had never possessed. From the opening scene-setting of "Belle" to the riotously oompah character piece "Gaston" to the climactic title song—performed by no less a footlight diva than Angela Lansbury—*Beauty* was the kind of musical that, live or drawn, had no longer seemed possible. Deliberately designed to follow through on all the promises of *The Little Mermaid*, it could at points seem derivative and shared with its predecessor some late-spotted action scenes less effective than the musical numbers.[3] Fortunately, it also contained a go-for-broke central production number that set spectators cheering once again. "Be Our Guest" was a deliberate tribute to classical animation and to the art of Busby Berkeley, echoing both *Snow White* and all those Warner cartoons where magazine covers and household utensils would come to life and perform when no one was around. Like *Singin' in the Rain* and the best parts of *Chicago*, it managed to evoke and honor and kid its predecessors all at the same time—in so doing imparting whiffs of the entire movie-musical experience.

Beauty and the Beast was far too successful not to prompt follow-ups, and none of its successors quite closed the circle on musical animation with such history-minded panache. *The Lion King*—an updated, more politically conscious *Bambi* (with echoes of *The Jungle Book*), and insanely successful—was something of a transition to more modern or even post-modern styles. With older Disney models becoming less of a reference point, there would now be superheroes (*Hercules*, *Tarzan*) and feminist heroines (*Mulan*, *Pocahontas*) that at points seemed so undifferentiated they could blend together. Then, effec-

---

[3] There was also the letdown not even Jean Cocteau could avoid: Beast is so compelling that any human replacement is anticlimactic. The rather florid blonde specimen here recalls Marlene Dietrich's reported take on *Snow White*: "That prince—looks queer. . . .You can't allow somebody who does Mickey Mouse to become a movie producer!"

tively, arrived the virtual discontinuation of drawn animation. For those who had lived their entire lives in the computer age, digital animation seemed far more credible than moving paintings, and in-jokes and cheeky humor became more prominent than musical sequences. The best of these new animated films were the equal of much of the classic Disney—the *Toy Story* and *Shrek* films, *Finding Nemo*, *Up*, *WALL-E*—and the music, nearly all of it written by Randy Newman, would have increasingly less pertinence.[4] While Newman's work was usually competent and sometimes inspired, the presence of songs in these films was more for obligatory purposes than anything else—acknowledging history without truly making use of it.

Animation's old and new co-exist oddly in the twenty-first century: because of home video, *Snow White* and *Pinocchio* and even the Silly Symphonies are present as never before, in part because Disney makes such a blasted big deal of rereleasing "new, improved" editions of them virtually like clockwork. Yet it is the very consciousness of them, for children above the age of four or thereabouts, that puts their musical nature in a rather bracketed configuration. Even as "Hi-Ho" and "Bibbidi-Bobbidi-Boo" will never die, most young viewers are now adjudged to have moved past the guilelessness and (alas) innocence such things seem to purvey. Films like *Enchanted* and *Tangled* and *Frozen* make consciously ironic use of the older models both in their music and their storytelling, never more so than when the live-with-animation *Enchanted* featured a trilling Amy Adams performing a sort-of "Whistle While You Work" reconfigured for household vermin. As for *Tangled*, its title alone showed the spin it was willing to put on Rapunzel, with a witch-mother—voiced by Broadway's Donna Murphy—who seemed more Mama Rose than Cruella. Much of this, it needs to be stated, was as entertaining as it was technically accomplished, albeit with a knowing virtuosity that carries less punch than the old straightforward songs-and-story format. They cost hundreds of millions now, and they make that and more on ticket sales and merchandising and home video—and ultimately it shouldn't be too surprising that it's all become too massive for anything winsome. Sleeping Beauty's dance with the mock-prince created by her woodland

---

[4] There should again be mentioned the splendid exception of *WALL-E*, with its videotape of *Hello, Dolly!* prompting the lovelorn robot's obsession with Michael Crawford's rendition of "It Only Takes A Moment." It can and should be argued that most of the historical influences bestowed by *Dolly!* have been negative and cautionary. This one is a marvelous exception, a neat demonstration of how even not-great musicals can produce indelible things.

friends is still adorable, and it's also something made long lifetimes ago. Fairy tales now demand a take that's wry, even cynical.

Much of the feature work discussed so far has been from Disney, a company founded on animation long before there were theme parks or mouse clubs or mega-merchandizing conglomerates. The non-Disney features can, without much stretching, seem analogous to the musicals not produced by Arthur Freed or MGM from around 1942 to 1958—not insignificant, necessarily, and also not terribly innovative, especially where the music is concerned. After the initial Fleischer pair of *Gulliver's Travels* and *Mr. Bug Goes to Town*, Disney had a monopoly on animated features for nearly two decades. Finally, with the Mister Magoo feature *1001 Arabian Nights* in 1959, other companies began to look in with an occasional try—*Gay Purree* (with a so-so Arlen/Harburg score), *A Boy Called Charlie Brown*, and a few others, including the aforementioned, emphatically-not-a-family-film-but-musical-nevertheless *American Pop*. In most or even all of them, the musical sequences were far less inherent than simply dutiful. The playing field became more crowded after 1986 and *An American Tail*, which boasted a high-profile ad campaign and executive producer (Steven Spielberg), subject matter (Jewish immigrant mice) that added a refreshing spin on the standard Disney anthropomorphism, and a decent musical score. While not unduly imaginative, it was successful enough to pave the way for more work from director Don Bluth and then others, right around the time Disney was scoring with its post–*Little Mermaid* renaissance. Two films in particular were especially ambitious in directly challenging the Disney dominance: Bluth's *Anastasia* for Fox and Dreamworks' *The Prince of Egypt*, both of which remade live-action classics and added songs and star voices.[5] *Prince*'s songs were highly publicized, being the work of Broadway's Stephen Schwartz—of *Godspell*, *Pippin*, and later *Wicked* fame—though it must be said that with the songs as with the visuals, the level of craftsmanship was more workmanlike than transcendent.

Both *Anastasia* and *Prince of Egypt* were reasonably successful, and there might have been more of the same but for a couple of factors. One was the sensation of *Toy Story*; while digital animation need not have made the drawn works seem naïve and obsolete, the march of technology tends to take no pris-

---

[5] Although *Prince of Egypt* was not *precisely* a remake of *The Ten Commandments*, Dreamworks still found it prudent to play down the similarities. At least it was better than that rotten miniseries.

oners. Far more egregiously, there was Fox's second attempt at a cartoon remake, and a reviled piece it was. Yes, there was indeed a cartoon version of *The King and I*, and never mind that this may have been the Rodgers and Hammerstein movie that least needed any kind of remake. Seldom, as an animated feature or a musical, has a film had such little reason to exist, and the error was compounded miserably with the decision to go Disney with a "cute" animal companion. Why didn't they just go all the way and let the damned monkey sing "Getting to Know You"? The failure of this *King and I* was predictable, fast, and for Fox somewhat mortifying, even as its position in cartoon purgatory became less solitary a bit later with the advent (possibly not the right term for a movie about Hanukkah) of Adam Sandler's *Eight Crazy Nights*. As a rule, feature-length animated musicals are too collaborative to qualify as vanity projects. This, however, was Sandler's baby, and stars of his stature (in 2002) could instigate major things. Hence, a theatrical film with the look of tacky cable-TV animation, with lots of vacuous, raucous music that naturally included Sandler's "Hanukkah Song," plus toilet jokes, slacker/loser humor, and all the other hallmarks of the Sandler oeuvre. It was, surely, the longest seventy-six minutes in animation history.

Lest the crud of *Eight Crazy Nights* give the wrong impression, song-propelled animation and potty wit need not cancel one another out. It may well be, in fact, that Sandler got the green light for his project only because of a predecessor that did those precise things really, really well. The animation looked like moving Colorforms, the humor was so base and nasty that even the title was pornographic, and the connections with the past—from *Steamboat Willie* and the Silly Symphonies onward—were breathtaking. One goes to a film entitled *South Park: Bigger, Longer & Uncut* with a certain set of expectations that naturally stem from its parent television series. There would be the cheeky kids spewing the expected obscenities, quite more than on Comedy Central; the funny and mean jabs at sacred cows of government, religion, and show business; the occasionally biting moments of satire; and, singularly enough, a somewhat conservative core. There might even be parodistic or pointed songs thrown in. And, it should be noted, all of these were present—but who could have known that Trey Parker and Matt Stone, and composer Marc Shaiman, would corral the musical elements so well? This, remember, was over a decade before Parker and Stone created the biggest hit on Broadway, *The Book of Mormon*—a show that would not have happened without this precedent.

The intent was clear from the first scene and "Mountain Town," which had Stan Marsh bopping through the village of South Park in a wickedly precise parody of "Belle" from *Beauty and the Beast*. It worked not simply as riff or satire but also as good exposition can in musical theater and film from *Show Boat* to *The Wizard of Oz* to *Hairspray*. While some of the songs were there mainly to be nervy or cheeky—one with an unprintable title that included the word "Uncle," plus the deathless "What Would Brian Boitano Do?"—the greater wonder was that most of them were essential, valid, characterful. As the plot recounted the escalating war between the United States and Canada, the songs advanced the action while subtly alluding to musicals past. (It helped, too, that Stan and Kyle and Kenny, and especially Cartman, all resembled Snow White's dwarfs.) "La Résistance" effortlessly took on *Les Misérables*, "Eyes of a Child" was a faux-uplift ballad out of the 1970s with its heart in a completely wrong place, and the epic "Blame Canada" hearkened back as far as the Marx Brothers and *Duck Soup*, while throwing in a pointed exhortation to assign culpability to "that bitch Anne Murray too." Shaiman's music was both smart and deft—prefiguring his work on *Hairspray*—and it was as if he and Parker and Stone were honoring all their cinematic ancestors at the same time they were trashing Disney, Canada, the Baldwin brothers, Saddam Hussein, gay Satan, Winona Ryder, and any number of greater or lesser targets. Far from being a piddling inanity like *Eight Crazy Nights*, or an autopilot piece like *Tarzan* or other lesser Disneys, *South Park* was, against all odds or expectations, a genuinely fine piece of musical cinema.[6] As mindful of its past as *Singin' in the Rain*, as skillfully crafted as *Gigi*, and as pointed in its targets as *Cabaret*. Let the point be emphasized one more time: who would've thought?

South Park: Bigger, Longer & Uncut was not the end of the line where musical animation was concerned, for there would be the incidental songs and invention of *The Simpsons Movie* and *Wall-E* and *Up* and all the rest. But there was a then-and-now aspect to *South Park* which, coupled with the near-death of drawn animation, made it both a summation and a fare-thee-well. The circle that started with *Steamboat Willie* had been now been completely closed.

---

[6] Lord knows what expectations were after "Blame Canada" was nominated for an Oscar, and Parker and Stone managed to attend the ceremony in character, and in style: Parker went in an exact copy of the plunged-to-the-navel Versace gown Jennifer Lopez had earlier worn to the Grammy Awards, while Stone opted for a more sedate Gwyneth Paltrow number. Alas, "Canada" lost to a dull *Tarzan* song by Phil Collins, denying the world what might have been a spectacular acceptance speech. With sparkle-encrusted flip-flops.

Along this path there had been *The Skeleton Dance* and Betty Boop and hippo pirouettes and Bugs and Elmer doing Wagner and household utensils channeling Busby Berkeley, and now, more than seventy years after *Willie*, the animation was made to look almost as rudimentary as it had back at the beginning. The digital age was approaching, with its beautiful and uncanny and often sterile look, and songs and music would soon, more frequently, seem less and less necessary. So it has continued, to the point where the old *Snow White* ways are kept in the past, save when a quick quote can elicit a fast laugh. How odd, then, that in a twilight moment of animated features, one impudent and nasty-minded little film ended up being so much more than a cash-in on a hit series. Without compromising or slighting their own sophomoric impulses, Trey Parker and Matt Stone managed to cap an entire genre. However longer and uncut it may wish to be, the *South Park* movie is a dazzling tribute to all those years of painted music-making that it also wishes to deride, virtually an animated *That's Entertainment!* Of course, it's also really cool and dirty, and if that's a problem, blame Canada. Anne Murray, too.

Chapter 11

Under My Skin
*Musicals and Race, Musicals
and Sexuality*

....

rustration with old film can adopt any number of guises. There is the
disenchantment of seeing something after many years and finding that
memory, either of specifics or merit, can play tricks. There may be the
letdown of a film that isn't quite good enough, or fails glaringly and unneces-
sarily. With silent and early sound film, there can be the near-tragic exaspera-
tion of something that no longer exists tantalizing with intimations of what
might have been. This last finds a connection with a Warner Bros. musical
called *On with the Show!* The title points to its being one of many backstage
stories made in the wake of *The Broadway Melody*, in fact, one of the first—
shot quickly and in theaters by late May 1929. It attracted wide attention because it was entirely in Technicolor, which was then rare, expensive, quite
imperfect, and here judged the best seen so far. The color made *On with the
Show!* an event and a hit, and now the frustration of history checks in: with the
exception of one brief clip recovered by a private collector, it survives only in
dim, contrasty black and white, the vaguest shadow of what had impressed so
many in 1929. Many big early musicals don't survive at all, so its very existence
is bounty; still, since the color was one of two factors to draw near-universal
praise, it's a bitter monochrome pill.

The other feature of *On with the Show!* liked by everyone is fortunately
extant, and even without the color it, or rather she, leaps off the screen. Ethel

Waters, at the time a young and slim star of nightclubs, recordings, and revue, was on the cusp of a crossover into primarily white entertainment. She appeared in *On with the Show!* only as herself, in performance onstage, but what performance: in a sea of hackneyed plot twists and an appalling performance or two, she steals it all, Technicolor or not. An hour or so separates her two songs, during which much of the movie evaporates. Her first appearance, introducing the peerless "Am I Blue?," she hits out of the theater. Later, she returns and gives a non-classic song, "Birmingham Bertha," a truly classic rendition, shrewdly cheeky in a way to put later divas to shame. Not much else in the film can rival this, and the closest is a tap quartet, the Four Covans, that appears twice. Like Waters, the Covans (two men, two women) are African American and denied any part in the script or the drama. For them, specialty performance would have been the only way to make it into a backstage film other than playing maids or valets. Musicals had started out with fake blackness, in the form of Al Jolson, and with *On with the Show!* the power and quality of the real thing was there for everyone to observe. While it would be a very, very long time until film began to give any sort of equal opportunity to players of color, musicals did sometimes show a little more respect, not least because these were performers of such quality that it would be insane not to employ them.

Musicals could also be a haven—some might say a benign closet—for another group usually left in the shade. It's well known now that gay and lesbian characters thrived onscreen in the days before the 1934 Production Code. If they were sometimes the butts of jokes and targets for scorn, in musicals, the men were often given a little more of a break. How long, after all, had a theatrical environment been a hospitable place for them? Designers, performers, assistants—they were there, people knew it, and the judgments tended to come down less harshly than in the outside world. *The Broadway Melody* featured a very conspicuous gay costume designer and, briefly, a big tough wardrobe mistress. As with the black artists in *On with the Show!*, it wasn't a lot—yet, compared with other film, there was a shade more fairness. In ways variously subversive or retro, it would continue, for both groups, for much of musical-film history.

The release of *On with the Show!* fell midway between two of 1929's most distinctive films. Neither was a conventional musical, and both were, in a year of wobbly technique and shaky aesthetics, quite advanced. Most pertinently, one had an entirely African American cast and the other nearly so. The famous entry in this pair is King Vidor's *Hallelujah!*, and the lesser status of the other is made apparent by its title: *Hearts in Dixie*. *Hallelujah!* is a problematic masterwork, its melodrama and stereotyping and Irving Berlin songs balanced with traditional hymns and such scenes of startling impact as a revival inside a crowded church where the singing and devotion become so intense that the faithful begin to pass out. As for *Hearts in Dixie*, it is known to some, not entirely fairly, as a Stepin Fetchit movie. Fetchit's persona and significance are always going to rate a great deal of argument, and let it be noted that though he is very much present in *Hearts in Dixie* he is not really the lead. (That distinction goes to Clarence Muse, an actor as opposed to a personality performer.) For an extremely early talkie, *Hearts* is technically impressive—more advanced in some ways than the more ambitious and ragged *Hallelujah!* And how easy it could be, ultimately how straw-man dead end, to evaluate either of these in terms of what they don't or can't do culturally. They are products of a white corporate system, in 1929 yet, and to expect too much out of either of them, to take umbrage at their narrowness and the inevitable patronizing, is to wrench history and perspective into places where they do not belong.[1] Both of these films were made fourteen years after *The Birth of a Nation*, and just a few months before the operetta with a *Birth of a Nation* heart known as *Golden Dawn*. It's something of a miracle that *Hallelujah!*, especially, was even made. However compromised, however wretched in individual moments and attitudes, both *Hallelujah!* and *Hearts* are bolder and more honest than most Hollywood film dared to be in 1929. Also, as with *On with the Show!*, they demonstrate the advantages sound film could give to African American artists.

Depression cinema and then the Production Code would limit the opportunities these actors had and confine them to all those roles, variously servile and buffoonish, that can make '30s and '40s film so depressing. On the rare occasion when they would break through, it was most often musically, with results so good that they inspire ingratitude for not occurring more frequently. Bill "Bojangles" Robinson and Louis Armstrong were the exemplars here, benign presences of staggering talent. Robinson's best-known film appearances were opposite Shirley Temple, and though the powers at Fox may not have

---

[1] Context is all, with the films in this chapter, and even some well-intended viewers will not always wish to make the necessary framing. It comes down, basically, to judging how many twenty-first-century demands to place on 1930 cinema. *Hallelujah!* and even *Hearts in Dixie* have moments of pertinence and honesty that should be counted positively, especially given the ways their performers demonstrate what they could achieve against *those* odds.

intended it so, the rapport of this tall older dark man and this little light girl made for something of a marvelous contrast to most of the racism of American film and American life. Their staircase dance in *The Little Colonel* is the one everyone remembers, and it must be said that it's not a particularly flashy sequence, nor all that extensive. It is also, quite plainly, remarkable, seemingly an improvised little moment of Robinson and Temple tap-dancing their way upstairs, accompanied by Robinson's twangy humming. (One of the tunes he hums is "Old Black Joe": compliance or sarcasm?) When Robinson reaches out his long arm to clasp Temple's hand, something significant is happening, and it's not some kind of Uncle Tom devotion. It's about two performers connecting, like Astaire and Rogers did or Hope and Crosby or Monroe and Russell, finding in their shared music an irresistible path to a very particular kind of joy. With *The Little Colonel* and the other films Temple made with Robinson, the resonance comes in the artless way some ingrained and hateful things are casually being ignored, even obliterated.[2]

At that same time and same studio, there was under contract a sassier second-string Temple named Jane Withers. She had zoomed to such fame as Temple's nemesis in *Bright Eyes* that she was then spun off into her own films as more of a chipper hellion than a dimpled darling. While her vehicles—some of them musical—lacked the gloss and care of Temple's, they were successful enough to put her quite high in popularity lists. One prime Withers specimen was a South-and-cottonfields period piece bearing the ominously rhetorical title *Can This Be Dixie?* Withers was firmly at the center of it, and at one point she was joined by a black chorus to perform a lively song-and-dance called, please be aware, "Pick Pick Pickaninny." No, it isn't just the title; it's the lyrics and staging, plus the queasy despondence felt while seeing what some people had to do in 1936 to stay employed. "Keep on pickin' or you'll lose that chicken," Withers chirps, and surely this is the way by which to gauge the magnitude of what Shirley Temple and Bill Robinson were able to achieve.

Nor did such a perilous diversion exist in a vacuum. Live minstrel shows were nearly extinct, by the time of sound film, and it is not to the musical's credit that it gave the entire minstrel tradition a falsely resuscitated kind of

[2] That's not to say that the Temple films were paragons of tolerance. Temple disguises herself in blackface in *The Littlest Rebel*—why not, with that title?—and *Dimples* concludes with Shirley as Little Eva in a hair-raising recreation of *Uncle Tom's Cabin*. Even Stepin Fetchit shows up, though at least Bill Robinson was spared that one.

currency. People like Al Jolson and Eddie Cantor would don blackface for slim or no reason, and the demented nadir of the whole phenomenon is the "When Jolson Meets Berkeley" spectacle in *Wonder Bar* called "Goin' to Heaven on a Mule." Nor did the tradition peter out with the fading of Jolson and Cantor's movie careers. Berkeley continued blackface into the 1940s with Mickey Rooney and Judy Garland, Bing Crosby dressed up like Uncle Tom to sing of Lincoln in *Holiday Inn*, and possibly the looniest extreme came in a burst of postwar Technicolor glamour in *The Dolly Sisters*. Betty Grable and June Haver perform "The Darktown Strutters Ball" straight, as it were, after which a bevy of Fox showgirls act out the song while made up in various café-au-lait hues. Some are done up in standard revue couture while others sport dice and cards, and one carries a watermelon muff. Grable and Haver then reappear as black-faced ragamuffins, Grable distending her lips and rolling her eyes. The whole exhibition is even more heedless than that fearsome last gasp of the tradition— the Joan Crawford-goes-mulatto number in *Torch Song*. Alongside these, even *Hearts in Dixie* can seem advanced.

Fortunately, the real thing was also happening. Not enough great perform-ers were being hired, the material was rarely the best, and some numbers were removed before showings in white Southern theaters. None of this staved off the magic: Paul Robeson and Hattie McDaniel in *Show Boat*; Bill Robinson and Jeni LeGon dancing in *Hooray for Love*, Cab Calloway in *The Singing Kid*, Louis Armstrong in *Pennies from Heaven* and, with Maxine Sullivan, singing "Jeepers Creepers" in *Going Places*. Calloway and Armstrong were also august presences in musical shorts, an area where artists of color could thrive. The only visual record of Bessie Smith in performance is her 1929 short *St. Louis Blues* and, amid a nest of stereotypes about gambling and loose morals, she comes through as an upper-case star. Sammy Davis Jr., a seven-year-old of mas-sive talent, appeared a little later alongside Ethel Waters in the two-reel *Rufus Jones for President*. Duke Ellington and his orchestra performed in features as well as shorts, and a youthful Billie Holiday turned up in an aggressively ar-tistic Paramount piece called *Symphony in Black*. Which factor tips the scale: dealing with disparaging circumstances, or having the opportunity to see these performers? Even socially unaware spectators could see that this was music-making of a rare order, at least in the theaters that deigned to run the films.

Was it the exigencies of wartime or was it simple good taste that permitted MGM and Fox to produce *Cabin in the Sky* and *Stormy Weather*? Yes, they both have their embarrassing moments, and the script of *Stormy Weather* can best be termed sorry, but as celebrations of talent these two films are astounding. Ethel Waters again, and Ellington and Robinson and Calloway and (too briefly) Armstrong, Lena Horne in both and Rochester and Katherine Dunham and Fats Waller and the Nicholas Brothers and many more, all in superb form. At a time when the notion of civil rights was starting to stir in America, here arrive two displays of artistry providing more genuine entertainment than nearly anything else Hollywood was doing, graphically if unwittingly demonstrating the relevance a musical can attain. Both respect their artists, by and large, and neither—taken, again, in their context—is demeaning.[3]

In *Cabin in the Sky*, a great part of the success comes from Vincente Minnelli's refusal to condescend to either the cast or the material, even when the MGM "Great White Father" attitude threatens to break in as early as the foreword (by Elmer Rice), which loftily announces a "story of faith and devotion." Fortunately, the more germane foundation of the project is Minnelli's awareness that Waters is a diva of the first rank and possesses an unparalleled gift for radiating sincerity and warmth: "Happiness Is Just a Thing Called Joe" has to be some kind of high-water mark of a singer really meaning a song. And she can get down too, jive-talking and jitterbugging and throwing off high kicks. It might be noted also that Waters's off-camera turbulence was a thing of wondrous magnitude, and the animosity she already felt toward Lena Horne was multiplied manyfold when she observed Minnelli taking special care with how Horne would be presented. This gives their showdown scene a distinct charge, and Horne's elegantly kittenish siren seems a world away from the coldly tense persona she would later assume.[4]

By contrast, *Stormy Weather* gives Horne little dramatic play and makes her the romantic interest of Bill Robinson, who was old enough to be her grandfather. Fortunately, *Stormy Weather* is like *Holiday Inn* or *Easter Parade*—the plot matters far less than the musical numbers that keep cascading out. Horne is a goddess in the title song, Waller mugs and sings "Ain't Misbehavin'," and by the

---

[3] The offensive "smiley-face" chorus-girl chapeaux in *Stormy Weather* can be excepted here. For something truly dismaying, see *Tales of Manhattan*, shot just prior to *Cabin in the Sky*. Ethel Waters, Paul Robeson, and Eddie "Rochester" Anderson are trapped in circumstances that can fairly be termed miserable, for them and the audience.

[4] As shot, Horne's entrance into *Cabin* was a show-stopper: the devil's siren, in her bubble bath, extols the virtues of sin in "Ain't It the Truth." Evidently it was cut after previews, perhaps in part because Horne's version followed a long set-in-hell rendition by Louis Armstrong and chorus; it may have just been too much "Truth." Horne later sang it on Broadway in *Jamaica*, less effectively than in the surviving *Cabin* footage where, no surprise, she's irresistible.

Sounds great, looks great: Lena Horne was one of the newer talents bringing pizzazz to wartime musicals. Another was pianist/vocalist Hazel Scott.
Their "Jericho" number was tacked on to give a much-needed lift to Vincente
Minnelli's *I Dood It*, although here Horne is wearing her goddess-gown from
another 1943 MGM musical, *Thousands Cheer*.

end, when the Nicholas Brothers fly over each other down a series of platforms,
it's nirvana. It was also the end of the line, in a way, since there would be no more
feature-length use of such talent for a long time. Part of this came with the
heightened presence and vigilance of the NAACP, under the powerful and often
judgmental Walter White. The intent was to project a positive image, which
producers of musicals sidestepped by hiring fewer black performers. Even as the
number of specialty artists decreased, blackface was still considered acceptable
and Walt Disney's *Song of the South* was a special, troubling case.[5]

---

[5] With its great animation and good tunes and patronizing attitude, *Song of the South* is a
title the Disney organization generally prefers to keep buried. It should be noted that even at
the time there were loud protests against it, and that James Baskett is so good (as both Uncle
Remus and the voice of Brer Fox) that he diminishes the cringe factor substantially. Once
again, it's the circumstances, not the performer.

Dramas, meantime, ventured out into bolder (for Hollywood) territory with *Pinky* and *No Way Out* and a few others; and finally, in 1954, there was Otto Preminger's *Carmen Jones*. What an odd, or at least unique, film, realistic yet fanciful in ways that go beyond usual filmed opera, both a spectacular stunt and a window to a newer age. It's meant as a novelty, an all-black modernization of a classic opera with laborious vernacular, yet it also has candor far beyond the "faith and devotion" of *Cabin in the Sky*, let alone the fakery of other musicals of its time like *White Christmas*. The material and approach are ever in constant tension: Bizet's music in a modern setting, a production that is vividly real when not soundstage stylized, and Dorothy Dandridge and Harry Belafonte, both singers, looking incredible and talking tough and then opening their mouths to give us voices supplied by others. The layers of artifice are so pervasive that it's something of a surprise that when "Beat Out Dat Rhythm on a Drum" rolls around, the voice coming from Pearl Bailey is that of Pearl Bailey. (Alas, Preminger knew little about shooting large musical numbers, so the dancers in "Rhythm," including people like Alvin Ailey, are glimpsed only briefly.) Much of the paradox can be seen in Dandridge herself: arrestingly beautiful and numbingly sexy even beyond that glimpse of her in zebra-print panties, yet with a reserve that tempers the all-out blowtorch approach. The effect is that of splitting the difference between Marilyn Monroe and Audrey Hepburn, perhaps while including some of the breakability of the real Dandridge. While most of the acclaim she got in 1954 zeroed in on how scorching she was, it's her subtlety that is as modulated as the finest Carmens onstage, Jones and otherwise.[6] It's fortunate, too, that the voice of the very young Marilyn Horne fits her so well, since the inevitable bump between the dialogue and the singing is glaring enough as it is. The edgy co-existence between the film's Bizet and its contemporary visuals is startling and compelling, and in some urgent ways Bizet must come in second. Thus is *Carmen Jones* a rarity among major movie musicals: its being a musical is, in some vital ways, quite beside the point.

Rock 'n' roll formally entered film a few months after *Carmen Jones*, which meant that more artists of color would promptly be on the screen. They were

---

[6] Dandridge contrasts interestingly with Broadway's first Carmen Jones, Muriel Smith, who can be seen onscreen in John Huston's *Moulin Rouge*. (Heard in that film, too, dubbing Zsa Zsa Gabor; later, she did Juanita Hall's vocals in *South Pacific*.) She's stunning, in a more statuesque fashion than Dandridge: fine Carmens come in many forms.

specialty artists, once again as earlier, but in look as well as sound it was quite a change. The 1930s had the debonair Duke Ellington; in 1956, it was Little Richard, singing "Good Golly, Miss Molly" in *The Girl Can't Help It*, seizing the screen with the same ferocity he used to pound his piano. This kind of immediacy seemed to connect far more with things going on in the "real world" in places like Little Rock and Montgomery than with rearguard films like *St. Louis Blues* and *Porgy and Bess*. By the 1960s, a notable divide was in place: big-budget musicals contained few black faces, low-price junk like *Ski Party* could be graced by someone as dynamic as James Brown, and television was far more relevant where musical artists of color were concerned. Then, in a time of blaxploitation films with great soundtrack albums, Diana Ross made her move onto movie screens. *Lady Sings the Blues* was as divided, in some ways, as *Carmen Jones*—a glossy, tailor-made *Funny Girl* showcase (complete with torchy "My Man") interwoven with horrifyingly real moments involving drugs and racism. Ross herself straddled these two worlds with starry aplomb, skilled in the songs, game in the drama, invoking her own persona far more than that of Billie Holiday. Though judged a success, Ross would be hindered by some of the same bad timing and bad judgment that hobbled Liza Minnelli. When she appeared in another musical, it was *The Wiz*, and that was that. For its part, *Lady Sings the Blues* served as a matrix for future endeavors like *What's Love Got to Do with It* and *Why Do Fools Fall in Love* and *Ray*—equal parts musical and biopic. With Laurence Fishburne and Angela Bassett as Ike and Tina Turner, and Jamie Foxx as Ray Charles, the power of the portrayals bridged that now-inevitable dubbing gap that occurred with the original artists supplying their own vocals.[7]

With cultural shifts, the rise of music videos, and the overall decline of musicals, there would not be many opportunities for artists, really, of any color. While *Fame* was kinetic and shiny and popular, deep in its heart it was something of a lower-voltage throwback to *Stormy Weather*. Given the enormous impact of *Thriller,* an earlier time would have seen a big-screen Michael Jackson vehicle almost immediately; by the 1980s such a thing was unfeasible.

---

[7] It would be a grand world if more actors in these bios could do their own singing, as with Ross, then Gary Busey as Buddy Holly, Sissy Spacek as Loretta Lynn, and Beverly D'Angelo (not Jessica Lange) as Patsy Cline. The point of these films, however, is that they're about unique singers, and a Joaquin Phoenix does not a Johnny Cash make, at least vocally. Objections to dubbing can be pretty ungrateful when there's a Bassett or Foxx, or a Marion Cotillard as Edith Piaf. And at least audiences were spared having to hear Jennifer Lopez imitate Selena.

The one exception was Prince—nervy, self-indulgent, exultantly subversive—in *Purple Rain*, which was so well received that he won an Oscar for his score. He then propelled himself into retro-Old Hollywood for *Under the Cherry Moon*, not a true musical but a calamity sufficient to kill any further cinematic impulses he may have nursed. There were also pop musicals like *Beat Street*, *Breakin'*, and *Krush Groove*, all looking toward the rise of hip-hop. (And to the mercifully short reign of Vanilla Ice.) Spike Lee created far more distinctive work than this, with films that could frequently tweak or prod older-style musical forms. *School Daze* was a deliberately malicious reconstitution of college musicals, and the later *Bamboozled* took on minstrelsy and blackface in the most barbed fashion imaginable. As with many of Lee's films, both of these were more talked about than financially and perhaps artistically successful—and both were the antithesis of the big musicals of an earlier age that won millions by playing it safe and being unchallenging.

The scrappy idiosyncrasy of *School Daze* and *Bamboozled* was something of an antidote to the corporate mindset that fashioned *The Bodyguard*, whose hit was mainly due to Whitney Houston's recording of Dolly Parton's "I Will Always Love You." This was filmmaking of a blandness to rival the glory time of the late 1930s musical, carefully constructed to take no chances whatever and offer nothing potentially offensive save Kevin Costner's haircut. As it turned out, it was also something of a finale, produced on what turned out to be the cusp of major media changes that would lessen the allure of film for many contemporary artists. Here is where the rise of niche cable programming and the Internet seem most pertinent: with everything that is available, legitimate or bootleg, who wants to go to a movie and see a current star grappling with some sort of unseemly plot? It didn't work for Rudy Vallee in 1929, nor Mariah Carey in 2001, and it would not be tried out on a Kanye West or an Usher later on. In the time of *Stormy Weather*, it was a revelation to see so many great performers together at one time—now, with awards shows and tribute specials, it's commonplace. Visibility has zoomed upward at the same time that, in a corporate sense, the playing field is still unfairly skewed where race is concerned.

Even with other types of musicals in abeyance, the breadth of black music and artists ensures them a periodic hearing in films as varied as *Hustle & Flow*, *Cadillac Records*, and *Black Nativity*. Also, in something of a class by itself, *Dreamgirls*. This holds less true for Latin artists, who for many years were stereotyped with a fervor almost equal to that for African Americans, and despite the enforced visibility that reflected President Roosevelt's Good Neighbor

Policy. American cinema had already had three bona fide Mexican stars, all starting in silents, moving into talkies, and occasionally making musicals: Ramon Novarro, Dolores Del Rio, and Lupe Velez. Later, from Brazil, there would be Carmen Miranda, who must occupy a place of honor in a movie Valhalla as possibly the most endearing performer who ever lived. Her success moved her for a time past the specialty niche into real stardom—though later, like other artists of color, she would be considered a dated throwback. During World War II, with Central and South American film audiences taking the place of the closed European markets, the studios were moved to produce films with titles such as *That Night in Rio* and *Pan-Americana*, albeit with Xavier Cugat's rumbas substituting for overtly authentic flavor. Soon, there would be Ricardo Montalban (Mexico), who danced, Fernando Lamas (Argentina), who sang, and also the delectable Estelita Rodriguez, recalled only by those willing to note that the factory of westerns, Republic Pictures, also turned out musicals with titles like *Cuban Fireball*.

Rita Moreno, who was often relegated to Latina-spitfire roles, made something of a cross-cultural breakthrough when she replaced Dorothy Dandridge as the Asian Tuptim in *The King and I*, yet some currents still flowed in the old ways when Moreno gave her Oscar-winning performance in *West Side Story*. Her Puerto Rican lover was played by the Greek-American George Chakiris and her Puerto Rican friend by the Russian-American Natalie Wood, whose Latin inflections could occasionally grow a mite cumbersome. Such falsity meant that the dynamism and power of *West Side Story*, its honesty, even, were at points undercut, despite the virtuosity of Moreno and Chakiris. In the decades since there has been the occasional *La Bamba* and *Selena* and *El cantante*—also, less distinctively, two Lambada films and not a whole lot else.

The year of *West Side Story* also saw that singular Rodgers and Hammerstein tribute to Chinese American assimilation, *Flower Drum Song*. If Asian artists and culture were even referenced in musicals before then, it was in something like that "Shanghai De-Ho" in the first *Anything Goes*, or the ornate extravagance Fred Astaire and Vincente Minnelli made of "Limehouse Blues" in *Ziegfeld Follies of 1946*. Genuine Asian lead performers—save for the mysteriously pan-Eurasian Yul Brynner—would seldom appear anywhere in film. *Flower Drum Song* did redress that balance with an authentically Asian cast, with the exception of Juanita Hall (black playing Asian, as she had also in *South Pacific*); plus, in the gorgeous person of Nancy Kwan, it had a great deal of bona fide oomph. Unfortunately, on film as on stage, it had as much quaint condescension baked into it as *Hearts in Dixie*, and later on, in a time of heightened sensitivity, it was small wonder that the show would require some major rewriting. Nor, in a time of few musical films and still-insufficient opportunities, has there been much else.

Gays, in musicals, have been a minority of a different sort. Coded and compromised on the screen, they have been an immense creative presence behind it and, often, in the audience. It might be noted upfront that many gay spectators do not always have the ferocity of devotion toward musical film that they do to musical theater. This is not that surprising. Broadway is itself a sort of closet in a way, special and exclusive and insider, while film is of necessity more egalitarian and, wretched term, family-friendly. Movies will seldom make as direct or frank an appeal to a more sophisticated gay audience as theater, even apart from what Warner Bros. did with Cole Porter's life. Until very recently, film drew in gay viewers via indirect or even furtive ways, and the entire concept of gay spectatorship and musical film is a specialized kind of dominion. Onscreen gay references in older film are generally a matter of inference and subversion, present for those who would see and be validated by them, and it lies in a separate principality from the various cults embracing Judy Garland or Doris Day or others. Glamour and spectacle and rebellion and that deviously nattering thing known as camp all factor into it, as do discussions of how much of it may have been intentional and what just might be inadvertent.

Jack Cole, for one, was never inadvertent. His dance routines, even in some appallingly routine movies (*The Thrill of Brazil*, anyone?) were meticulous and well researched and, for the most part, quite carnal. Even in his own rigorous field, Cole was known as a stern taskmaster, demanding and profane and as hard on his dancers as he could be, sometimes, on himself. (Entire troupes of gifted dancers blew out their knees executing some of his trademark deep bends.) There are few Cole numbers not immediately recognizable as his work: certain colors and motifs are favored (he loved pink), the women move in certain ways—especially Cole's most frequent muse, Gwen Verdon—and the men show more skin. It was neither rare nor shocking for gay choreographers to be in charge of major films in the 1930s or '40s or '50s; besides Cole, there were Hermes Pan and Charles Walters and Robert Alton and others. Where Cole's numbers stood apart was in their overt sexuality; more than anyone of his generation, he split the difference between sensuality and smartness in a way that might pass the censors but still retain a wealth of implication. Decorous, it might be said, yet potentially filthy—and thus quite fitting for a man whose reported after-hours hobby was creating pornographic needlepoint.

Because of Marilyn Monroe, Cole will always be best known for "Diamonds Are a Girl's Best Friend" in *Gentlemen Prefer Blondes*, a film that also contains the sequence which, if not his greatest, is surely both his most relevant and insolent. Indeed, in the many decades since Cole conceived and shot "Ain't There Anyone Here for Love?," few have been able to see this number as anything other than an epic celebration of man-on-man physicality. And, fortunately, the only viewers oblivious to its effect were the US censors, who were so preoccupied with cleavage that they registered not so much as a complaint.[8] Rarely do old musicals get so upfront with their subtext: Jane Russell, a big woman dressed in black to resemble a benevolent dominatrix, strolls among a large group of undressed men while bemoaning their lack of interest in her. Supposedly they're the US Olympic team doing their exercises, which allows Cole to have them dressed in skin-colored trunks and nothing else. It's a dance number without dance, with wrestlers, divers, and musclemen paying not the slightest attention to the bemused glamour girl in their midst. At one mind-boggling point, Russell ambles through a double line of athletes waving their derrieres at her while she idly swings a couple of tennis rackets. Even straight audiences gasp. Cole, who died in 1974, must still be laughing.

Granted, Cole presents an extreme case of the knowing-insider way musicals might speak to their audiences about gay sexuality. In the early days of musicals, seldom was anything this outrageous—although it should be mentioned that in a 1929 flop called *Glorifying the American Girl*, the modern-dance pioneer Ted Shawn saw to it that a couple of Follies numbers featured far more men than was usually the case, and with far less to wear. More commonly, there would be gay characters on the screen, none more conspicuous than in that watershed, *The Broadway Melody*, in which a stereotypical, temperamental gay designer is played by a fussy-toned actor named Drew Demarest. He coos and giggles, and at one point has a run-in with a butch wardrobe woman played by the massive Blanche Payson, who was a cop before she went into films. None of this is subtle, nor enlightened save in the general sense of acknowledging gay people to be a prominent part of the theater. Accepted, too, even when there is some ridicule. The designer is harassed by some of the

---

[8] Give the Brits credit, though—their censors caught it, so the number was removed for *Blondes*'s initial UK run.

show's wealthy investors, but he's still one of the key people in a major production. Once again, it's not difficult for modern observers to take the retrospective view and bemoan the derogatory tinge; what is less easy, and probably more appropriate, is to note that in a time of next to no visibility, a film like *The Broadway Melody* was making millions of people aware of a fact of life that otherwise was getting little mention anywhere. However frilly or annoying or marginal the Demarest character might be, he seems to be good at his job, and over the next few years—even, subtly, after the Production Code kicked in—backstage films would have the occasional gay costumer or dance director.[9]

By the 1940s, gay or proto-gay characters on the screen were less prevalent and more dangerous: the gothic women and ambiguous men of film noir. For musicals a gay [male] identity was reflected less through character than design, ambience, disposition. It was at this time that the Arthur Freed group at MGM became informally known as "The Fairy Unit" because of the number and visibility of personnel making stylistic statements in films like *Ziegfeld Follies* and *Yolanda and the Thief* and *The Pirate*. All three were directed by Vincente Minnelli, whose own sexuality seems to have been as complicated as the visual schemes of his most ornate films: tagged as gay soon after his arrival at MGM (the green eye-shadow helped), he dated Lena Horne then embarked, with Judy Garland, on the first of three marriages. Minnelli's work on the screen shows a fascinated deployment of detail and décor, the design aesthetic of brittle inner-circle Manhattan cocktail parties where gay men and lesbians would have thrived. (Party scenes are a Minnelli hallmark.) The color and highstrung attention to detail not only don't resemble '40s musicals at other studios; they don't look like what anyone else was doing at MGM. Indeed, *Yolanda and the Thief* (like, to a lesser extent, *The Pirate*) may be more plausibly viewed as objet d'art than as cohesive entertainment.

Minnelli's one rival in this type of visual foregrounding was Mitchell Leisen, who worked at Paramount and, like Minnelli, had been a designer before assuming directorial chores. Like Minnelli he was often, and scathingly, derided as a fey homosexual, and some of his more macho colleagues—Billy

---

[9] The word "gay" refers mainly, where musicals are concerned, to men. Lesbian figures were notably less present. Beyond the *Broadway Melody* wardrobe woman, there was the fascinatingly offbeat *I Am Suzanne!*, which blended live performers with marionettes. One of its numbers is set in hell and shows a woman puppet sent to the inferno as punishment for preferring male attire. Why did they include such a vignette? Because, in late 1933, they could.

Wilder in particular—sneered at his abilities. Despite this, he had a long run of successful and often very good films, also a marriage plus relationships with women as well as men. His success plus his visual bent led Paramount to assign him *Lady in the Dark*, a job he tackled with an aesthetic so delineated it can be plucked off the screen and fondled. This is a film of surfaces, setting off its furnishings and costumes and hairdos and Technicolor with such incessancy that Maria Montez's south-sea fantasies look ascetic in comparison. The madness of the visuals constantly swamp the music and psychology—and, even apart from Mischa Auer as a giddy fashion photographer, the thing cannot be read as anything other than very gay, in a particularly extreme '40s kind of way.

By decade's end and afterward, musicals' gayness generally became more austere, with the glorious exception of Jack Cole. A film like *My Fair Lady*, for example, had a gay director (George Cukor) and designer (Cecil Beaton), but little in the way of overall gay complexion. Later, the bisexuality of *Cabaret* was certainly bracing, after which little followed, in that out-yet-oppressed time, to make much of a dent. *Mame*, in fact, seemed to deliberately sidestep the whole issue by implicitly setting up Lucille Ball as a gay icon then undercutting the whole notion with dull and unintentionally amusing caution. The one gay-musical aesthetic that did become more evident was that of veneration. Whether or not there were genuine ties between Judy Garland's death and the Stonewall Riots, adulation for Garland only increased after her death. Then, as gay spectatorship became more visible, a synergetic pass of the torch saw the older reverence give way to the newer exuberance. This was manifested in the way newer icons—Garland's own daughter and Diana Ross and especially Bette Midler—all made deliberate claims on the affection of gay spectators. This, of necessity, was staked out in concert venues and television appearances, since movies offered rare or no opportunities. It was notable too that Barbra Streisand, with her flamboyance and early years singing in gay clubs, often seemed less than willing to relate to that segment of her base, though *Funny Lady*, with its sidekick played by Roddy McDowell, at least acknowledged that gay men were essential to backstage life. Although a more activist gay profile was not present in mainstream film, it was referred to intriguingly in one scene in *The Rose*: Bette Midler as The Rose goes to a gay club that features impersonations of Streisand, Ross, Mae West, and...Bette Midler as The Rose. "That drag queen's doing me!" Midler yells delightedly, then proceeds onstage for a group performance of Bob Seger's "Fire Down Below" in a madly communal pageant of simulation and homage.[10]

Given the disco obsession of the later 1970s, it was inevitable that both straight and gay disco worlds made it onto film. For straights, it was *Saturday Night Fever*. For gays—and talk about uneven dance-floors—it was *Can't Stop the Music*. Instant artifact, instant camp, instant testimony to the misbegotten excesses of its producer, Allen Carr. Like Carr himself, *Can't Stop the Music* was gay without thinking anyone knew, which was quite an achievement for a musical starring the Village People and directed by Nancy Walker. With their "Macho Man" mock-stereotypes, the Village People were themselves a singular phenomenon of the pre-AIDS era, and it's possible that an entertaining and witty film could have been crafted out of their improbable ascension and crossover fame. Unfortunately, Carr was coming off the enormous hit of *Grease*, so flash and one-dimensional exuberance took the place of even the most rudimentary cultural or sexual nuance. Rarely does subtext rise to the surface with the inadvertent violence it does in *Can't Stop the Music*, so much so that the jokes started before the film prints were even dry. The signal moment, the item for the archives, was that "YMCA" number, in which Valerie Perrine functioned essentially as Jane Russell had in "Ain't There Anyone Here for Love?"—a beauty surrounded by hot men, but without Jack Cole's wry brilliance. In a time when musicals had little currency—*Grease* was the massive exception proving the rule—Carr's folly seemed more of a dead-end relic, more of an irrelevance, than even *Mame* or *Paint Your Wagon*. Worse, it took the essential falseness of many musicals and ratcheted it up to cosmic deceit.[11]

In a sane world, *Can't Stop the Music* might have been followed, a few years later, by a brighter and more forward gay musical. There was, indeed, Blake Edwards's *Victor/Victoria*, with its "be nice to gays" attitude and odd commingling of stylishness and slapstick. Then, after that, a long deathly silence. The human toll of the AIDS crisis was horrendous, and the artistic toll was not limited simply to the enormous numbers of performers and creators cut down. Because of the pan-

---

[10] Too bad, then, that homage cannot also be directed, in *The Rose*, toward the decision to eliminate the lead character's bisexuality. In a "mainstream" world, such deletions are not at all uncommon—even in *Chicago*, Mama Morton was far more forward on the stage. Speaking of musicals with Queen Latifah, that "racial uplift" number added to the *Hairspray* movie was way unnecessary, part of film's eternal need to sugarcoat the wrong things.

[11] While the flop of *Can't Stop the Music* put a major crimp in Carr's momentum, the worst was yet to come: he was the one responsible for that Rob Lowe/Snow White duet of "Proud Mary" on the Oscars. After that, no more career.

Can't or won't? The wonder that is *Can't Stop the Music*, with the Village People, Valerie Perrine, Bruce Jenner, Steve Guttenberg, and way too much badly used supporting talent. In an awful way, however, it sort of *was* the movie music of the '80's.

demic and the seeming indifference to it by appallingly large parts of the government, the public, and even the entertainment industry, the whole notion of gay culture was set back for years. When it did begin to come back, the magnitude of the tragedy was such that few viable works by or about gay men did not concern themselves in some way with loss or death. Fortunately, there began the rise of independent queer cinema, in which—at least once in a blue moon—even musical ideas would be part of the mix. The Canadian *Zero Patience* was nothing less than a rumination, with songs and dances, on the entire epidemic, most specifically the flight attendant suspected to have been largely responsible for spreading the virus. Credit them, at the very least, with chutzpah and imagination.[12]

[12] In a less creative (not to say less respectable) vein, there also was an occurrence that may have been inevitable: a gay-porn musical, bearing the overreaching title *Romeo & Julian*. While

By the twenty-first century, with love daring to speak its name and marriage on the horizon, a mainstream film finally decided to be a gay musical, with ambiguous results that had little to do with sexuality. Surely it would have been great for the film industry to correct that old Warner Bros. mistake called *Night and Day*. The notorious fake biography of Cole Porter had been an abomination on nearly every front, and here, in 2004, was a bright opportunity to take a more frank look at Porter and his music and boyfriends. The most intriguing aspect of the project was its time-bend conception: the standards would be performed in old-new fashion by pop and rock and jazz singers ranging from Alanis Morissette to Elvis Costello to Mick Hucknall of Simply Red. This was the idea of producer-director Irwin Winkler, for whom this project was a long-nourished dream, and it was the beginning and end of inspiration. If *De-Lovely* was more honest than *Night and Day* about Porter's sexuality, it trod just as many wrong paths, at points with less showmanship. Its slack pacing and unattractive look put Winkler's affinity for musicals on a par with someone like Sidney Lumet, and few of the artists were presented with either style or grace. (Hucknall's rendition of "I Love You" crossed the line into the overtly weird.) Like Cary Grant, Kevin Kline made a Porter considerably glamourized (and butchened, as it were) from the real thing, and once again his marriage was misrepresented with a Linda (Ashley Judd) who was twenty-one years younger instead of eight years older. *De-Lovely* was like a new-millennium version of the Porter/Minnelli *The Pirate*: enterprising and adventurous and ultimately canceling out much of its own laudable intent. It also managed to insult its audience when, at one point, Porter and Linda go to a screening of *Night and Day* and chuckle about all its falsehoods. In 2004, this was akin to having George W. Bush snicker over the various ineptitudes of James Buchanan or Herbert Hoover.

Before and after *De-Lovely*, artists further outside the mainstream continued to craft more worthy gay-themed musical work. Here as elsewhere, *Hedwig and the Angry Inch* was both paradigm and exception, and there was the more genteel *Camp*. A sort of a more-inside predecessor of *Glee*, it told of a bunch of kids who prefer the Tonys to the Super Bowl, as observed during

---

it did indeed contain a song score, the general aura was neither serious nor parodistic, let alone Shakespearean. Both leads were doubled in voice, not body, and such choreography as was on display was not of the dance variety.

musical-theater summer camp. In an early scene, a busload of adolescents did a singalong to Sondheim's "Losing My Mind," after which the gay quotient became somewhat more guarded.[13] The problems of the gay kids, transvestism included, receded in favor of more standard backstage-teen-angst doings, but at least they were being acknowledged. Besides some good musical sequences, *Camp*, with its double-edged title, was in its way a genial path-blazer, raising a point that for 2003 was somewhat revolutionary: show queens can be of every age, gender, and preference.

Lower-budget and less timidly gay than *Camp*, *Were the World Mine* placed its own teen backstage drama in a more fantastic and Shakespearean realm, that of an all-male prep school production of *A Midsummer Night's Dream*. Cast as Puck, a misfit gay teen comes up with his own equivalent of the play's love potion, and this time it makes everyone gay. After a predictable amount of same-sex havoc, some worthy lessons are learned and the course of true love finally runs smooth. While most of the songs—from folk-lyrical to rock—were part of the *Dream* play, a few were performed outside it, mostly in fragments. The intent was worthy, some of the moments (especially musical) were quite lovely, and the difficulty of being an independent musical film made for a great deal of unevenness. Reality and fantasy were not always coupled with ideal smoothness, and the "we all need to get along" message of tolerance near the end became, predictably, a trifle heavy-handed. This is the kind of film that will almost inevitably be caught between independent rock and big-studio hard place: it would benefit from the luxury of more time and care and rewrites and production values, yet is too idiosyncratic (and Shakespearean and musical and gay) to rate a nod from companies able to provide those assets. At that, it evoked more feeling and carried greater significance than a mammoth piece like *Across the Universe*, at perhaps 1 percent of the cost.

In the end, a film like *Were the World Mine* must inspire both gratitude for what it attempts and a frustration different from that with which this chapter opened: the vexation that more bold and quirky musicals, gay or straight, of any or all colors, aren't being attempted. Like *Cabin in the Sky*, to name one, *Were the World Mine* was a film outside much of the mainstream, compromised by what were, at the time of its creation, unavoidable things. That does not negate its achievement nor the accomplishments of most musicals by or for or about

---

[13] It was a nice touch, at any rate, that Sondheim himself made a cameo at the very end, a benign cross between deus ex machina and show-biz Santa.

or in celebration of minorities. Even at their most frivolous, they can be messengers: they make declarations and they deliver major talent, even as it can be exceptionally easy to get annoyed with them for not going far enough. Since the world is never an ideal place, it is generally better to appreciate the good and great things these films do manage to impart, often in spite of daunting odds. As for the annoyance, there will always be far more suitable places where it may be directed. A viewing of *Can't Stop the Music* will vividly bear that out, and fast.

Chapter 12

Put 'Em in a Box

....

L ong decades before people were making grotesque asses of themselves
on reality television, they did so less advertently on a long-running
show called *Candid Camera*. "People caught in the act of being themselves" was the slogan, which translated as commoners and patsies set up and
humiliated while a hidden camera captured it for the world. On one show in
the mid-1960s, the stunt somehow managed to focus on movie musicals—
specifically, what people abhor about them. The premise was simple: what if
real life was like musicals? How would regular people react if some of their
fellows just burst into song? Producer Allen Funt planted his cameras and
mikes in a busy diner somewhere in the New York area and engaged actors to
play waitresses and countermen. The customers, apparently, were real and
unsuspecting, and whenever one came in and placed an order, it would start—
solos and duets and ensembles about the food, about the joy of life in general,
about anything, and with instrumental accompaniment. Unlike many of
Funt's traps and gimmicks, this one was less embarrassing than actively,
weirdly amusing, the customers less annoyed than dazed and flummoxed. It
was as if *The Sound of Music* was trying to sit in a viewer's lap, as witty a way
as any to point out musicals' essential unreality. For neither the first nor last
time, television scored some easy points in its ongoing, co-dependent battle
with musical cinema.

Television had no sooner begun its reign, around 1948 or thereabouts, when it was clear that its extraordinary overlap with film would make for a competitive environment. Each had its own cards to play—TV with its convenience and accessibility and immediacy, movies with quality and production values. How easy it was, around 1950, for movies (radio too) to make sneering putdowns of television, with its drab visuals and amateur-night programming. "That's all television is—nothing *but* auditions," says nasty Addison DeWitt in *All About Eve*, and many of the early shows and performances bore that statement out rigorously. Most of them were live, and in no stage performance would so many people see so many mistakes and dropped lines and props. And still they watched, and bought sets, and increasingly stayed away from movies. With the rise of television and the divestiture of the theater chains, film was given a one-two punch such as to make movies more make-or-break than they had ever been. A big film might still be an event—an *Annie Get Your Gun* very deliberately offered the very things television could not—yet the midrange Hollywood product suffered vastly, musicals more than most.

How well, after all, was musical performance suited to television. People like Kate Smith would be on, singing every weekday, and beginning in 1950 there was Ed Sullivan on Sunday night, always with the most current people. For some, it was akin to the best of a movie musical, the song and variety without the dumb plot scenes in between. Even aside from the regular programming, music could come in insistent form—commercial jingles or a peculiar phenomenon called Snader Telescriptions. These were TV's equivalent of the movies' musical shorts and the grandparents of music video—films of singers or musicians performing one song, shot for use by local stations as fast airtime filler. If, say, a boxing match ended in a fast knockout, up might pop Gale Storm singing "Isn't It Romantic" or even, still playing his guitar long after *Gold Diggers of Broadway*, Nick Lucas. More imposingly, there was the crossover of people like Bob Hope and Dean Martin and Jerry Lewis, as popular on the small screen as on the big. Most pointedly, by 1950, there was the direct competition of musicals themselves. NBC's *Musical Comedy Time* presented live one-hour cutdowns of famous shows, some of which had been filmed (*Louisiana Purchase*) and others not (*Miss Liberty*, *Revenge with Music*). There might not be color or ornate sets and large choruses, but how easy and nice it was to stay home, put on a bathrobe, and sit back to watch the singing comic Bert Wheeler repeating his stage and film role in *Rio Rita*, or Nancy Walker in *Whoopee*, or Jackie Gleason in *No, No, Nanette*. While movies were plusher and prettier, they also were far less convenient.

The film industry reacted predictably—bigger productions and bigger screens and 3-D and sex—and still the encroachment would not go away. What big screen could have been more impressive, after all, than the experience of that live, earth-moving 1953 duet with Ethel Merman and Mary Martin? By 1954 there was color—at least for a tiny percentage—and the big musical productions were being called "spectaculars." Even with the hype, they were indeed good, some of the time. *Lady in the Dark* with Ann Sothern was more faithful to the show than that film had been, and in its way quite better. *Peter Pan* with Mary Martin bypassed film completely, going straight to television, as did Rosalind Russell in *Wonderful Town*. Inevitably, there were new productions as well—a musical *Our Town*, with Frank Sinatra as the Stage Manager introducing "Love and Marriage," packed more punch than the movies Sinatra was making around the same time. Variety shows, too, continued without cease—*Your Hit Parade* and the rest, presently *American Bandstand* and all the other ways young audiences could find their own music. And few films short of *The Ten Commandments* (or, more to the point, *The King and I*) were as much of an event, in early 1957, as Rodgers and Hammerstein's *Cinderella*, starring Julie Andrews. Against all this competition, the demographics of musical film could only shrink. Even some good ones—*The Band Wagon* or *A Star Is Born* or *Les Girls*—would lose large amounts of money, and studios began dropping their contract players left and right. Many of their musical performers ended up going to live theater or, naturally, live television.

By the middle of the 1950s, the dynamic had become even more arresting: old films were now being shown on television. Except for the rare reissue (*GWTW, Snow White, King Kong*) or return engagement, this was the first time in film's history that the bulk of its product did not, in effect, go away and die. At first, in the early 1950s, it was the independently produced films, including a few minor musicals along with any number of westerns and crime films. Then it all started—first RKO, then Columbia and Paramount and Universal and Warner Bros. Finally, MGM, following that first, devastatingly effective network showing of *The Wizard of Oz* in 1956. Old movies, old stars, old musicals, and none of it necessarily optimal on a small screen, which was guaranteed to diminish the effectiveness of spectacle or great cinematography. The color films could look especially weird, the monochrome prints giving the impression that many musicals were set amid epidemics that caused black lips. And, ever, commercials without number and cuts without cease or mercy. Programmers at local TV stations became an especially savage lot after they realized that a 100-minute musical could fit into a 90-minute time slot (including commercials) if songs were deleted.[1]

With all the drawbacks and with TV's undifferentiated aura, the bounty of film being run on TV was staggering. Forgotten titles became magical, and people whose names or reputations had long gone away were suddenly more vivid on TV than ongoing tube personalities like Merv Griffin or Gisele Mac-Kenzie. Maurice Chevalier was only known in the 1950s for being, well, not young anymore—and here he was in *The Love Parade*, rakish and adorable. Deanna Durbin was a fresh teenager, unpretentious and cute and what a singer! Ruby Keeler, by then a retired California housewife and mother, was suddenly young and pretty and, with those loud taps, as endearing as ever. Keeler's demi-Svengali, Busby Berkeley, was the real discovery: even on a small screen those compositions were eye-poppingly unlike anything in the musical cinema of later decades. No wonder a major Berkeley renaissance started in the 1960s.

Films on TV also had their disorienting aspects. The oldest of them seemed so alien, with their obsolete protocols and odd formality, that they enhanced that *Singin' in the Rain* notion of early talkies as a quaintly extinct age with no bearing on anything afterward. Imagine, for instance, falling asleep with the TV on, then, after midnight, waking to find oneself plunged into the arabesques of *The Great Gabbo* or even *Golden Dawn*. Or Warner Bros.' train-wreck revue, *The Show of Shows*, at once akin to current variety shows and at the same time eons away from anything viable. (Plus, in the black-and-white of its original and now-lost Technicolor, so grainy as to seem broadcast from another galaxy.) A *Top Hat* would run one day on Million Dollar Movie—it might even run every day for a week—and it would be smart and crisp, if a shade brittle. Then, the following week, something like *On with the Show!* might turn up, looking like a cave painting. Small wonder that the concept of camp became a fixed notion around this time, with some of these musicals as eager, inadvertent contributors. Newer films on the home screen could have their own problems as well—anything made after 1953 was likely in some sort of widescreen

---

[1] Any avid watcher of movies on TV, from the 1950s to the 1980s, likely has a horror story of things cut out of a musical. Exhibit A: if ever a musical's reputation rests on one big number, that musical is *The Harvey Girls*—and, yes, "On the Atchison, Topeka, and Santa Fe" was cut out of one New Orleans run, circa 1978. Angela Lansbury cued the song and Channel 6 cut to some commercials. When the movie resumed, the train had left the station.

process that could not, in pre-letterbox days, be telecast intact. So a *King and I* or *Gigi* would play on network TV with half its picture missing—panned and scanned, reframed and re-edited. With, it is needless to say, full-to-the-brim interruptions to pitch coffee and cigarettes and toothpaste. The new accessibility and visibility of these films raised the public consciousness in a way that can fairly be called revelatory; the other side of the coin is the extent to which they were vandalized and cheapened. The Lord giveth and taketh.

There was also the plus and minus, in TV's newer programming, of parody. Occasionally, in variety specials or series, there would be mementos or satires of old musicals, done usually with incomprehension and the same condescension such shows would display toward silent film or, for that matter, anything non-sacred. Spoofs were made of operettas and backstagers, and except for Sid Caesar and his team these were jokey and dumb, with insufficient point or specificity or wit. Then, in vivid contrast, came Carol Burnett. With her talented castmates and writers and costumer Bob Mackie, Burnett arguably did more than anyone else in television to keep old musicals alive before the start of the home video age. She wasn't only a transcendent comedian and fine singer and gifted mimic—she was a movie buff who could brag on just how many times, during a stint as a movie palace usher, she had seen Doris Day in *On Moonlight Bay*. Where other programs were vague in their targets, Burnett went in for detail and concision. She and her cohorts could be simultaneously respectful and wicked toward the likes of "Sonja Honey" or "Hester Williams" or, on one epic occasion, a sidesplitting iteration called *The Doily Sisters*. She was assured enough to tread even on the hallowest ground with a spot-on replay of Judy Garland's tremulous emotionalism, as well as a mean, hilarious riff on *That's Entertainment, Part II* which featured yesteryear's stars coming back as saggy and senile travesties of their young selves. Surely there were few people in the mid-1970s, at least outside of gay bars, who had much recollection of Joan Crawford's *Torch Song*—but Burnett did, with a bushy-eyebrowed takeoff so sharp that it infuriated Crawford herself. Best of all, Burnett and her associates knew that these films had been loved, and that now, frayed as their edges might be, they were still worth the time and the respect, even the devotion.

Awareness and respect of a vastly different sort kicked in around 1980 with the nearly simultaneous rise of home video and cable television. Old musicals, especially the classics, were now available on VHS tape (Beta and videodisc too, for a while), either to be rented or, for the voracious and acquisitive, bought. Many of the classics from the Freed Unit were soon released, as were

Something for the boys: Vicki Lawrence and Carol Burnett, entertaining the troops as "The Doily Sisters." *The Dolly Sisters* offered such an abundance of material that this was the only movie parody, in the entire history of *The Carol Burnett Show*, to run a full hour. Even the "Forties doing World War I" hairdos were spot-on.

the Astaire/Rogers oeuvre and some of the others. One could watch "Good Morning" or "The Carioca" over and over, or fast forward through the duller plot scenes of a *Follow the Fleet* to get to the gold of "Let's Face the Music and Dance." Finally, it was no longer about staying up for a 2 A.M. Late Show run, even as such became more doable with home VCRs with timers. While there were many elusive titles that weren't released and no longer turned up on TV, availability was such as it had never been before, albeit with widescreen films still only in that wretched pan-and-scan form.

Around this same time came the birth of MTV, and a few years later VH1, in which new music and (relatively) fresh or gifted performers were spotlighted in mini-productions of variable creativity. Sometimes the imagination and craft could be breathtaking, just as the cynicism could, often enough, be quite numbing. The editing became ever quicker, the sexism could be borderline appalling, and the steals or homages from old movies were numerous and sometimes clever. Logically enough, it all marked the approximate time when singing became less an end in itself than a component of presentation, and when live performances began to resemble film instead of the other way around. With a performer of modest vocal gifts like Madonna, music videos were a godsend, an inestimable cornucopia of image and reinvention and an opportunity to channel divas past. "Material Girl" was a knowing recreation of both the style and substance of the Marilyn Monroe–Jack Cole "Diamonds Are a Girl's Best Friend," both sassy (which Madonna usually was) and witty (which she sometimes attempted to be). If it made younger spectators a bit fuzzy on the divergences between Monroe and Madonna, it also served as a signpost to older work that, even for jaded kids, might be worth a visit. It also led the way to more reborn reimaginings, and sometimes the actual icons themselves would turn up in clips or recycled appearances. If Paula Abdul wanted to do a "Singin' in the Rain" knockoff alongside the original Gene Kelly routine, technology could make it happen. For better and worse, for respect and cannibalization, the art of popular musical performance was being irretrievably altered. Often, at least, it was to the good, not least because the newer stuff sometimes made some of the older work seem more germane.

There were also periodic returns to the 1950s idea of televised versions of Broadway shows, which had otherwise faded away by the mid-1970s. While many were straightforward stage productions, as on PBS's *Great Performances,* there were also some specially created works to take up some of the slack for all the things big-screen film was failing to do, just as *The Muppet Show* thrived when other variety shows were tanking. Less expectedly, given the time, there was the 1993 CBS-TV film of *Gypsy,* starring Bette Midler, which gained nearly as much attention, with possibly more acclaim, as it would have in movie theaters. Contractually mandated to be completely faithful to the original script, it was competently done, suitably cast, and in certain ways a kind of atonement for a film version that had angered the show's fiercer partisans. Nevertheless, the good ratings and Midler's awards could not keep it from following the same path that so often plagues modern musicals: little or no follow-up. For a while there was fanciful talk of a Cher *Mame,* then a long silence as network television began to cede its creative primacy to cable channels and commence a long and lucrative fascination with the notion of glorified game-shows known as reality programming.

Was it inevitable, or simply shrewd, that musical performance became one of the most sacred aspects of reality TV? For tens of millions who loved karaoke and had forgotten or never seen *The Original Amateur Hour*, *American Idol* became a national obsession. Nobodies with good voices, or wannabes with no voices at all—anyone might be given the chance to make or break on a national stage, then be judged by both experts (Paula Abdul once again) and a fiercely partisan general public. It was *42nd Street* for the post-modern age, contrived and silly and, for many, mesmerizing, with its interchangeably loud power ballads and occasional odd re-dos of older standards. Here, suddenly, were instant stars and, quite promptly, fast has-beens, and the outreach was such that it managed to embrace twenty-first-century film as well. Two of the show's more telegenic contestants, winner Kelly Clarkson and finalist Justin Guarini, were starred in *From Justin to Kelly*, as astute and rapturously received and financially successful a musical as *Glitter*. Far, far more viable was the fate of an *American Idol* also-ran, Jennifer Hudson, whose performance in *Dreamgirls* and subsequent Academy Award delineated the gulf between momentary fame and solid achievement. Even here, though, some fanatics saw Hudson's Oscar as a consolation prize for not winning the top *Idol* slot: such is the looking-glass world of popular culture in the twenty-first century.

More expensive, if not as lucrative, were the more conventional musicals still making it to television: an entertainingly multicultural remake of *Cinderella*; expedient and often-undercast re-dos of *South Pacific* and *Bye Bye Birdie* and *The Music Man*; an adequate third TV version of *Once upon a Mattress*; a remake of *Annie* that turned out so well that its director, Rob Marshall, was able to move on to *Chicago*. Along with these, prompted by the briefly sensational *Allie McBeal*, was the phenomenon of special "musical" episodes of TV series—mostly sitcoms, always meta-commentative, and few ever reaching such delirious levels as *The Simpsons*'s hysterically astute parody of *Mary Poppins* or its musical version of *A Streetcar Named Desire*. Then, from out of virtually nowhere, came a pair of smash Disney Channel trifles graced with the generic titles *High School Musical* and *High School Musical 2*. These were as energetically flimsy as they sounded—*Grease* for the cell-phone generation— and suddenly teenage girls (and a few boys too, especially the kind who grow up to revere Sondheim) were swooning over the same clichés that had enchanted their ancestors back in the days of *Sunny Side Up*. While the characters were the sketchiest cartoons and the echoes of earlier films were less homage than theft, this pair, plus the big-screen third entry, was as exactly right for its time as *Rio Rita* or *The Sound of Music* had been for theirs. The same formulas can work over and over as long as the chemicals are up for a slight remix.

When *Glee* started, it was as if all those musical sitcom episodes had cross-pollinated with the better parts of *High School Musical*, plus such teen-angst fare as *My So-Called Life*. At a time when high school glee clubs seemed about as current as hula hoops or "Just Say No" buttons, producer Ryan Murphy came up with something irresistibly new by—the persistence of history, once again—going all the way back to *The Broadway Melody* and *Babes in Arms*.[2] Instead of the talented unknowns played by Bessie Love or Mickey Rooney, there were the sweetly self-directed Rachel and the unapologetically gay Kurt. Regional competitions took the place of big-time theater or vaudeville, and the smarmy stage-door Johnny types gave way to the hilariously evil cheerleader coach Sue Sylvester. Modest little song routines would, Berkeley-style, turn into the most polished extravaganzas, mainly set to current or recent pop hits, plus a smattering of classics. Meanwhile, the characters would have their greater or lesser traumas and amours, acquiring various lessons on life and hormonal restraint along with musical polish. For a while, in its early episodes, it seemed the most bracing kind of update possible, an adolescent *Chicago* with almost as much talent as exuberance. The cast, of newcomers and a few pros, seemed to have ability nearly without limit, with an occasional guest like Gwyneth Paltrow also demonstrating definite, sometimes unexpected, aptitude. Not everyone was taken with it, not an unexpected reaction given that it was more musical and more gay than had ever been seen in series television.[3]

As with all fast-hitting series, the decline of *Glee*, when it came, was inevitable, fueled by simple repetition, over-familiarity, and—most crucially—too narrow a window onto the musical past. (Also real tragedy, in the form of the sudden death of cast member Cory Monteith.) It was understandable that the show would seldom reach far back into the lore of theater or film; the rare

---

[2] There was also a singular TV ancestor to be invoked: the fast-canceled, visionary *Cop Rock*. Yes, it was silly and deserved most of the jokes made at the time. More to the point, it was far too off-kilter to succeed in a time of literal police dramas—and more ingenious and daring than just about any other kind of musical on film or TV in 1990.

[3] A foul tweet about *Glee* from Bret Easton Ellis was a sad corrective to the notion that things have indeed gotten consistently better. It was the opinion of the *American Psycho* auteur that while *Glee* was a good enough show, watching it was akin to stepping "into a puddle of HIV." Sometimes the bad old days are neither forgotten nor gone.

performance of something like "Puttin' on the Ritz" was more a surprise than anything else, without real framing or context. When the kids would mount an entire show, it was most frequently the simplest, most superficial kind of bubblegum: *Rocky Horror* or *Grease*. Even Rachel's ongoing deification of Barbra Streisand was erratically presented—Lea Michele's full-bore rendition of "Don't Rain on My Parade" could only be diminished by having the *exact* same musical arrangement and intonations Streisand had used in the *Funny Girl* film. All of this pointed, unfortunately, to an abrogation of responsibility: instead of setting trends, *Glee* was as content to follow them as all those nobodies on *American Idol*. It might be necessary, for example, to show that these kids' musical sensibilities had been formed in part from their exposure to the trifling oeuvre of Britney Spears—yet there was no irony to be had, no indication that the success of someone like Spears might be a triumph of the meagerest sort, style blatantly lacking substance. And there were two entire shows devoted to her music! By the fourth season, the well of inspiration had become sufficiently thin for there to be excessive devotion to viral Internet ephemera like "Gangnam Style." While this may have been true to the narrow repertorial options of a real glee club in Lima, Ohio, on a show with this much potential and so many noble possible sources it was small and coarse. The best of *Glee* honored its antecedents by bringing their attainments into a new century and toward a new audience; the worst of it trashed its past, less through disrespect than by simple expedience, a short attention span, and a lack of awareness. That's television.

   Glee, loved and loathed, had sufficient success to draw some inevitable emulation. Thus was produced *Smash*, an even more specific throwback to the *42nd Street*s of a prior century. It was, in fact, the most detailed backstage saga witnessed by a large audience since *On with the Show!* or *The Band Wagon*: genuine if phony show-must-go-on stuff with back-stabbing and financial woes and talented understudies and, most bracingly, new and often fresh songs, many of them by the same Marc Shaiman whose work had been such a wonder in the *South Park* movie. Certainly, the pretext of a musical about Marilyn Monroe was grindingly unimaginative and the foundation was so wobbly that the show started to be in major trouble from early episodes onward, its second-season cancellation seen as only slightly less inevitable than a sunset. Contributing to the crash, surely, were some cartoon plot turns, fake attempts at relevance, and some *Glee*-like excess that turned a trip to an Indian restaurant into a deranged Bollywood extravaganza. (Three redundant words, granted.)

Fortunately, there was also in evidence a crisp, heritage-minded professionalism that could sometimes make outrageous details at least momentarily plausible. At one point, the show even found time for a moving kind of torch-passing: Walter Huston had introduced "September Song" on Broadway, and three-quarters of a century later on *Smash*, his granddaughter Anjelica performed it in a sweetly tentative voice and a complete awareness of how nicely history can operate when it is well attended and wisely heeded.

In the eternally recycling maw that is television, nothing lasts, save possibly in boxed sets. Big musical productions, once a mainstay, have gone from live to tape to film to digital and streaming, and now rarely occur save as halftime or awards shows or Pay-Per-View concerts. (The unevenly cast live *Sound of Music*, in 2013, was a major and highly rated exception.) The Internet has appropriated much of the slack and energy from music videos, leaving cable stations like MTV and VH1 to the gauche detritus of reality programming and jaded game shows. Variety shows, which once seemed permanent, suddenly vanished, just as westerns and miniseries and competition shows and the *Glee*s and *Smash*es can and do all pass away. Not even the old movie musicals run on TV anymore, with the fortunate exception (and imaginative programming) of Turner Classic Movies. Technology and climate and people move on and change, and still it is the nature of both physics and art that very little has truly vanished entirely. Musicals, remember, are blessed with an immutable bottom line: on television and most especially on film, they are permanent, for all their seeming flimsiness, and the best they give is genuinely irreplaceable. No matter how much they are neglected and misunderstood, or copied or deployed inappropriately, they somehow manage to survive. To console, to mentor, to exhilarate. For those who allow themselves to connect with them, they can serve on any level ranging from junk food to antidepressants, and then on to oases and even houses of worship. Sometimes they can seem extinct on movie screens, and often on television as well and, really, that's just part of their act. Illusion, after all, is something musicals can do extremely well. Better, in fact, than anything or anyone else.

Epilogue
Dream Dancing

....

In 1977, before *The Wiz* opened, there was a great deal of talk and speculation about its being the film to bring back musicals.

In 1980, before *Xanadu* opened, there was a great deal of talk and speculation about its being the film to bring back musicals.

In 1986, before *A Chorus Line* opened, there was a great deal of talk...etc.

In 1996, before *Evita* opened, ...etc. etc.

In 2002, before *Chicago* opened, there was a great deal of talk and speculation about its being the film to bring back musicals. This time, for a while, it happened.

In 2012, before *Les Misérables* opened, there was a great deal of talk about its use of live singing. There was next to no speculation about its bringing musicals back.

The film version of *Les Misérables* was as close to roadshow as could be possible in an age of multiplex and digital projection. It had a theatrical pedigree of exhaustive longevity, literary pretentions, an Oscar-winning director, an extended running time, a starry cast, and that indefinable air of "prestige" previously encountered in works as successful as *My Fair Lady* and as disastrous as *Porgy and Bess*. As with *Chicago*, it was produced on a careful budget that was about one-third the size of most superhero extravaganzas, and if the response did not reach the *Sound of Music* stratosphere, it was, by all standards, a major worldwide hit.

As the makers of *A Chorus Line* or *The Phantom of the Opera* could attest, an enormously popular show does not necessarily make for a financially successful movie. *Les Miz* was, obviously, unlike them in that regard. Both its profitability and the passion of its adherents might seem to be an extremely good indicator that more musicals, hopefully worthy and lucrative ones, might follow. Unfortunately, the great success of *Les Miz* has always operated in the realm of extreme idiosyncrasy. It did, and does, stand alone. It operates outside of accepted trends and does not offer emulative paths. (The closest equivalent is *Miss Saigon*, from the same creators, and it would not have its predecessor's staying power.) In its English-language version—greatly expanded from the original oratorio-like French incarnation—*Les Miz* was, in subject matter and cast and effect, a big show. It was, in fact, a modern, more serious, operetta. Much of its phenomenal success came from that very size, or more properly from the way its size connected with its big tunes and emotions. So suavely did it accomplish its intentions that millions of people who would not be caught dead at an opera were swept along by a piece with no spoken dialogue. For them, it came to define musical drama. For others, it seemed less compelling than self-important, its musicality less of lyricized Victor Hugo than of insistent pomposity and, even, facile sludge. It was, in fact, as polarizing a show as any in the history of musical theater—and the film continued this *Sound of Music* divide with commendable alacrity. Many who found most musicals trivial were riveted by its seriousness and passion, especially as embodied by Anne Hathaway's extraordinary commitment, which extended to a harrowing head-shaving that was as onscreen-real as the singing. On the con side, for many who traditionally loved musicals, there was in *Les Miz* a great deal of hype and bustle and noise, plus such add-ons as a relentless hand-held camera, a *Camelot*-like reliance on close-ups, and a fine actor, Russell Crowe, without a proper singing voice. For those many adherents observed leaving movie theaters in tears, these were, conversely, pros rather than cons. (Crowe excepted.) In a larger sense, in what might be termed the cavalcade of historical continuity, there was far less of a substantial nature.

Musical as it was, successful as it was, *Les Miz* operated solely in its own sphere. It would have few if any imitators, it could not be hawked at Comic-Con, and it had no potential connected to that voracious be-all of twenty-first-century entertainment: franchise. There would not be a *Les Miz 2: The Survivors* or *Fantine: The Early Years*. Nor would it be equipped to function as a *Sound of Music* bellwether for musical trends, spurring on many others. The truth about

Les Miz could perhaps be detected in all those news reports extolling the bravery of its live singing as if it were a cinematic innovation. Many musicals—including *all* of them, back in the earliest time—had used on-set performance, just as previous works had dealt with history, tragedy, large emotions, and a large canvas. The fact that many thought *Les Miz* innovative in any of those particulars attested less to taste than to convenient enthusiasms, the eagerness to embrace the hard work of likable performers, and the disposability, in many twenty-first-century views, of older film.[1] "The single greatest musical of all time!" was the overreaching claim of some myopic reviews, and of course it was not so. The unfortunate fact is that film, in this present day, is not positioned to follow the tenets of musical film as listed earlier in these pages. The only history *Les Miz* adds to, or learns from, is that of commercial endeavor—a hugely successful show that became a hugely popular movie, money begetting money. Otherwise, the historical grasp, the learning from antecedents, is negligible. This is not the fault of *Les Misérables* specifically, nor does it slight its achievement or the love given it by millions of partisans. It is, instead, a reflection of the nature of film in the second decade of a new century, with its permanent-yet-disposable character, its steady misconstrual of history, and the fact that the art of the musical plays a small and extraneous and marginal role in the way contemporary film functions.

An acclaimed director like Quentin Tarantino will derive inspiration and material from groups and genres of film previously held to be so disreputable that they are still informally known by pejorative names: spaghetti westerns, blaxploitation, chop-socky. In Tarantino's hands, the old tropes are reconstituted, commented upon, transformed, and in the process acquire a one-off respectability. Musicals, on the other hand, exist in brackets. Many years ago, major directors had stabs at Tarantino-esque musical reinvention—Scorsese with *New York New York*, Coppola with *One from the Heart*—with little success and no ongoing implication, and there has been little since then. Transformation, where musicals are concerned, is not necessarily impossible, but it is so extraordinarily difficult that even latter-day masters have trouble doing it. Bob

---

[1] One case in point, among many: that 2011 Oscar sensation *The Artist*. Engaging and even beautiful in many ways, it also had a vast misunderstanding of much of the time and history it was attempting to depict. And, crucially, it was received by an uncomprehending public completely unconversant with the greatness of silent film, the true nature of the transition to sound, and the nature of early movie musicals. What could have been a devastating tribute and recollection ended up, instead, a genial flight of fancy. C'est la vie.

Fosse had no true follow-up to *Cabaret*, and Rob Marshall should not have followed up *Chicago* with *Nine*.

In its own, hyper-aware way, *Chicago* had reflected and respected its past, just as a stage show like Stephen Sondheim's *Follies* (probably the single greatest show to not be filmed) intertwines yesterday and today with harsh brio. Unfortunately, popular cinema has little inclination for such resonance. The ahistorical demeanor of *Les Misérables* was one of the reasons it succeeded—along with its being, on several levels, so nonescapist a piece of escapism. Diversion, after all, ain't what it used to be. Violent action sequences, relentless digital effects, even extended riffs on flatulence—all are the modern production numbers that have taken the place of *American in Paris* ballets or "Do-Re-Mi." Too much has happened in the world and in the audience for things to be otherwise. A culture that can flourish on work that merits the adjective "dystopian" will not produce anyone on the order of Julie Andrews.

Except. Except. . . . Musicals don't die, not even when neglected or lampooned or laminated or willfully misunderstood. In no way will *Les Misérables* be the last, just as *Glee* and *Smash* will hardly remain television's final comment. More is possible, more has been planned and announced, and more will happen. Remakes of older works—especially shows that weren't filmed right the first time—are inevitable, and it is at very least reasonable to expect, or hope, that some of them will get major things right. If they do not do so, the public will know; when they do pull it off, they will join the A list with the greats. There will ever be at very least the possibility of capable performers, gifted writers and composers, decent material, perhaps even directors of talent who are conversant with the names Mamoulian and Minnelli. It will never again be as it once was, and it should not be: in that "was" time there was much dreck, alongside too much fine work treated far too casually. Will there ever again be a *Swing Time*? Likely not, and there should not be. Nor will there be another Chevalier or Streisand or Kelly or Waters or even Grable. Nor another "Lullaby of Broadway" or "On the Atchison, Topeka, and the Santa Fe." Only one is possible, except in the case of the Nicholas Brothers. These films and these moments and these people were wonderful, and their contributions—the ways in which they matter—are such that their existence need not simply be framed in the past tense. The circumstances that helped them to occur and to thrive are gone, and yet their effect is such that they endure and continue, readily available to serve as hope and indication and inspiration. If *The Wizard of Oz* is not proof of these things, nothing is.

"As sentimental as *Little Women*": Such was *Time*'s assessment of the final scene of *The Wizard of Oz*. For sure, many Ozians have been known to weep when Judy/Dorothy says that last line. Why not, then, give the final bow to Judy Garland, and to Ray Bolger, Jack Haley, Clara Blandick, Frank Morgan, Charley Grapewin, and Bert Lahr? And, though they're not seen here, Billie Burke, Margaret Hamilton, and Toto too.

One of the beauties of a work like *Singin' in the Rain* is that it makes it possible to think past that rueful attitude of "They don't make 'em like that anymore." No, they don't, and can't and won't. Yet, as long as they can be seen and loved, they can be learned from. They can indicate opportunities and paths. The surroundings and contexts change, as do the people on both sides of the screen; and even with all that, some fundamental and everlasting truths remain. There will always be diversion, there will always be music, and there will always be a need to express and live beyond the ordinary confines of mundane communication. This is where musicals come in, at least when they are doing their job. When people of wisdom and talent know how to deploy everything they've received from them, musicals can still be great and precious. In the meantime, their loony, magnificent cornucopia bounty remains to entice and beguile and stimulate. Nor can cynicism deflate them, not even when it seems, once again, that they're the tree falling in the forest that no one hears. They are still heard, and they're still there, passing along "Isn't It Romantic?" through the countryside or dancing to "Singin' in the Rain" despite that downpour or mocking the razzle-dazzle of the judicial system or blaming Canada. Plus all the other things they can do. They've had their times in the sun and out of it, and they keep surviving. Their absence is always temporary, their heritage is everlasting, and they do it without making it look hard, even in heels. They transform themselves without losing their identities, they bless and sustain without losing their sense of humor, they find ways to thrill and annoy and captivate, often all at the same time. In their past and in our present, they've given more than can be comprehended, and the esteem they have earned is at points beyond measure. To repay them with simple, heartfelt gratitude is not nearly enough, but let it serve for the moment. Thanks for the memory.

Acknowledgments

....

Neither musicals nor books about them occur in a vacuum. If the creation of this book did not have precisely the collaborative spirit of a *Wizard of Oz*, it did depend, immensely so, on the help and advice and feedback and opinions of others. To which please add: care, physical and emotional feeding, love, support, stress relief, sympathy, prayers, and humor. My humble and heartfelt thanks, then, to all who offered insight and counsel and shared thoughts and suggestions and provided encouragement and sustenance. With the full knowledge that I am forgetting to mention a name or two, for which I apologize in advance, I must mention the following friends, family, colleagues and institutions.

My gratitude must first extend all the way to Rio de Janeiro, where the fantastically helpful Aureo Chiesse Brandão spent an extraordinary amount of time and effort to support this project, especially from the standpoint of illustrations. Image matters as much as sound in these films, and Aureo's contributions in this area have been unstinting, inspiring, and deeply appreciated.

Closer to home, there are my wise and ever-caring and perceptive friends and associates in New York City: Joseph Gallagher, Marc Miller, Moshe Bloxenheim, Steven Lowenthal, Eric Spilker, Edward and Mary Atwood Maguire, Karen Hartman, Joe McElhany, John and Roseann Forde, Adele Greene, Bob Gutowski, Matthew Kiernan, Rick Scheckman, Kirk de Gooyer, Connie Coddington, Marie Moser, Glen Leiner, Joseph Radon, Edward Walters, John

Canemaker and Joe Kennedy, Ataman and Jayne Burt Ozyildirim, Brian Gaud-ino, Vince Giordano, Bruce Goldstein, Scott Levine. In New Jersey: Ron Hutchinson and all those who make The Vitaphone Project a fantastic organization; and Bill Grant, my wellspring of sense and support, and his family. In Connecticut, two terrific couples: Lou and Sue Sabini, and Chip Reed and Chris Fray. In New York State: the Reverend Amy Gregory and Bill Phillips, Jay Blotcher and Brook Garrett, James Layton, Jack Theakston, and Gerry Orlando and the entire membership of the marvelous Syracuse Cinephile Society. In Pennsylvania: Beverly and Payson Burt, Kristin and Payson "Hank" and Lilea Burt, Laurie and Bill and Will and Drew Baltrus, Janet Kovacs, Phyllis Priester, David Litofsky, Jay Schwarz. In Washington, DC, and environs: Dwight Blocker Bowers, Dorothy Green, Jenny Paxson, Karen Deppa, and Charlie Green. In Atlanta: Lee Tsiantis, Dennis Millay, and Christopher Connelly and James Goodwyne. In Massachusetts: Richard Finegan and Ralph Celentano. In California: Marty Kearns and Ken Richardson, Debra Levine (bravo Jack Cole!), Marilee Bradford and Jon Burlingame, Robert McKay, Michael Schlesinger, Peter Fitzgerald, George Feltenstein, David Chierichetti, Andrew Masullo. In Texas: Karen Latham Everson and her family. In Sweden: Jonas Nordin. In Australia: Paul Brennan. In the United Kingdom: old friends Diane Allen and the Reverend Francesca Rhys, and Andrew Henderson. And, of course, a loving call-out to my entire Louisiana family: my one-and-only-and-wonderful sister, the Reverend Peggy Foreman; Jared and Meredith and Luke and Andrew and Nathan and Zachary Foreman; my brothers in all but a technical sense, the Reverend Ned Pitre, Keith Matherne and Spencer Gauthreaux; Belle and Denise and David Thibodeaux, Keith Caillouet, Audrey Turner, Annette Autin Champagne, Diana Cangemi, Darren Guin, and all my relatives and dear friends and classmates of long and loving standing. Many others also, of course, and my thanks to them and you all.

With sadness and with love, I acknowledge the recent loss of some wonderful friends and family: Earl Carter, Henry Fera, Vince Vitale, Albert Wood, Patricia Rothrock, James "Jimmy" Barrios, Jerry Crowe, Ruth Woodruff, Jean Lococo, Marietta Sabini, Loretta Haddad, Amy Breaux. They have left, and yet in my work and my mind and heart they are never gone.

Since I wrote that first edition of *A Song in the Dark* back in the early-mid-1990s, the availability of films and information has been massively transformed. With the Internet and DVD and YouTube and all the attendant resources, reams of film and background and commentary have been placed within the reach of nearly anyone. This can only be considered cause for celebration—yet I must offer the most heartfelt appreciation to the libraries and archives that hold the prime sources of the films themselves (on *real* film, yet), the original documents, and much more: the Library of Congress, the Margaret Herrick Library of the Academy of Motion Picture Arts and Sciences, the UCLA Library, and especially the Film and Television Archive, the Doheny Library at the University of Southern California, the Museum of Modern Art, the George Eastman House, the Museum of Radio and Television, the British Film Institute. Also, I salute and thank the other archives and libraries outside the United States and around the world, including those whose uncatalogued holdings will no doubt keep turning up some hitherto lost treasures.

Naturally, many rounds of applause must be directed to my editor, Norman Hirschy, whose perception and circumspection and persistence and rigorous good sense were instrumental—not to mention crucial—in making this project come into being. And my sincere gratitude also to Joellyn Ausanka, Lisbeth Redfield, and everyone at Oxford University Press whose work and help caused *Dangerous Rhythm* to be a real and concrete thing.

Finally, I must offer a few words of appreciation to all the people who have spoken and written to me about my previous books, *A Song in the Dark* and *Screened Out*, and about my work on DVD and television. Your words and good wishes have sustained and heartened me more than I can ever say. This book is, quite appropriately, dedicated to my father, but it is truly for all of you as well. Thank you and—to those of you cited (or unmentioned!) here—God bless you all, and bravo.

Richard Barrios
Pennsylvania,
December 2013

Source Notes

....

Introduction: All That Jazz

10 "They Both Reached for the Gun." *New York Times*, March 23, 2003.

Chapter 1: Everything's Been Done Before

17 *New York Times* editorial on Vitaphone, August 8, 1926.

26 Marilyn Monroe and *Pink Tights*: various Monroe biographers have recounted the genesis of this project. An elaborate and optimistic pre-production ad for *Pink Tights* may be seen in James Robert Parish, *The Fox Girls* (New Rochelle: Arlington House, 1971), p. 608.

Chapter 2: Where Do They Come From (and Where Do They Go?)

37 *The Desert Song*: I am grateful to Scott Levine and Andrew Masullo for their graphic reactions to this fascinating film.

39 "Something different..." Sentiments to this effect, by such publications as *Film Daily* and the *New York Post*, appeared in a digest of reviews of *The Desert Song* printed in *Film Daily*, July 1, 1929.

55 *Chicago*: Among the critics voicing objections to the film, perhaps the most eloquent was Margo Jefferson, "*Chicago* and the Future of the Movie Musical," *New York Times*, February 28, 2003.

Chapter 3: Seeing's Believing

57 "I have nothing," Billy Wilder: quoted in Ed Sikov, *On Sunset Boulevard: The Life and Times of Billy Wilder* (New York: Hyperion, 1998), p. 470.

57 Shirley MacLaine on Wilder's aversion to musicals: *Private Screenings* interview with Robert Osborne, Turner Classic Movies, 2003.

62 *Song of the Flame*: As with a number of early musicals, this is a lost film. However, the soundtrack survives, as does (in the Warner Bros. collection at USC) a transcription of the dialogue and lyrics.

63 *Madam Satan* and DeMille's bosses: Robert S. Birchard, *Cecil B. DeMille's Hollywood* (Lexington: University Press of Kentucky), p. 246.

75 "After *Cabaret*...": Pauline Kael, "Grinning," *The New Yorker*, February 19, 1972.

76 *Moulin Rouge!*: "The horror" comment was made to the author by a confidential source.

76 *Chicago*: The circumstances surrounding the deletion of "Class" are recalled by Rob Marshall in the audio commentary on the DVD; the number itself is also on the DVD.

Chapter 4: People

80 "Long shots": *Photoplay*, October 1926.

84 "My gosh..." Fred Astaire, *Steps in Time* (New York: Harper, 1959), p. 183.

93 "Saint Dorothy": *The New Yorker*, October 30, 1978.

94 Dorothy Lamour: Ms. Lamour starred in Coward's *Fallen Angels* in 1974 at the Beverly Dinner Theater in New Orleans.

Chapter 5: The Art of the Possible

106 *Kismet*: Although other sources have said that Stanley Donen took over the film after Minnelli's departure, the film's star, Ann Blyth, recalled that it was Richard Thorpe. Interviewed by Robert Osborne at the TCM Classic Film Festival, April 2013.

107 Arthur Freed's output: Hugh Fordin, *The World of Entertainment: Hollywood's Greatest Musicals* (Garden City, NY: Doubleday, 1975) offers an extensive history of Freed's career as a producer.

109 "Never make...": numerous sources in print and online have attributed this quote to Pasternak without giving its precise source. It appears, for example in Jeanine Basinger, *The Star Machine* (New York: Alfred A. Knopf, 2007), p. 270.

112 Jack Cole: I am particularly grateful to Debra Levine for her meticulous research on, and well-placed enthusiasm for, Cole. Her essays may be found at artsmeme.com.

115 "She could do…": quoted in John Kobal, *People Will Talk* (New York: Alfred A. Knopf, 1985), p. 597

116 "A story told…": quoted in David Denby, "Cutups," *The New Yorker*, May 28, 2001.

118 "Imitation Lubitsch…": Andrew Sarris, *The American Cinema: Directors and Directions 1929–1968* (New York: Dutton, 1968), p. 161. This assessment comes under the heading of "Less Than Meets the Eye."

Chapter 6: Music Makes Me

120 "Over the Rainbow": accounts of the song's near-deletion have appeared in numerous works. The best-researched account, and the source of the Mervyn LeRoy quote, is in John Fricke, Jay Scarfone, and William Stillman, *The Wizard of Oz: The Official 50th Anniversary Pictorial History* (New York: Warner Books, 1989), p. 118.

121 "When you're doing": Harold Arlen, quoted in Lewis B. Funke, "Arlen the Tunesmith," *New York Times*, July 4, 1943.

125 *Lady in the Dark*: The fate of "My Ship" is recounted in David Chierichetti, *Mitchell Leisen: Hollywood Director* (Los Angeles: Photoventures Press, 1995), p. 179.

125 Songwriters: For a detailed early account of the nature of their work, see "Westward the Course of Tin-Pan Alley," *Photoplay*, September 1929.

129 "Sweet Leilani": Mason Wiley and Damien Bona, *Inside Oscar: The Unofficial History of the Academy Awards* (New York: Ballantine Books, 1988), pp. 81, 88.

130 "Thanks for the Memory": Chierichetti, *Mitchell Leisen*, pp. 110–11.

136 Berlin and "Cheek to Cheek": Laurence Bergreen, *As Thousands Cheer: The Life of Irving Berlin* (New York: Viking, 1990), pp. 344–45.

Chapter 7: With Plenty of Money

Many of the financial figures in this chapter come from two sources: for the Warner Bros figures, the William Schaefer ledger, in the Schaefer collection at the Doheny Library, University of Southern California; and the Eddie Mannix (MGM) ledger, at the Margaret Herrick Library of the Academy of Motion Picture Arts and Sciences. Additional figures are to be found in Donald Crafton, *The Talkies: American Cinema's Transition to Sound 1926–1931* (Berkeley: University of California Press, 1997), pp. 547–52; Aubrey Solomon, *Twentieth Century-Fox: A Corporate and Financial History* (Lanham, MD: Scarecrow Press, 2002), pp. 216–60; Mark A. Vieira, *Sin in Soft Focus: Pre-Code Hollywood* (New York: Harry N. Abrams, 1999), pp. 220–21; Boxofficemojo.com; and the Internet Movie Database (IMDB.com).

139 "I want quality…" quoted in Mark Vieira, *Irving Thalberg: Boy Wonder to Producer Prince* (Berkeley: University of California Press, 2010), p. 91.

143 *Dancing Lady*: frequent citations have been given of its status as the model MGM commercial product. A detailed study of its production (including the saga of "Everything I Have Is Yours") is given in Ronald Haver, *David O. Selznick's Hollywood* (New York: Alfred A. Knopf, 1980), pp. 136–48.

144 "In its era...": Esther Williams with Digby Diehle, *The Million Dollar Mermaid* (New York: Simon & Schuster, 1999), p. 117.

149 *The March of Time*: there is an extensive account of this unique disaster in this author's *A Song in the Dark: The Birth of the Musical Film*, 2nd ed. (New York: Oxford University Press, 2009), pp. 326–30.

152 John Gregory Dunne, *The Studio* (New York: Random House, 1969).

Chapter 8: I Get the Neck of the Chicken

156 "Did Lucille Ball...": Pauline Kael, "A Brash Young Man," *The New Yorker*, March 11, 1974.

157 *Captain of the Guard*: A report of the Canadian/French controversy was given in *Variety*, April 16, 1930.

157 *A Song in the Dark*: see review in the *New York Times*, June 29, 1995.

158 *Paint Your Wagon*: a history of this film's genesis may be found in James Robert Parish, *Fiasco: A History of Hollywood's Iconic Flops* (Hoboken, NJ: John Wiley, 2006), pp. 61–79.

167 *Porgy and Bess*: see A. Scott Berg, *Goldwyn: A Biography* (New York: Alfred A. Knopf, 1989), pp. 478–88. Special thanks to Lee Tsiantis, Corporate Legal Manager at Turner Broadcasting System, Inc., for helping to clarify the tangled status that has prevented this film's exhibition.

Chapter 9: Turn on the Heat

174 *The Broadway Melody*: for a report of the enthusiasm greeting this film, and Bessie Love's performance in particular, see Herbert Howe, "The Girl Who Walked Back," *Photoplay*, May 1929.

176 *Gigi*: detailed accounts of its production can be found in Fordin, *The World of Entertainment*, pp. 453–95, and Stephen Harvey, *Directed by Vincente Minnelli* (New York: Museum of Modern Art, 1989), pp. 139–48.

186 *Singin' in the Rain*: see Fordin, *The World of Entertainment*, pp. 347–62, for an especially helpful recounting of this film's creation, especially as regards the standpoint of Arthur Freed. Also, see Earl J. Hess and Pratibha Dabholkar, *Singin' in the Rain: The Making of an American Classic* (Lawrence: University Press of Kansas, 2010).

Chapter 10: Painting the Clouds

198 *The Little Mermaid*: "Under the Sea" ovations were a frequent occurrence, including at an opening-night screening attended by the author in San Francisco, November 17, 1989.

Chapter 11: Under My Skin

209 *Cabin in the Sky*: the entire "Ain't It the Truth" number, with vocals by Armstrong, Horne, and chorus, may be found on the Turner Classic Movies/Rhino soundtrack, for which producer Marilee Bradford contributed helpful and extensive liner notes.

215 Gay characters: see this author's *Screened Out: Playing Gay in Hollywood from Edison to* Stonewall (New York: Routledge, 2002).

Chapter 12: Put 'Em in a Box

228 *Torch Song*: Crawford's negative reaction to Burnett's "Torchy Song" spoof is discussed in Bob Thomas, *Joan Crawford* (New York: Simon & Schuster, 1978), pp. 267–68.

232 "A puddle of HIV": The full tweet from Ellis, in April 2011, was "I like the idea of 'Glee' but why is it after every episode I feel like I've stepped in a puddle of HIV?" It was sent out to over 142,000 Twitter followers, retweeted ad infinitum, and reported on extensively. Shortly after the first tweet, Ellis followed up with "No, I wasn't drunk last night. I was watching Chris Colfer [Kurt on *Glee*] sing 'Le Jazz Hot' and felt like I had suddenly come down with the hivs."

Epilogue

237 "The single greatest musical...": The quote (by an unnamed Fox TV critic) was part of the television ads for *Les Misérables* that ran (interminably) on network television (and very often during *Glee*) in late 2012 and early 2013.

Selected Bibliography

Books on Musical Film

Altman, Rick. *The American Film Musical*. Bloomington: Indiana University Press, 1987.

Altman, Rick, ed. *Genre: The Musical; A Reader*. London: Routledge & Kegan Paul, 1981.

Bradley, Edwin M. *The First Hollywood Musicals: A Critical Filmography of 171 Features, 1927–1932*. Jefferson, NC: McFarland, 1996.

Cohan, Steven. *Hollywood Musicals, The Film Reader*. In Focus: Routledge Film Readers. New York: Routledge, 2001.

Cohan, Steven. *Incongruous Entertainment: Camp, Cultural Value, and the MGM Musical*. Durham, NC: Duke University Press, 2005.

Delamater, Jerome. *Dance in the Hollywood Musical*. Ann Arbor, MI: UMI Research Press, 1978.

Dunne, Michael. *American Film Musical Themes and Forms*. Jefferson, NC: McFarland, 2004.

Feuer, Jane. *The Hollywood Musical*. Bloomington: Indiana University Press, 1982.

Fordin, Hugh. *The World of Entertainment: Hollywood's Greatest Musicals*. Garden City, NY: Doubleday, 1975.

Furia, Philip, and Michael Lasser. *America's Songs: The Stories behind the Songs of Broadway, Hollywood, and Tin Pan Alley*. New York: Routledge, 2006.

Furia, Philip, and Laurie Patterson. *The Songs of Hollywood*. New York: Oxford University Press, 2010.

Grant, Barry Keith. *The Hollywood Film Musical*. Hoboken, NJ: Wiley-Blackwell, 2012.

Hemming, Roy. *The Melody Lingers On: The Great Songwriters and Their Movie Musicals*. New York: Newmarket Press, 1986.

Herzog, Amy. *Dreams of Difference, Songs of the Same: The Musical Moment in Film*. Minneapolis: University of Minnesota Press, 2009.

Hirschhorn, Clive. *The Hollywood Musical*. New York: Crown, 1981.

Hischak, Thomas. *Film It with Music: An Encyclopedic Guide to the American Movie Musical*. Westport, CT: Greenwood Press, 2001.

Hischak, Thomas. *The Oxford Companion to the American Musical: Theatre, Film, and Television*. New York: Oxford University Press, 2008.

Hischak, Thomas. *Through the Screen Door: What Happened to the Broadway Musical When It Went to Hollywood*. New York: Oxford University Press, 2004.

Kennedy, Matthew. *Roadshow! The Fall of Film Musicals in the 1960s*. New York: Oxford University Press, 2013.

Knight, Arthur. *Disintegrating the Musical: Black Performance and American Musical Film*. Durham, NC: Duke University Press, 2002.

Kobal, John. *Gotta Sing Gotta Dance. A Pictorial History of Film Musicals*. London: Hamlyn, 1971; rev. ed., London: Spring Books, 1983.

Kreuger, Miles, ed. *The Movie Musical from Vitaphone to 42nd Street: As Reported in a Great Fan Magazine*. New York: Dover, 1975.

Mast, Gerald. *Can't Help Singin': The American Musical on Stage and Screen*. Woodstock, NY: Overlook Press, 1987.

McVay, Douglas. *The Musical Film*. New York: Barnes, 1967.

Mordden, Ethan. *The Hollywood Musical*. New York: St. Martin's Press, 1981.

Mundy, John. *The British Musical Film*. Manchester: Manchester University Press, 2007.

Mundy, John. *Popular Music on Screen: From Hollywood Musical to Music Video*. Manchester: Manchester University Press, 1999.

Sennett, Ted. *Hollywood Musicals*. New York: Harry N. Abrams, 1981.

Springer, John. *All Talking! All Singing! All Dancing!* New York: Citadel, 1966.

Stern, Lee Edward. *The Movie Musical*. New York: Pyramid, 1974.

Vallance, Tom. *The American Musical*. New York: Barnes, 1970.

Woll, Allen L. *The Hollywood Musical Goes to War*. Lanham, MD: Rowman & Littlefield, 1983.

Books on Individual Films

Carringer, Robert L., ed. *The Jazz Singer*. Madison: University of Wisconsin Press, 1979.

Fricke, John, Jay Scarfone, and William Stillman. *The Wizard of Oz: The Official 50th Anniversary Pictorial History*. New York: Warner Books, 1989.

Fumento, Rocco, ed. *42nd Street*. Madison: University of Wisconsin Press, 1980.

Harmetz, Aljean. *The Making of* The Wizard of Oz. New York: Alfred A. Knopf, 1977.

Hess, Earl J., and Pratibha Dabholkar. *Singin' in the Rain: The Making of an American Classic*. Lawrence: University Press of Kansas, 2010.

Kaufman, Gerald. *Meet Me in St. Louis*. London: British Film Institute, 1994.

Knox, Donald. *The Magic Factory: How MGM Made "An American in Paris."* New York: Praeger, 1973.

Rushdie, Salman. *The Wizard of Oz*. London: British Film Institute, 1992.

Seymour, James, ed. *Gold Diggers of 1933*. Madison: University of Wisconsin Press, 1980.

Wollen, Peter. *Singin' in the Rain*. 2nd ed. London: British Film Institute, 2012.

Other Works on Film

Ankerich, Michael G. *The Sound of Silence: Conversations with 16 Film and Stage Personalities Who Bridged the Gap between Silents and Talkies*. Jefferson, NC: McFarland, 1998.

Balio, Tino, ed. *The American Film Industry*. Madison: University of Wisconsin Press, 1976.

Bandy, Mary Lea, ed. *American Moviemakers: The Dawn of Sound*. New York: Museum of Modern Art, 1989.

Basinger, Jeanine. *The Star Machine*. New York: Alfred A. Knopf, 2007.

Bordwell, David, Janet Staiger, and Kristin Thomson. *The Classical Hollywood Cinema: Film Style and Mode of Production to 1960*. New York: Columbia University Press, 1985.

Crafton, Donald. *The Talkies: American Cinema's Transition to Sound, 1926–1931*. Berkeley: University of California Press, 1997.

Doherty, Thomas. *Pre-Code Hollywood: Sex, Immorality, and Insurrection in American Cinema, 1930–1934*. New York: Columbia University Press, 1999.

Eyman, Scott. *The Speed of Sound: Hollywood and the Talkie Revolution*. New York: Simon & Schuster, 1997.

Geduld, Harry M. *The Birth of the Talkies: From Edison to Jolson*. Bloomington: Indiana University Press, 1975.

Gomery, Douglas. *The Coming of Sound: A History*. New York: Routledge, 2005.

Higham, Charles, and Joel Greenberg. *The Celluloid Muse: Hollywood Directors Speak*. Chicago: Henry Regnery, 1971.

Katz, Ephraim. *The Film Encyclopedia 6e*. New York: Harper Collins, 2008.

Kobal, John. *People Will Talk*. New York: Alfred A. Knopf, 1985.

Mast, Gerald, ed. *The Movies in Our Midst: Documents in the Cultural History of Film in America*. Chicago: University of Chicago Press, 1982.

O'Brien, Charles. *Cinema's Conversion to Sound*. Bloomington: Indiana University Press, 2005.

Parish, James Robert. *Fiasco: A History of Hollywood's Iconic Flops*. Hoboken: John Wiley, 2006.

Sklar, Robert. *Movie-Made America: A Cultural History of American Movies*. New York: Vintage Books, 1975.

Solomon, Aubry. *Twentieth Century-Fox: A Corporate and Financial History*. Metuchen, NJ: Scarecrow Press, 1988.

Walker, Alexander. *The Shattered Silents: How the Talkies Came to Stay*. New York: William Morrow, 1979.

Weis, Elisabeth, and John Belton, eds. *Film Sound: Theory and Practice*. New York: Columbia University Press, 1985.

Biographies, Autobiographies, and Books on Individual Artists

Astaire, Fred. *Steps in Time: An Autobiography*. New York: Harper, 1959.

Berg, A. Scott. *Goldwyn: A Biography*. New York: Alfred A. Knopf, 1989.

Bergreen, Lawrence. *As Thousands Cheer: The Life of Irving Berlin*. New York: Viking, 1990.

Birchard, Robert S. *Cecil B. DeMille's Hollywood*. Lexington: University Press of Kentucky, 2004.

Chierichetti, David. *Mitchell Leisen: Hollywood Director*. Los Angeles: Photoventures Press, 1995.

Clarens, Carlos. *Cukor*. London: Secker & Warburg, 1976.

Croce, Arlene. *The Fred Astaire and Ginger Rogers Book*. New York: Galahad Books, 1972.

Fricke, John. *Judy Garland: A Portrait in Art and Anecdote*. Boston: Bullfinch Press, 2003.

Goldman, Herbert G. *Jolson: The Legend Comes to Life*. New York: Oxford University Press, 1988.

Harvey, Stephen. *Directed by Vincente Minnelli*. New York: Museum of Modern Art, 1989.

Haver, Ronald. *David O. Selznick's Hollywood*. New York: Alfred A. Knopf, 1980.

McElhany, Joe, ed. *Vincente Minnelli: The Art of Entertainment* (Contemporary Approaches to Film and Television Series). Detroit: Wayne State University Press, 2008.

Milne, Tom. *Mamoulian*. London: Thames & Hudson, 1969.

Mueller, John. *Astaire Dancing: The Musical Films*. New York: Wings Books, 1985.

Rubin, Martin. *Showstoppers: Busby Berkeley and the Tradition of Spectacle*. New York: Columbia University Press, 1993.

Spivak, Jeffrey. *Buzz: The Life and Art of Busby Berkeley*. Lexington: University Press of Kentucky, 2010.

Thomas, Bob. *Thalberg: Life and Legend*. New York: Doubleday, 1969.

Turk, Edward Baron. *Hollywood Diva: A Biography of Jeanette MacDonald*. Berkeley: University of California Press, 1998.

Vieira, Mark. *Irving Thalberg: Boy Wonder to Producer Prince*. Berkeley: University of California Press, 2010.

Walker, Alexander. *Joan Crawford: The Ultimate Star*. New York: Harper & Row, 1983.

Weinberg, Herman. *The Lubitsch Touch*. New York: Dover, 1977.

Williams, Esther, and Digby Diehl. *The Million Dollar Mermaid*. New York: Simon & Schuster, 1999.

Miscellaneous Books

Bordman, Gerald. *American Musical Theatre: A Chronicle*. 2nd ed. New York: Oxford University Press, 1992.

Jauss, Hans Robert. *Toward an Aesthetic of Reception*. Trans. Timothy Bahti. Brighton, Sussex: Harvester Press, 1982.

Kreuger, Miles. *Show Boat: The Story of a Classic American Musical.* Rev. ed. New York: Da Capo Press, 1990.

Lissauer, Robert. *Lissauer's Encyclopedia of Popular Music in America: 1888 to the Present.* New York: Paragon House, 1991.

Mordden, Ethan. *Broadway Babies: The People Who Made the American Musical.* New York: Oxford University Press, 1983.

Selected Periodicals

Billboard

Close Up

Exhibitors Herald World

Film Daily

Harrison's Reports

Los Angeles Times

Motion Picture Herald

Motion Picture News

The Nation

New York Herald-Tribune

The New York Times

The New Yorker

Photoplay

Time

Vanity Fair

Variety [Weekly]

Selected Websites

arts meme. www.artsmeme.com

Box Office Mojo. www.boxofficemojo.com

Internet Movie Database. www.imdb.com

Rotten Tomatoes. www.rottentomatoes.com

Vitaphone Varieties. www.blogspot.vitaphone.com

Index

The year in parentheses following a film title designates that film's year of release. In the instances involving a stage show being filmed, the year refers to the film. (Exceptions are so noted.) Numbers in italics refer to illustrations, and the letter "n" followed by number signifies the numbered footnote on the page number preceding it.

31901055541298